THE WIDENING GULF

THE WIDENING GULF

Northern attitudes to
the independent Irish state
1919–49

DENNIS KENNEDY

THE
BLACKSTAFF
PRESS

BELFAST

First published in 1988 by
The Blackstaff Press Limited
3 Galway Park, Dundonald, Belfast BT16 0AN, Northern Ireland

Printed in England by
Billings and Sons Limited

British Library Cataloguing in Publication Data
Kennedy, Dennis, 1936–
The widening gulf : northern attitudes to
the independent Irish state, 1919–49.
1. (Republic) Ireland. Attitudes of
Unionists of Northern Ireland, 1919–49.
Northern Ireland. Unionists. Attitudes
1919–1949 to (Republic) Ireland
I. Title
941.7082

Library of Congress Cataloging-in-Publication Data
Kennedy, Dennis, 1936–
The widening gulf : northern attitudes to
the independent Irish state, 1919–49 / Dennis Kennedy.
p.   cm.
Bibliography: p.
Includes index.
$20.00 (U.S. : est.)
1. Northern Ireland — Politics and government. 2. Ireland –
Politics and government — 1922–1949. 3. Ireland — Politics and
government — 1910–1921. 4. Ulster Unionist Party — History.
5. Public opinion — Northern Ireland. 6. Nationalism — Northern
Ireland — Public opinion. 7. Home rule (Ireland) — Public opinion.
8. Irish question — Public opinion. I. Title.
DA990.U46K463   1988   88–6134
941.5082'2—dc19   CIP

ISBN 0-85640-396-2

CONTENTS

INTRODUCTION

> The rights of the minority must be sacred to the majority. . . it will only be by broad views, tolerant ideas and a real desire for liberty of conscience that we here can make an ideal of the Parliament and the executive.[1]

Thus Sir James Craig, shortly to become the first Prime Minister of Northern Ireland, speaking in Belfast in February 1921. For good measure he went on to say that Unionists in the North were very much bound up in the rest of Ireland. They must hope not only for a brilliant prospect for Ulster, but a brilliant future for Ireland.

The reality turned out to be very different, in terms both of relations between majority and minority in Northern Ireland, and of relations between the two parts of the island. But in the early months of 1921 it was possible for the predominantly Protestant Unionist community in the north-east of Ireland to feel a degree of optimism and generosity. The Government of Ireland Act 1920 was shortly to give them the opportunity to avoid incorporation into a self-governing nationalist, and largely Catholic, Ireland. Instead the new state of Northern Ireland would remain in legislative union with Great Britain, though it would have its own devolved parliament and executive.

It was not an ideal solution to the age-old problem of Ireland and Britain, bedevilled for centuries by the presence in Ireland of a very substantial minority who did not share the growing aspirations of Irish nationalism, and who vehemently opposed any modification of the legislative union between the two countries, established by the Act of Union of 1800. By 1921, however, the Unionist community of about 900,000, concentrated in north-east Ulster, had accepted that some limited form of independence, or Home Rule, for most of the island was inevitable. The price of their own salvation from such a fate was the abandonment of their fellow Unionists, around 300,000, outside the north-east, and the acceptance of limited devolution within the United Kingdom for their own six-county state.

Unionism in nineteenth-century Ireland had developed essentially as a reaction to sporadic moves by Irish nationalists of various hues – but increasingly Catholic and Gaelic – to dismantle the Union of 1801 in favour of some form of legislative independence. Unionists were not one homogeneous group, but a series of groups, identifiable by religious denomination, by economic and social standing and, particularly in the north-east, by geographical concentration. To varying degrees they exhibited many of the attitudes later explicitly enunciated by organised Unionism – fear and distrust of Catholicism, a conviction that the economic welfare of Ireland depended on legislative union with Britain, a rejection of, or an indifference to, any romantic concept of a Gaelic Irish nation, and a converse belief in the supreme virtues and importance of the British Empire.

It was a rejection of the growing intensity of the nationalist demand for Home Rule in the 1870s and 1880s, led on the parliamentary side by the outstanding figure of Charles Stewart Parnell and backed by a vigorous and often violent Land War aimed at the overthrow of landlordism, that helped fuse the various elements of Unionism into a coherent political force. The agrarian violence of the Land War had helped provoke a resurgence of the Orange Order, the ultra-Protestant movement that had had its origins in sectarian violence in rural Armagh a century earlier. The Orange Order bound its members together in lodges pledged to defend the Protestant religion, the Protestant constitution and the Protestant monarch. Combining as it did all classes of Protestants in Ireland, it was well suited to form the basis of organised political Unionism in the 1880s.

In 1885 there emerged another factor vital to the stimulation of organised opposition to Home Rule. This was the realisation that the Liberal Party, under the leadership of William Ewart Gladstone, was moving towards an accommodation with Irish nationalism under Parnell. When Gladstone came to power in 1886 he told the ministers in his new Government that he proposed to examine the possibility of a 'legislative body to sit in Dublin'.[2] Thereafter, a main preoccupation of organised Unionism was the need to win the argument at Westminster. Initially at least, that argument was based on the theoretical threat posed to a whole range of interests in Ireland and Britain by the envisaged creation of an Irish parliament. This in turn was based on a series of assumptions as to how such a parliament would act. It was

2

assumed it would limit or extinguish the religious liberties of Protestants, that it would inevitably damage the Irish economy, and that its very existence would prove to be a source of weakness to Britain and the Empire in times of international tension or conflict.

Some evidence was at hand to support such contentions. Irish nationalism was by then closely identified with Catholicism. In 1911 John Dillon MP, one of the leaders of the Irish Parliamentary Party, declared that the Irish race was the right arm of the Catholic Church, and the Irish 'the most Catholic nation of the whole earth'.[3] Such statements, perceived by Unionists as threats to themselves, could be linked to the new papal decrees of Ne Temere and Motu Proprio which asserted church authority on secular affairs.[4] The economic interests of the Northern Unionist industrialists, of their workers and of the Southern landlords would have only minority representation in an Irish parliament. In addition there was the belief that legislative independence would inevitably mean fiscal independence and that could mean a threat not just to Irish Unionist interests, but to Britain's supply of cheap food. However, the threat to Britain's security was the first plank in the platform of Unionism presented in Britain itself. Unionists could cite the separatist tradition in Irish nationalism, from Wolfe Tone onwards, which had sought to take advantage of England's every difficulty, as Major John MacBride and others had done at the turn of the twentieth century through the Irish Brigades in the Boer War.[5] They could point to opposition by the Irish Parliamentary Party at Westminster to British military actions.

But these were all hypothetical arguments, based on assumptions as to how an independent Irish parliament might act. They were also arguments put forward, at least until 1912, in the belief that Home Rule could be resisted and prevented. By then the Parliament Act of 1911, curtailing the power of the House of Lords, had removed the last obstacle to the passage through Westminster of a Home Rule measure for Ireland. In effect this meant that all of Ireland was due to be placed under a subordinate legislature in Dublin by 1914 at the latest. Only the well-organised and highly motivated Unionists of the north-east of the island could retain a genuine hope of thwarting Home Rule, if not for the whole island, then for their corner of it, and if not by argument and persuasion, then by other methods. The lengths to which they were prepared to go were indicated in the organisation and arming of the Ulster Volunteer Force, the illegal importation of guns, and the setting up of a provisional government.

The outbreak of the First World War in 1914 overtook both the Home Rule Act and the Unionist opposition to it. But by then Irish Unionism was already becoming Ulster Unionism, and partition was emerging as the only way to reconcile the massive Catholic and nationalist demand for Home Rule with the equally determined Ulster Unionist rejection of it. The general election called in December 1918, immediately after the end of the war, saw a sweeping victory for the new and more extreme nationalist movement, Sinn Féin, in all of Ireland outside north-east Ulster. In January 1919 this led to an embryonic partition when the Sinn Féin members elected to Westminster refused to take their seats and set up instead Dáil Éireann in Dublin as an Irish parliament, electing an independent Irish executive. These institutions were not recognised by the Government of the United Kingdom of Great Britain and Ireland, and the Unionists took no part in them.

Ulster Unionists were no longer reacting just to their fears of a measure of devolution for Ireland or part of it, but to the reality of an Irish political entity that at least purported to be an independent state. The full significance of the claim of the nationalist members elected in December 1918 to be 'an independent Constituent Assembly of the Irish Nation'[6] may not have been immediately appreciated by Unionists, but they were soon faced with the reality of a Dáil Éireann that met and set up an alternative administration. Behind the Dáil was an Irish Republican Army that was far from theoretical, and in time too there were Sinn Féin courts administering justice.

After 1919, and quite explicitly so after the Provisional Government was set up early in 1922, the independent state, or statal institutions based in Dublin, embodied Irish nationalism and became its visible, physical manifestation. Unionist responses were therefore not just to a theoretical nationalism, or to their own assumptions about that nationalism, but to the reality of institutions and eventually of a practically independent state, acting in the name of Irish nationalism.

4

In theory, and partly in practice too, the partition of 1921, the creation of the Northern state, the acceptance of the Anglo-Irish Treaty and the founding of the Free State in 1922 resolved the conflicting claims of Unionism and nationalism and provided a settlement. In theory at least, much of the whole negative basis for Unionism as a reactive force was therefore removed, leaving it free to develop positive attitudes and policies towards the running of the new devolved unit, towards the nationalist minority within it, and towards the other entity now created on the island. Craig's speech and other statements in 1921 indicated an awareness that this new situation existed, and that the settlement of 1921–2 was a foundation on which to construct something positive, not just a rampart behind which to continue the struggle.

Yet the subsequent Unionist attitude was indeed to regard the settlement as a defensive rampart. The rights of the Catholic minority, 430,000 strong and almost 34 per cent of the population of Northern Ireland, were less than sacred to the majority – broad views and tolerant ideas were in short supply. And Unionists went to great lengths to distance themselves from the rest of Ireland and from any concept of Gaelic nationalism.

Why did this happen? Was it simply that Unionists, having secured their position of dominance within the partitioned area, saw no need for generosity and were largely motivated, anyway, by traditional hostility towards Catholicism and nationalism? That was no doubt partly the case for some Unionists. But the question remains as to why there was no evolution of Unionism. For succeeding generations the Unionist political organisation retained the almost total support of the majority community in Northern Ireland. The posture of that organisation and the attitudes of most Protestants hardened rather than softened towards both their Catholic neighbours and the idea of Irish nationalism. In fact, Unionism as a political philosophy remained little more than a response to Irish nationalism. This response was not just that articulated by political spokesmen; it was also the response, in terms of opinions and attitudes, of the Protestant community. Election results repeatedly showed that the majority shared the views of organised Unionism on the political priorities within the Northern state.

But this is to say little more than that Unionists were Unionist.

More interesting is to seek the extent to which, and the ways in which, this Unionism remained basically a reaction to Irish nationalism, and to what extent it continued to draw strength and cohesion from widely held perceptions of the nature and characteristics of that nationalism as it became embodied in the new Irish state. Unionist statements and speeches of 1919–49 indicate how the political leaders of the Protestant community in Northern Ireland remained obsessed by the threat of nationalism and their distaste for it. Such speeches were, naturally, widely reported in the newspapers of the time. As well as being a prime source for the opinions of influential and representative men, and for accounts of the actions of Government and political organisations, the three daily Unionist papers published in Belfast, and to a lesser extent the array of weekly papers published throughout Northern Ireland, offered frequent editorial comments on the Southern state and events within it. These newspapers were also the windows through which the vast majority of Northern Unionists viewed the nationalist struggle from 1919 onwards. For most they were the only sources of information. Thus a reading of these papers, particularly for the vital early years immediately after the end of the First World War, gives a good picture of the events in Ireland as Unionists perceived them.

In the circumstances of the Protestant community in the northeast of Ireland at that time there are exceptional reasons for paying particular attention to the Unionist newspapers. They were widely read in a highly literate society and were, through editors, staff and ownership, closely integrated into the Unionist community. Editors and proprietors could be, and were, politicians up to government level. They were influential lay members of church committees; journalists at all levels were often active members of the Unionist Party, of the Orange Order and of the Masonic Order.

As sources for a factual history of the period these newspapers have clear limitations. But as aids to understanding Unionists' perceptions of both what was happening to them and what was going on in the island, they are invaluable. What was going on was both dramatic and confusing. The Unionist papers followed in detail the parallel paths of development after the general election of December 1918. There was the novel situation of an 'illegal' parliament sitting in Dublin, setting up an executive or government and, in the course of 1919, starting to wage war against the Government in London and its administration in Dublin, and its agents and anyone else in Ireland who remained loyal to it.

On a wider plane there was the continued effort to solve the Irish dilemma by parliamentary, constitutional means. The Government of Ireland Bill was published early in 1920, proposing partition, with two subordinate parliaments in Belfast and Dublin. As that Bill progressed through Westminster, Unionists accepted it and prepared to put its provisions into practice through an election in May 1921, and the opening of the Northern Ireland Parliament in June 1921. All this was against the background of widespread rebellion, with considerable violence, throughout most of the rest of the island. By that time the IRA, the army of the illegal Southern state, was already engaged in violence in the area that was to become Northern Ireland. That activity had become part of severe inter-communal violence, with attacks on the Catholic minority, and the expulsion of Catholic workers from the Belfast shipyards and other places of employment. In response, the Dáil in Dublin had launched an economic boycott of Belfast and other Northern towns that was to last two years, enforced by IRA violence.

By mid-1921 the British Government found itself, on the one hand, shepherding the new state of Northern Ireland into existence under the Government of Ireland Act, while on the other, first signing a cease-fire with the forces fighting against that Act in the rest of the island, and then proceeding to renegotiate the Act as far as that part of Ireland was concerned.

All this was happening in the second half of 1921. In that period violence and conflict between the two groupings were increasing sharply. And London was, at the same time, having separate and constructive relations with each. The violence of the IRA inside, and against, the new Northern state intensified, and the Dáil's economic boycott was extended. Nor did this bizarre and contradictory situation end when a settlement was achieved between London and Dublin early in 1922 and a Provisional Government took over a largely independent Southern state. It was only in the middle of 1922, when the confusion of a civil war between

7

factions of the Sinn Féin movement in Dublin was added to the existing fractured mosaic, that Northern Ireland was freed from what its Unionist population had seen as a combined military, economic and diplomatic assault on its very existence.

The dramatic impact of these turbulent years on the Unionist community is conveyed in the pages of the Unionist newspapers. These also portray the continued anxieties of that community over the ensuing two decades, as the nature of the new Southern state evolved, seeking to develop radically its relationship with Great Britain and its own constitutional status, while at the same time pursuing the nationalist goal of a united and independent island.

To examine the impact of these events on the Unionists of Northern Ireland is not to justify Unionist actions, or to offer an apologia for Unionism. But it does raise serious questions as to the extent to which other players in the Irish scene, not least nationalist Ireland, contributed to the tragedy of Northern Ireland itself, and to the widening gulf between North and South.

NOTE ON TERMINOLOGY

Newspapers and politicians of the period referred variously to the two parts of Ireland as 'the North', 'Northern Ireland', 'the north of Ireland' and 'Ulster'; or 'the South', 'the Irish Free State' and 'Éire'. In the face of such diversity no attempt has been made in this book to impose any uniformity and no significance is attached to the use of any term.

Lord Craigavon is referred to as Sir James Craig prior to January 1927 and thereafter as Lord Craigavon.

Under the Constitution of the Irish Free State the head of government was designated the President of the Executive Council, but invariably referred to by Northern sources as the prime minister. Similarly, the Chairman of the Dáil was usually called the Speaker in Northern newspapers.

PART ONE

I
LOOKING OVER THE FENCE

In 1919, and for most of the period up to 1949, newspapers were the principal medium by which the people of the north of Ireland learned of events beyond their immediate personal locality. It was in newspapers that issues relating to political developments were discussed and opinions formulated. Broadcasting from London began only in November 1922 and from Belfast in September 1924. The first daily radio news bulletin from Belfast did not commence until 1928. News broadcasts were scant in the 1930s, and the outbreak of the Second World War meant the virtual suspension of regional broadcasting.[1]

Meanwhile, newspapers flourished in the region. What circulation figures there are suggest that by 1921 altogether more than 140,000 copies were being sold by the three main Belfast Unionist papers: the *Belfast News-Letter*, the *Northern Whig* and the *Belfast Telegraph*. The fourth daily paper, the *Irish News*, catered almost exclusively for the Catholic–nationalist community. Most provincial towns had weekly or twice-weekly local papers. Of the Unionist papers the *Belfast News-Letter* was the oldest, in fact one of the oldest in the British Isles, having been founded in 1737. The *Northern Whig* dated from 1824 and the *Belfast Telegraph* from 1870.

There was a highly literate population to read them. The 1911 census showed that in the whole nine-county province of Ulster the rate of illiteracy in the population over nine years of age was only 8.7 per cent. Within that average the rate for Catholics was 14.7 per cent, with much smaller figures for the Protestant denominations – Church of Ireland 6.1 per cent, Presbyterian 2.6 per cent and Methodist 1.9 per cent. For Belfast the figures were lower again – 3.5 per cent for Church of Ireland and 1.9 per cent for Presbyterians.[2]

The *Telegraph*'s circulation was much larger than the others: in 1920 it claimed sales of at least 70,000 copies, in 1930 of 74,000 and in 1940 of 96,000. After the Second World War daily sales soared, reaching 159,000 by 1950.[3] The Telegraph group, owned by the Baird family, was the most powerful, publishing several weekly papers and an *Irish Daily Telegraph* intended for circulation outside the range of the evening paper and as far away as Dundalk, Co. Louth, and Sligo in the west.

In the early 1920s the *Whig* claimed on its masthead that it had the 'largest sale of any Ulster morning newspaper', which was probably around 30,000 copies. In 1922 the *News-Letter* claimed daily sales of 34,000.[4] By 1935 it boasted that its 'nett sales far exceed that of any other Ulster morning paper'.

The families that owned these three newspapers were powers in the land and particularly prominent within organised political Unionism. At the head of the *Telegraph*, until his death in 1934, was the larger-than-life and much lionised figure of Sir Robert Baird. In 1886 – the same year Gladstone introduced the first Home Rule Bill – Baird had taken control of the group, founded by his father and uncle in 1870. By all accounts a forceful personality with considerable business acumen and a readiness to embrace technical innovation, he built a powerful empire based on the *Telegraph*. He was very much a press baron, involved in civic and public life. He held high office within the Orange Order, being Deputy Grand Master of Ireland and also of Scotland. His great personal interest was the Masonic Order, in which he held numerous offices, and he was largely responsible for the founding of the Masonic Press Lodge in Belfast in 1917. His role as a significant figure in the Unionist community was recognised by a knighthood, bestowed in June 1921 on the occasion of the opening of the new Northern Ireland Parliament by George V. He was described at his death, by a subsequent editor of the *Telegraph*, as 'not only the best-known, but in many respects, the greatest Ulsterman of his day'.[5] He was succeeded in the chairmanship of the *Telegraph* by his brother, Major William Baird. He too maintained a daily presence in the paper's offices and exerted his own strong influence on its content.

When George V knighted Baird in 1921, he bestowed a similar favour on the head of another Belfast newspaper family – Trevor Henderson, managing director since 1914 of the

News-Letter, a post he held until he retired in 1928. Though much less a public figure than Sir Robert, Sir Trevor had been particularly active within the Unionist political organisation. He had been secretary of a Unionist club in Belfast, he held office in constituency organisations and he was a member of the Standing Committee of the Ulster Unionist Council. After him control of the *News-Letter* went to two nephews – James Henderson and Captain R.L. Henderson. James Henderson was to remain on the board until his death in 1963. He too served as a member of the Standing Committee of the Ulster Unionist Council. Other members of the Henderson family were prominent in both journalism and Unionism in Belfast.[6]

Unlike the Bairds and the Hendersons, the family that owned the *Whig,* the Cunninghams, was not primarily a newspaper family. Their original business was stockbroking and they had extensive interests in property and commerce in Belfast. The *Whig* had been a radical paper in the nineteenth century, strongly pro-tenant right, and strongly anti-Orange. But it swung firmly Unionist in 1885 and remained so under the Cunninghams.

Again unlike the other two families, no Cunningham was knighted in 1921. But they did gain a Senator – Samuel Cunningham was appointed a member of the new Northern Senate in 1921 and sat until 1945. He was chairman of the *Whig* from the early 1920s until his death in 1946. His elevation to the Senate, and also to the Privy Council, was recognition of his prominence in the Unionist organisation, mainly in west Belfast, and in the Orange Order. He too was a member of the Standing Committee of the Ulster Unionist Council and had been since the Home Rule crisis days of 1912. Like most, though not quite all, newspaper proprietors and journalists in Unionist Belfast, he was a Freemason, and a founder member of the Belfast Masonic Press Lodge.[7]

If ownership of the three main papers serving the Protestant community was solidly Unionist, the links between editors and journalists and the Unionist establishment were even more striking. Thomas Moles, editor of the *Telegraph* from 1924 to 1937 was an example of this. Moles joined the *Telegraph* from the *Armagh Gazette* in 1902 and became its chief leader writer and political commentator in 1909. It was said of him that he was the only journalist who knew in advance of the Ulster Volunteer Force gun-running at Larne, Co. Antrim, in 1912, and who witnessed it and indeed took part in it. Like Baird, he was an enthusiastic Orangeman and Mason, and he was also an active political pamphleteer in the critical years before the First World War. In 1917 he was nominated by the Ulster Unionist Party to serve on the secretariat of the Irish Convention in Dublin – an unsuccessful attempt to solve the Ulster problem by mediation and discussion. But the remarkable aspect of Moles's career was that he combined editing his newspaper with membership of two parliaments. He sat as a Unionist at Westminster from 1918 to 1929 and in the Belfast parliament from 1921 until his death in 1937. In the new Northern parliament he was elected chairman of the Committee on Ways and Means, which meant occupying the post of Deputy Speaker. So for a period of five years, from 1924 to 1929, while he was editor of Northern Ireland's largest newspaper, he was a member of two parliaments and Deputy Speaker of one. Even then he continued to dictate, for the columns of the *Telegraph*, his own political commentary on the day's business in the Northern parliament.[8]

Moles was succeeded as editor in 1937 by John Sayers, one of two brothers who had long held senior positions under him. John Sayers had been a leader writer since 1914 and assistant editor since 1924. He died in 1939, and was succeeded by his brother R.M. (Bertie) Sayers, who remained in the chair until 1953. Both brothers were firmly within the circles that constituted the Unionist establishment, circles that had their centres in the Unionist Party, the Orange Order, the Masonic Order, and the Ulster Reform Club – the gentleman's club in Belfast that brought together the industrial and commercial leadership of the Protestant community.

The *Whig* too, for a time, shared its editor with the two parliaments. Robert John Lynn, knighted in 1924, had joined the *Whig* in 1903, had become a leader writer, then editor in 1913, remaining in that post until 1928 when he was removed by the Cunninghams. Lynn was elected to Westminster in 1918 and served until 1929. He also sat in the Northern Ireland House of Commons from 1921 to 1945. In 1937 he succeeded his fellow journalist Moles as Deputy Speaker in Belfast. At that time he was also managing editor of the Presbyterian Church's weekly paper, the *Witness*.

14

Under his editorship the *Whig*, while staunchly Unionist, was much less orthodoxly so than the *Telegraph*. Instead it followed Lynn's own brand of Unionism. This was fiercely 'loyal' on all essential points, yet ready to be critical of the Government and of Craig personally over particular issues such as the temperance question, or the cost of administration. Frequently, especially in 1921 and 1922, the *Whig* found itself to the right of the Government in its demands for much stricter enforcement of law and order against Sinn Féin and the IRA. This readiness to attack the establishment on specific issues was perhaps a continuation, in muted form, of the *Whig*'s earlier radical tradition. Certainly it still presented itself as 'The People's Popular Paper – for the housewife, for the farmer, for the labourer'.

Lynn's dual parliamentary membership, plus extensive involvement in company directorships, eventually proved too much and the Cunninghams parted company with him in 1928.[9] Their choice of his successor was remarkable – he was Willy Armour, son of the Revd J.B. Armour, the veteran Presbyterian Home Ruler. Armour had joined the *Whig* as a reporter in 1923 on his return from India, where he had worked in the Education Service. A highly educated and cultured man, he soon emerged as a specialist writer.

Though his term as editor lasted only two years, Armour is of considerable interest, partly because he was far from an orthodox Ulster Unionist in both his background and his views, and also because he subsequently wrote about his editorial experiences, in his book *Facing the Irish Question*, published in 1935. By his own account he was both a Home Ruler and an Imperialist. As a student at Oxford he had supported Home Rule, while his job in India, as editor of the *United Provinces War Journal*, was a propagandist post on behalf of the Empire. His writings after his period with the *Whig* were strongly anti-Unionist.

Even more so than Lynn before him, Armour lived up to the *Whig*'s motto, *Pro Rege Saepe, Pro Patria Semper* (often for King, always for country). He was a sharp critic of aspects of Northern administration – on agriculture, public transport and other matters. Indeed, the immediate cause of the end of his editorship was a motion of censure against him for breach of privilege of the Northern Ireland Parliament over criticism of the siting of a new bridge in Derry.

However, as editor Armour never questioned the basics of Unionism, and when an election was called during his tenure in May 1929, the *Whig* duly supported Craig. Armour later defended this position on the grounds that in Northern Ireland the Government was not only the administration, but 'like much else in the province, personified Crown, Constitution and everything human and divine'.[10] For his own part, he said, he had no wish to upset any one of these things, so the only course was to support the Government. Any change would have been for the worse. Besides which, he argued, while a newspaper could be of service in upholding principles, government was not its function.[11] Nevertheless, at times Armour displayed considerable impatience with aspects of Northern life. On 24 June 1929 an editorial by him in the *Whig* was strongly critical of what it called 'groove-like attitudes' and complained that for Protestants there was a feeling of impropriety attached to the smallest criticism of officials or policy. As a result they had had to approve of every absurdity and every stupidity.

When the Cunninghams terminated Armour's contract in spring 1930, they allowed him a period of notice, during which he addressed his own farewell to readers of the *Whig* through the editorial column. On 3 May 1930, in his final piece headed 'Finis', he wrote of his friend President Tomas Garrigue Masaryk of Czechoslovakia, quoting his dictum that no state or policy could prosper unless the groundwork be moral. The leader continued:

> We confess that the one thing that has been borne in on us in the last seven years has been the need for an absolute standard. There is a difference between right and wrong, between truth and false-hood, between justice and injustice. There are evils which cannot be evaded, and that, unattended, spread like dry-rot through all society to its ruin.

This final plea for fair play shows a strong flavour of Toc H, the worldwide spiritual and philanthropic movement that had sprung out of First World War experiences, and in which Armour was deeply involved. But it also shows a disillusionment with Unionist rule in Northern Ireland that was normally never hinted at in the columns of the *Whig*.

After Armour, the Cunninghams went outside Ireland for their next editor and brought over an Englishman, Frank Adams from Stoke-on-Trent, to head the *Whig*. Adams is remembered as a good editor, who rapidly assimilated to Unionism, and when he parted company with the Cunninghams around 1939, he went to Stormont as the Northern Government's first information officer. He was in turn replaced by another Englishman, John Hunt, who came from the *Yorkshire Post*. In the best tradition of the *Whig*, Hunt was sharply critical of the Belfast Corporation and was sued for libel by a number of members.[12] Hunt was replaced in 1943 by Bruce Proudfoot, a Scotsman who had joined the *Whig* in 1925. He had come to Ireland then, he said, believing in Irish unity but soon came to accept the validity of the Unionist position, and he served as editor for the rest of the *Whig*'s life. It closed in 1963.

Relations at the *News-Letter* between the proprietors – the Hendersons – and their editors were evidently much more harmonious. The entire period from 1919 to 1949 saw only two editors – William Geddes Anderson up to 1928, and Harry McKee from then on. Anderson was a Scot, whose position in the *News-Letter* in the crisis years of 1913–14 brought him especially close to Sir Edward Carson and Craig and the Unionist leadership. Harry McKee was a Belfast man who had joined the paper as a sub-editor in 1904 and had moved to London as London editor in 1916. Under him the *News-Letter* gave almost unswerving support to the Unionist Party and its incumbent leadership in the Northern Government. McKee's twelve years in London had brought him into close contact with the Westminster Unionists, notably Carson and Craig in the period 1916–21, and his marked association with Craig remained for many years. He reported the Treaty negotiations from London and he had a major scoop in 1925 when he revealed the recommendations of the Boundary Commission Report. His career in journalism was remarkably long: he retired in 1954 after fifty years with the *News-Letter*, twenty-six of them as editor.[13]

The fact that two editors, Moles and Lynn, from leading Belfast newspapers could combine their journalistic functions with Unionist membership of both the Northern Ireland and Westminster Parliaments, indicates the extent to which it was accepted that the press was part of the mobilised Protestant community in the North – which Unionism undoubtedly was in 1912–22 and even beyond. Inevitably there must have been the closest possible liaison between Craig and his Government, and the *Telegraph* under Moles. An indication of the extent of this is found in connection with the Budget speech of the Minister of Finance John Milne Barbour in May 1936. A letter from Sir Wilfrid Spender, then Secretary of Finance, to the editor of the *Telegraph*, still Moles, confirms that the *Telegraph* would, as in previous years, be given an advance text of the speech. The background is given in Spender's 'Financial Diary' for mid-May 1936. As a result of a row over a Budget leak in Britain, Craig had ruled that no advance information on Barbour's speech should be made available to the press. Spender's account goes on:

> In view, however, of the representations made by Mr Milne Barbour that the Telegraph was entitled to get some consideration for its support of the Government, the Prime Minister agreed to my giving the editor of the Telegraph a special concession.[14]

The concession was only, of course, a matter of hours to allow the *Telegraph* to print details of the Budget in its last afternoon edition, just after the speech had been made. The *News-Letter* evidently begrudged this and Spender adds that 'the rather petulant criticism in the News-Letter on the 15th inst.' was probably partly due to resentment that the *Telegraph* had been facilitated.

Budgets apart, there was no doubt co-operation between the *News-Letter* and the Government too. In January 1935 all the Belfast Unionist papers carried reports of appeals for help from Loyalists in the Free State to the Northern authorities, and for their transfer to the North. A cutting of one such article from the *News-Letter,* in Cabinet papers held in the Public Record Office of Northern Ireland, has attached a note from Wilson Hungerford, secretary of the Ulster Unionist Council, to Craig, which makes it clear that Craig had seen a draft of the article before publication, that Hungerford had helped in its preparation, and that McKee, the editor of the *News-Letter* 'had promised a two-column spread'.[15]

There was intense commercial and journalistic competition among the Belfast papers, particularly between the *Whig* and the *News-Letter*, who were in a constant battle for circulation. Yet none of them strayed far from orthodox Unionism towards a more moderate or liberal viewpoint – apart from the *Whig*'s aberrations under Armour. The firm control exercised by Unionist owners and senior journalists may account for this, but it may also suggest that there was simply no market within the Northern

Protestant community for anything other than orthodox Unionism. The *Whig*'s sorties into 'radical' positions, whether under Lynn in the 1920s or in later attacks on the Belfast Corporation in the 1940s, were in no sense attacks upon Unionism or deviations from it, even though particular bodies such as the corporation or individuals like Craig himself or the Government collectively might be the targets.

The attitude of these Belfast papers in terms of journalistic organisation towards the rest of Ireland was somewhat strange. In the period up to the Second World War none of the three appointed staff correspondents in Dublin. This was despite the fact that in the early 1920s, and particularly from the advent of Eamon de Valera to power in 1932 up to the war, Dublin generated a vast amount of news adjudged of major interest to Northern readers. All three relied almost entirely on stringers, working out of either the *Irish Independent* office, or that of the *Irish Times*. Staff reporters were despatched to Dublin regularly for only two events – the General Synod of the Church of Ireland and the Dublin Horse Show. (Sometimes the St Patrick's Day dog show also merited a staff presence.) But elections, the Dáil, even the long-running evolution of the Free State's constitutional relationship with London, were all left to the 'moonlighting' of Dublin journalists.

It was only the really exceptional event in Dublin that moved the news desks in Belfast to despatch their own correspondents. The opening of the first Dáil in the Mansion House in January 1919 was one such occasion. Bruce Proudfoot, later editor of the *Whig*, recalls being sent twice to the Dáil in the 1920s – once to cover the introduction of the Cosgrave Government's Public Safety Act in 1927, and soon after, the entry of de Valera and Fianna Fáil into the Dáil.[16]

Apart from the extensive reporting of events of direct relevance to the North, such as elections or Dublin's relations with London, the Northern papers tended to restrict their reporting of the Southern scene to Budgets, to occasional stories on the disastrous state of the Free State economy, to compulsory Irish in schools, and to the plight of Southern Loyalists. Even this last was generally reported on the basis of statements and debates in London, mainly in the House of Lords with Lord Carson foremost, rather than on any direct investigation in the Free State itself. There was also a tendency

19

to report in detail interviews given by William T. Cosgrave, de Valera or other Southern leaders to American or British journals, while no attempt seems to have been made by the Belfast papers to seek such interviews themselves.

Looking back in *Facing the Irish Question* on his seven years with the *Whig*, Armour recalled how everything he had written had been from a Northern angle: 'I rarely even looked over the fence,' he said. At one point he gives an account of meeting Cosgrave, President of the Executive Council, when he accompanied an Ulster-American friend on a visit to Cosgrave's office. He comments on how impressed he had been by Cosgrave, but there is no evidence that he ever reported anything of this meeting in the *Whig* or that he sought to use the opportunity to arrange his own interview with Cosgrave. His explanation was that he knew then – in 1926 – that there were certain trees in the Northern Garden of Eden which were unsafe to touch:

> . . . among them justice for Irish men and good will. . . Now, unless I have completely misread from a distance the Ulster Protestant Press, the only thing which a prudent editor actually can safely comment upon and remain 'loyal' is the unhappy plight of the Irish Free State.[17]

Commenting on the 'unhappy plight' of the Free State was certainly a characteristic of all the Belfast Unionist papers. So much so that the Moderator of the General Assembly of the Presbyterian Church in 1924, the Revd R.W. Hamilton, publicly criticised both politicians and papers in the North for ridiculing the leaders of the South, instead of encouraging and admiring them. He was sorry to say the Northern papers played to the gallery far too much.[18]

A reading of the Belfast newspapers from 1919 to 1949 confirms that they were selective in their coverage of Southern news. There was extensive reporting and commenting on the dramatic developments of the period of violence from 1919 until the Truce, and of the Treaty debates and the run-up to the Civil War, and the Civil War itself. Thereafter it is possible to group the areas of coverage under several headings, with little or no variation among the three main papers. Indeed, not only were the preoccupations of the *Telegraph, Whig* and *News-Letter* similar as regards the South, there was from time to time a remarkable similarity of language in editorial comment. The major theme for the entire period was the constitutional evolution of the Free State away from the position agreed in the Anglo-Irish Treaty of 1921. Up to 1925 much that was written in this regard was concerned with the Boundary Commission and what was seen in the North, quite correctly, as Dublin's great hope that the eventual outcome would be a substantial border revision and the probable end of Northern Ireland.

After 1932, de Valera's explicit moves to eliminate all vestiges and symbols of British rule attracted a great deal of attention, and were mainly responsible for very extensive coverage of Southern affairs for most of that decade. In the year 1938, for example – admittedly a year of exceptional interest – the *Whig* published approximately eighty editorials on Free State topics, and that total does not include frequent comment on the general constitutional position of the North in which Southern aspects were mentioned. A topic closely related to the evolution from Free State to Republic was the continued existence and periodic revival of the IRA. This, and any other tendency to lawlessness or anarchy such as arose out of the fascist Blueshirt movement of the 1930s, was widely reported and commented upon.

A third theme was the position of the Protestant or Unionist minority in the Free State. Initially, particularly in 1922, the reports were of the threat to their continued survival in the face of murder or expulsion. Later the concern was with their economic welfare, with the progressive removal of what were seen as the safeguards built into the Treaty and the Free State Constitution – such as the right of appeal to the Privy Council in London as the supreme judicial authority. One aspect of the hardship visited on the Southern Protestants, the 'imposition' of the Irish language upon them, was itself a regular preoccupation of the Belfast papers. Southern attempts to create a Gaelic civilisation, through the language, sport and culture generally, were clearly welcome raw materials for Belfast leader writers anxious to ridicule the Free State.

Similar ammunition was also to hand in the condition of the Free State economy. Apart from the basic contrast between what the *Whig* termed 'the greatest nation the world has ever seen', that was Britain, and 'a little huxtering state', there was repeated comment on the disparities North and South. The Free State's Budget provided an annual story, usually about soaring taxation and deficits. Comparisons of tax levels and costs of basic services, such as the post, were common.

Apart from these major themes – the move towards a Republic, the threat of violence, the position of the minority, the Irish language, and the economy – the Northern papers turned to other topics. The personality of de Valera was one, the Catholic nature of the Southern society and state another, though this occurred less frequently than might have been expected.

Newspapers were not the sole source of information and opinion on the Free State available to Northern Protestants. Their own churches operated in all of Ireland, ensuring at least some personal contact with Southern Protestants on committees or at conferences. Regular transfer of bank, railway and other staff meant that a small number of individuals or families actually had experience of living in both parts of partitioned Ireland. Other families left the South to settle in the North and they too would have provided a picture of the Free State for neighbours and friends. Trinity College Dublin and St Columba's public school continued to attract Northern students, as did the Masonic schools. Despite the decline in trade across the border, and the discouragement to travel presented by the customs checks, some still travelled regularly to the South for holidays or business, or sporting or cultural activities.

Nevertheless the daily newspapers were, for the great majority, the most powerful factor in establishing a view of the South. Detailed examination of the various areas of Southern coverage provided by these papers, under the headings suggested, gives a comprehensive idea of how Northern Protestants perceived the Free State and the general thrust of Irish nationalism embodied in it. For the crucial period from 1919 up to 1922, when violence was at its height in both North and South, and when the Northern and Southern entities and their respective executives and parliaments were being created in a time of chaos and turmoil, the pattern of events as reported daily in the Unionist papers of Belfast was the pattern as perceived by their readers. Not surprisingly that perception differs greatly from the standard nationalist history of a War of Independence. It differs in that the perspectives from which the events were viewed were entirely different, with the result that individual acts, or series of acts,

22

could have a significance for Northerners that was not apparent in the South to the nationalistically-minded majority.

That the Unionist newspapers, like most papers, were biased goes almost without saying. In June 1922 Sir Nevil Macready, General Officer Commanding British forces in Ireland, remarked that the newspapers North and South were giving an entirely distorted or biased view of nearly every incident in Belfast.[19] In January of that year General A.R. Cameron, the Commanding Officer in Belfast, wrote to Craig expressing his concern about the biased reporting by the Unionist press of events in the city. No one reading it would realise, he said, that Loyalists had, in many cases, started the trouble.[20]

A much stronger denunciation of the Belfast papers is contained in *Facts and Figures of the Belfast Pogrom* by G.B. Kenna, published in Dublin in 1922. The writer describes the Unionist papers as a 'monstrous, lying press' and says a vast deal of responsibility for what had happened in the city should undoubtedly be laid at the doors of the three Belfast Orange newspapers and their confederates abroad.[21] The book repeats accusations made at Westminster against the *News-Letter* in particular for publishing four anti-Catholic letters on 15 and 16 July 1920 which, it was alleged at the time, had provoked the expulsion of Catholic workers. In fact, given the usual lack of prominence accorded letters to the editor, these undeniably inflammatory letters probably reflected rather than fomented a widespread view among the more militant Orange classes. The book itself has to be regarded as part of the propaganda war.

By modern standards all three Unionist papers were extremely serious. They reported incidents at great length, using copious eye-witness accounts, and almost invariably following the official, or Government, line where violence was confirmed. Thus a very detailed account in the *Telegraph*, 13 December 1920, of the sacking of Cork by the Auxiliaries as a reprisal, describes the destruction and the horror of the night of terror, but gives no indication as to who might have been responsible. One day later, the paper gave a full report of the allegations against the Crown forces made at Westminster, highlighting the Government statement that there was no evidence that Crown forces had started the fires.

The Belfast papers would clearly be unreliable as a major or single source for the actual events, particularly the violence, of the period. But so too would the nationalist *Irish News*, or the Dublin papers. The three Unionist papers in Belfast provide a corrective to other newspaper sources and, more valuably, portray the picture of events as they were seen by the Unionist community at the time.

Two other publications, the *Church of Ireland Gazette*, and the *Witness* published by the Presbyterian Church in Belfast, provided weekly reading for a more limited circulation. The *Gazette* concentrated largely on church affairs, with only the occasional editorial comment or letter to the editor dealing specifically with political issues. The *Witness*, on the other hand, was a broadsheet that looked like a newspaper and was very similar in many respects to the *Whig* or the *News-Letter*, and free with its comment on major political matters. The *Witness* ceased publication in 1941, having been managed in its later years by the former *Whig* editor, Sir Robert Lynn.

The only significant dissenting voices from within the broadly Unionist–Protestant community during the period came from the *New Northman* and *Lagan*. The *New Northman* was published quarterly from 1932 to 1941 by the Students' Representative Council of Queen's University, being both preceded and succeeded by the less political *Northman*. *Lagan*, which described itself as a collection or miscellany of Ulster writing, appeared annually for four issues only from 1943. The *New Northman* was essentially directed at the university and presumably had a very restricted circulation. But in the late 1930s it dealt with the more fundamental philosophical questions confronting thinking Protestants and other intellectuals within the Northern state. *Lagan* was a literary magazine which no doubt reached only a tiny intellectual minority. But its pages also contain questionings of the nature of Northern society and the identity of Ulster Unionists and Protestants.

24

2

VIOLENT AND TREMENDOUS CHANGES

> Then came the Great War. Every institution, almost, in the world was strained. Great empires have been overturned. The whole map of Europe has been changed. The position of countries has been violently altered. The modes of thought of men, the whole outlook on affairs, the grouping of parties, all have encountered violent and tremendous changes in the deluge of the world, but as the deluge subsides and the waters fall short we see the dreary steeples of Fermanagh and Tyrone emerging once again. The integrity of their quarrel is one of the few institutions that have been unaltered in the cataclysm which has swept the world.[1]

Winston Churchill's irony captures the enduring stubbornness of the Ulster problem, and also indicates the frustration and exasperation felt by those who had to try to deal with it. But it would be wrong to assume that in 1918 the deluge receded from an Ulster and an Ireland unchanged by the intervening years. For in Ireland too the modes of thought, the whole outlook, even the grouping of parties, had encountered violent change between 1914 and 1918. The nature of the campaign for Irish self-determination had been fundamentally altered, both in goal and in method.

Far from being suspended for the duration of the war, as Prime Minister H.H. Asquith had hoped in 1914, the Irish question evolved rapidly. The Easter Rising in Dublin in April 1916 had reopened it dramatically. It had led to a radical realignment of nationalist forces, and to a resumption of political contacts and negotiations, culminating in the Irish Convention of 1917–18, called by the British Government in an unsuccessful attempt to find an accommodation between the Unionists of Ulster and Irish nationalism.

The First World War, as England's difficulty, provided the opportunity for the Rising in 1916 but it also provided a new background to, and a new context for, the Irish question. British patriotism, pride and belief in the Empire as a force for good in the world reached new heights, not least among the Unionists of

Ireland. The war, the victory, and the sacrifices made in achieving it, framed the culture of the period. That period did not end abruptly in November 1918 – fighting continued in Russia and the Middle East. The Peace Treaty was not signed at Versailles until the middle of 1919. In the course of that year many thousands of Irish soldiers returned from war service. Local authorities, particularly in north-east Ulster, busied themselves with war memorials. Military titles and military uniforms remained long in vogue.

History now portrays the First World War as a far from heroic undertaking. But the public rhetoric of the period, the popular culture too, presented the war as both heroic and moral. The British viewpoint was that the war was between civilisation and decency as embodied in the Empire, on the one hand, and the deadly enemy of those virtues – German or Prussian militarism. As the *Northern Whig* told its readers on 12 November 1918: 'The world has at last been freed from this monstrous incubus of militarism, and in President Wilson's striking phrase, has been made safe for democracy.' Ulster Protestants identified strongly with this victory of right and freedom. However, participation by Irishmen in the war was considerably less than by other regions of the United Kingdom. The *Official Report on Recruiting* notes that only 6 per cent of the male population of Ireland was enlisted, while the figure for England was 24 per cent. The absence of conscription was obviously an important factor, though the report also points out that emigration meant the male population of Ireland tended to be under eighteen or over fifty.[2]

Recruitment among Unionists was almost certainly higher than among other sections. Geographically, Ulster contributed well over half the total – 75,000 out of about 130,000. Of 86,000 recruits enlisted in Ireland between the outbreak of war and January 1916, more than 32,000 came from Belfast and the counties of Antrim and Down. The figures for Belfast and Dublin for the same period were 26,883 and 16,726 respectively.[3] The grouping of the Northern regiments into a small number of divisions, most notably the grouping of the UVF recruits into the 36th Ulster Division, strengthened the identification of the Protestant community in the North with Ulster's participation in the war. It also ensured that a major battle like the Somme had tremendous impact on the same community. On the first day of July 1916 the Ulster Division suffered some 5,000 casualties, including 2,000 dead. The opening day of the Somme was also the original date of the Battle of the Boyne, and there was a quick appropriation of the Somme into the Orange tradition. Church parades marking the Somme anniversary on the first Sunday in July became, and remain, a major event in the Orange marching season and incidents from the Somme featured on Orange banners.

The Somme, and the heavy sacrifices made by Ulstermen at it, came barely two months after the Sinn Féin Easter Rising in Dublin. This was a conjunction that helped cement the Unionist view that their own supreme loyalty had been in contrast to the treachery of nationalist Ireland. This, despite the fact that nationalists too contributed many men and many lives to the British cause. Of the 40,000–50,000 Irishmen who died in the First World War, at least half of them were in all probability from nationalist Ireland rather than Unionist Ulster. But the Rising, the subsequent swing in nationalist opinion to Sinn Féin, and the widespread opposition to conscription obscured that contribution. By 1918 Ulster Unionists saw nationalist Ireland's behaviour only as treachery, in stark contrast to their own heroic contribution. The Somme and the Easter Rising had become the twin symbols of loyalism and treachery. In November 1918 Sir Edward Carson told the Ulster Unionist Council that he was proud of the part Ulster had taken in the war. But he feared the term 'Ireland' had become one almost of reproach among the people of Great Britain and the Empire.[4]

A year later, on 12 November 1919, the *Belfast News-Letter* commented on Armistice Day disturbances in Dublin:

> They [Sinn Féin] have no respect for the brave men who gained the victory of right and freedom, no sense of gratitude to their deliverers and no sense of remorse for the assistance they gave the enemy. They wanted Germany to win, and thus placed themselves in opposition to the opinion of the civilised world.

The idea that Irish nationalists might not fully share the ideals the British Empire stood for was not new. Before the First World War one of the main arguments against self-government for Ireland was that such an arrangement would weaken the Empire at its very heart. In 1912 Andrew Bonar Law, then leader of the opposition in the Commons at Westminster, wrote that the Unionist Party was hostile to Home Rule because in time of war it would be 'a source of weakness that might be fatal to us'.[5] Carson, writing in the same year, saw the same danger:

27

We have to consider not only the speeches of avowed enemies of the Empire, like Major MacBride and the Irish Americans, but we have also to remember the attitude adopted upon all questions of foreign policy by the more reasonable nationalists of the type of Mr Dillon.[6]

The Irish Parliamentary Party, said Carson, had consistently opposed every warlike action British Governments had found to be necessary.

Major John MacBride, later executed as one of the leaders of the 1916 Easter Rising, had fought against the Empire alongside the Boers in South Africa. In 1912 Carson was still able to draw a clear distinction between MacBride, an avowed enemy of the Empire, and more moderate nationalists. Only such as MacBride, he seemed to anticipate, would actually take sides against Britain in a war. This view seemed to be confirmed when John Redmond, the leader of the Irish Parliamentary Party at Westminster, pledged his, and nationalist Ireland's, support at the outset of the war.

The main thrust of constitutional nationalism in Ireland throughout the nineteenth century had been for Home Rule, not total separation. It was not anti-British in so far as it did not regard partnership within the British Isles and the Empire as incompatible with Irish aspirations. In 1913, when Home Rule had passed the House of Commons, and was in theory on the way, John Redmond's brother, Captain William Redmond MP, saw such a partnership stretching ahead 'for all time':

> Thirty years have seen the grievances of Ireland removed one by one, and today sees the representatives of Ireland, in the face of the outstretched hand of friendship from Great Britain, no longer bitter, but ready and willing on the basis of the Home Rule Bill to enter the future on terms of friendship and goodwill for all time with the people of England, Scotland and Wales, and the whole Empire.[7]

Three years later when Home Rule under the precise terms of that Bill looked less certain, John Redmond was to write that the war had united in common cause

> . . . the defence of England against a mighty danger, and the defence of the principles for which Ireland, to be true to herself, must ever be ready to raise her voice or draw her sword.[8]

Ireland's honour, he wrote, and Ireland's interest were both now involved in the same cause. Human freedom, justice, pity and the cry of the small nationality, crushed under the despot's heel, appealed to her. It was for these her sons were fighting, and for these she would stand in the new place of influence she was winning in the world's councils. There, acting with and through her sister democracies, Canada, Australia, New Zealand, South Africa and Great Britain, her spirit would help to bend the British Empire to a mission of new significance and humanity.[9]

That was the official voice of Irish nationalism at the outset of the war, even though there was substantial opposition to it. The Irish nationalism that fought and won the general election of 1918 was radically different. Its heroes had taken up arms against Britain and the Empire in 1916, in collusion with the German enemy; one of its number, Roger Casement, had been executed for conspiracy with the Germans. The 'German plot' of 1918 was taken as further evidence that Sinn Féin was in alliance with the enemy.[10] From a historic nationalist perspective this transformation might seem less dramatic than it did to Ulster Unionists at the time. Separatism, as distinct from Home Rule, had always been the goal of some strands of nationalism, and armed struggle had, at regular intervals, been the method adopted to try to achieve it. Given the blocking of Home Rule and the growing likelihood of partition, it was not very surprising that armed struggle would again be tried. As Dorothy Macardle, the prime chronicler of Irish Republicanism, has it: 'The irresistible force of resurgent nationalism was advancing; the immovable obstacle of British Imperial interest stood in its path.'[11]

But in 1919 Ulster Unionists felt that they were faced with much more than resurgent nationalism. The demand now was for a Republic, which by definition meant severance of Ireland from the United Kingdom and the Empire. On 14 July 1919 the *News-Letter* declared that Irish nationalism was now revealed as a revolutionary separatist movement, inherently hostile to Great Britain and the Empire – citing as evidence the campaign against conscription at the height of the war. This demand for a Republic, involving the dissolution of the United Kingdom, the heart of the Empire, was indeed revolutionary. The methods already adopted to pursue it – rebellion in wartime, agitation against and refusal of conscription, plotting with the enemy – were also both revolutionary and treasonable.

It is clear that from 1918 on Unionists saw Sinn Féin's nationalism as revolutionary on an even grander scale. It had become for them, and so they increasingly sought to present it, not an end in itself, but a means of attacking the Empire. Sinn Féin, the Unionists insisted, were fighting not just to make Ireland free, but to dismember the Empire. A favourite theme that was to become an obsession in the Unionist press was the anti-conscription campaign of 1917 and 1918, not just in Ireland but elsewhere in the Empire. On 22 January 1919 the *Whig*, in a comment on the first Dáil's appeal to the free nations of the world, said the Sinn Féiners had grasped the essential fact of Ireland's strategic position. They wanted to get Ireland into their own hands just because by this fact they would be able to deal Britain a mortal blow.

The idea that Sinn Féin was more concerned with destroying the Empire than with freeing Ireland sounds far-fetched, and no doubt did so to many at the time, particularly in Britain. But it was put forward in the shadow of the First World War with memories fresh of the treachery of Easter 1916 and the contacts between Sinn Féin and the German enemy and of the campaign against conscription. All these were actions harmful to the Empire in its time of greatest difficulty, and possibly mortally so. What made it believable to Ulster Unionists, and to a somewhat wider audience in Britain, was the Catholic dimension. There was a historic Protestant perception of the Catholic Church as hostile to the Empire, dating back to the seventeenth century and the Glorious Revolution. And there was the almost total identification of Catholicism with Irish nationalism. But there was more to it than that, as the *Belfast News-Letter* repeatedly pointed out during 1919, 1920 and 1921.[12] The Catholic Church had also organised opposition to conscription during the war, not only in Ireland, but in Quebec and in Australia.

This Catholic opposition to conscription was portrayed as the Catholic Church working against the British Empire at its hour of greatest need. The Catholic Church was joining forces against good, against liberty, democracy and freedom. At that time, to those familiar with British history, particularly of the seventeenth century, when Britain had championed liberty and popular freedoms against repressive Catholic monarchy and the Counter-Reformation, this was not surprising. In Ulster, where the events of the seventeenth century were remembered more vividly than anywhere else and where the view of the Catholic Church as a threat to personal liberty was already deeply ingrained, the argument fell on fertile ground. On 1 November 1921 the *News-Letter* spelled it out: 'What is going on in Ireland is part of the anti-British campaign inspired, organised and directed by the Roman Church.' Earlier, on 2 August 1919, the same newspaper, commenting on Irish-American propaganda, noted that the most powerful and most implacable force behind this was the Catholic Church:

> The Bishops and priests are more active than ever they have been. They think they have now a great opportunity of striking a blow at the British Empire, and they are using it to the utmost.

Going on to comment on opposition to conscription in Quebec and Australia during the war, it said:

> The British people will be wise if they assume that the Vatican will always be hostile to them, and that efforts to conciliate it are a failure.

In Belfast great significance was read into the fact that the Catholic Church decided in May 1920 to proceed with the beatification of Oliver Plunket, whom Unionists termed an Irish rebel, and who had indeed been hanged for treason in Ireland in the seventeenth century. The fact that the Irish bishops had travelled to Rome for this ceremony and had there visited the graves of the exiled Irish chiefs O'Neill and O'Donnell was taken as symbolic support for present-day Irish rebellion. It was all part of 'the venomous, anti-British agitation which the Roman Church is fomenting and sustaining in all parts of the world', said the *News-Letter* on 29 May 1920. Other evidence, it seems, was to hand to prove that the Vatican was anti-British, not just with regard to Ireland. In August 1919 the British Government made public details of peace proposals put forward by Pope Benedict XV in August 1917. On 14 August 1919 the *News-Letter* commented that these revelations confirmed the opinion already held in all Allied countries that the chief object of the peace proposals had been to bring about a peace favourable to Germany.

Far from being involved in a local difficulty over nationalism and self-determination, the Ulsterman saw himself once more in the vanguard of a much greater and wider struggle. It was the Siege of Derry and the Battle of the Boyne all over again, it was the Great War continued – a view confirmed not just by the fact that British soldiers became involved in fighting Sinn Féin, but even more so by the fact that soldiers returning to civilian life in Ireland from service in the war were targets for harassment and even assassination by Sinn Féin. For good measure the Belfast papers occasionally threw in the modern bogey of Bolshevism to supplement the Romanist menace. This too helped place what was happening in Ireland in a larger context and helped present events in Ireland as a major threat to the Empire.[13]

Such a presentation was extremely important to Unionists in 1919 as they sought to persuade British public opinion to take serious note of what was happening in Ireland. They had need too of arguments to bolster their own standing with British public opinion, for their own heroic view of their behaviour during the war was not universally shared. Their stubborn refusal to reach any accommodation with Home Rule at a time when such a settlement was seen as vital to Britain's war effort had won them few friends. In 1918 no one in Britain rejoiced to see the 'dreary steeples' re-emerging.

The radical transformation in the Irish question that had occurred during the war years was not immediately obvious. But those years had indeed dramatically changed the context within which Unionist resistance to nationalism was formulated and expressed. Before 1914 the Ulster Unionists were the main negative element in Britain's Irish problem. They were the obstacle to a settlement and in 1912 they had become the rebels, taking up arms to oppose both constitutional nationalism and British authority. By 1919 these roles were becoming blurred. The Somme and Ulster's war contribution had drawn personal congratulations in 1918 from George V to his 'loyal Ulster subjects'.[14] That message was to Carson and the Ulster Unionist Council, the very people who had been organising disloyalty in 1912–14. Irish nationalism, on the other hand, was now represented by Sinn Féin, the traitors of 1916, the friends of the Germans and the enemies of the Empire.

That was how the Ulster Unionists saw the situation in 1919 and that was how they hoped others, particularly the British Government and public, would see things too – recognising the Unionists as the supreme Loyalists. The Somme and the sacrifices of war would surely help British opinion see the true nature of the Ulster position, help it realise at last that the 'rebellion' of Ulster in 1912 was in fact an act of ultimate loyalty – defying British authority in order to preserve the integrity of the United Kingdom, and prevent a foolish and critical weakening of the heart of the Empire.

In the more narrowly Irish context, Unionist views had considerably hardened during the war years. As one of the more outspoken members of the new Northern parliament put it in 1921, explaining why Ulster would never accept an all-Ireland parliament:

> It is because we know the antecedents of these men who would control an All-Ireland parliament. If our objections were strong in 1912, they are a thousand-fold stronger today. From 1916 onwards we have seen Sinn Fein in all its ugliness, and much as we disliked the old Nationalist Party and the old Nationalist methods, we dislike Sinn Fein more, and we have no more intention of placing our liberties under a Dublin Parliament than we have of placing them under Ali Baba and his forty thieves.[15]

3
DANGEROUS FOOLS

The general election of December 1918 confirmed the transformation of Irish nationalism. Sinn Féin, having won a handful
of seats in by-elections before the dissolution, came back with 73
out of the 103 Irish seats. Parliamentary nationalists dropped
from 68 to 6, 5 of them returned for Ulster constituencies. The
Unionists won 26 seats, 23 of them in north-east Ulster.[1] This
landslide in seats, rather than votes, was not necessarily a totally
true reflection of opinion in the country, for many seats were
uncontested and there was evidence of widespread intimidation,
but it constituted, nonetheless, a political revolution. Nationalist
Ireland was now represented by a party pledged to the achieve-
ment of an independent Republic and led by de Valera – one of the
commanders of the 1916 rebellion. Moreover, that party would
have at least a two-to-one majority over all others in an all-Ireland
parliament.

Sinn Féin had fought the election, claiming it stood less for a
political party than for 'the old tradition of nationhood'.[2] It
asserted the inalienable right of that nation to self-determination
and sovereign independence, and declared its intention of appealing to the Versailles Peace Conference on these grounds. It had
also declared that it would make use of 'any and every means
available to render impotent the power of England to hold Ireland
in subjection by military force or otherwise'.[3] The manifesto
stated Sinn Féin's intention of setting up a constituent assembly in
Dublin, on the basis of the election returns, as the supreme national
authority. On 21 January 1919 the assembly of the first Dáil in the
Mansion House in Dublin, and the ambushing and killing of two
Royal Irish Constabulary constables at Soloheadbeg in Tipperary,
marked the beginning of the implementation of the manifesto. The
first event attracted much more attention than the second.

The Northern papers gave extensive coverage to the meeting in
the Mansion House, coverage which indicated not just Unionist
interest, but considerable anxiety. It reflected too what was to be

34

one of the main weapons used by Unionists in their attack upon Sinn Féin and the Dáil – that of ridicule. 'A ridiculous fanfaronade, a miserable simulacrum of a parliament, a combination of the grotesque and the dangerous', was how the Belfast Presbyterian weekly, the *Witness,* saw it on 22 January 1919. The only qualities its members had were 'a little knowledge of poetry, a little love of dark Rosaleen and a little knowledge of the Irish language'. On the same day the *Belfast News-Letter* reported that the Sinn Féiners met in Dublin 'and went through the farce of establishing a Republic'. The members had added to the absurdity of the proceedings by conducting them in the Irish language. And the *Northern Whig* described two documents issued by the Dáil – the draft constitution and the appeal to the free nations of the world – as 'long-winded declarations characterised principally by their childish obliviousness of facts and their excessive vagueness'.

But behind the ridicule lay a realisation that the events in Dublin had serious implications for the future of Ireland. The *Whig* went on to comment that the pronouncements of the Dáil, however vague, were in effect a declaration of war. It was easy, the *Whig* said, to see the elements of ludicrousness in these various documents, but it would be a mistake to treat Sinn Féin as a bad joke on the strength of them. The *Witness* had no doubt that many of the Sinn Féiners were fools but, it continued, 'they are dangerous fools, and cunning and resourceful at that. We await with interest, not unmingled with anxiety, as to new events.'

These early press reactions to the first Dáil illustrate two essential elements in the Northern response to the whole Sinn Féin movement. On the one hand the pretensions to nationhood, to forming a national parliament and an independent government, were not to be taken seriously. The charade of playing them out appeared foolish to Unionists and certainly had to be presented as such to British opinion in the wake of a war fought, in part at least according to the rhetoric of the day, to secure the rights of small nations. But at the time it was an already established part of the Unionist case that Irish nationalism, as practised by Sinn Féin, was extremely dangerous. It was a real threat to the Empire and to the United Kingdom itself and had to be taken very seriously indeed.

The claim to national self-determination in the atmosphere of 1919 was potentially a most powerful one. The initial Unionist response, inherited from earlier all-Ireland Unionist opposition to Home Rule, was that no Irish nation existed. As late as 28 February 1920, the *News-Letter* was bluntly declaring:

We deny the claim of nationality; Ireland never was a nation. . . We object to partition because we object to being divorced from full representation in the Imperial Parliament, not just for ourselves alone, but for our country.

But for some time this denial of Irish nationhood had been living alongside a two-nations approach. On 19 September 1919, the *News-Letter* quoted with approval from an article published in Britain:

Ireland is inhabited by two distinct nations, or at least nationalities. . . The larger is composed of Celts, whether by race or assimilation. . . the others of Saxon descent. The ethnic character of the two races is as violently opposed as is well nigh conceivable. They are not less widely separated in their religion. . . No attempt to deal with the Irish problem can succeed which does not start by recognising this fundamental fact.

In March 1920 the Ulster Unionist Council agreed not to oppose the new Government of Ireland Bill embodying partition and two Home Rule parliaments in Ireland. Thereafter, Unionists were more anxious to stress the distinctiveness of the two Irish entities and their peoples than they were to disprove the existence of an Irish nation. Self-determination had become as dear to the heart of Belfast as it was to that of Dublin. The historian James Winder Good, no admirer of Ulster Unionism, had already seen the likelihood of this in 1920. The emergence of the idea of self-determination, he wrote, actually strengthened the Ulster case, though nationalists of all shades of opinion had closed their eyes to this.[4] In July 1921, when Craig and de Valera met in London following the Truce, Craig responded to de Valera's statement that his only demand was for self-determination for the Irish nation by saying that that was all he himself wanted for the six counties.[5] That same month, on 4 July, the *News-Letter* quoted with approval a comment on the new Belfast parliament:

It is the whole case of the people and the Parliament of the Six County area that there are two Irelands – the Protestant, Loyalist and Saxon-blooded and Saxon-minded Ireland, and the Roman Catholic, Nationalist and Celtic Ireland.

But by that date the two Irelands were divided not just by race, nationality or religion, but by a mounting wall of violence. The *Whig* had clearly considered the statements of Dáil Éireann on 21 January 1919 'a declaration of war' in the context of war by Irish nationalism against British authority. The shooting at Solo-headbeg on that same day is now looked back upon as the first act in the Anglo-Irish War but few attached such significance to it at the time. Rather, it was regarded as yet another 'outrage', and given scant space in the Northern press. Tipperary was a long way from Belfast and the victims were local men. The connection between armed action in Tipperary and parliamentary secession in Dublin was not made. Two months later, in March 1919, a Sinn Féin raid on Collinstown air base near Dublin made more impression. No one was killed but the taking of arms and ammunition prompted the *News-Letter* on 21 March 1919 to comment that 'ruthless warfare was planned.'

By the end of March 1919 it was clear that widespread violent action was taking place over a large area of the country. The perception of it, certainly from Belfast, was not of a war of independence in support of the Dáil, but as the *News-Letter* described it on 1 April, as a campaign of murder and terrorism to intimidate the people into supporting Sinn Féin. The war was not seen as Sinn Féin and the Dáil against British rule but as armed gangs of Sinn Féin taking action against anyone who did not support the movement. Attention was captured, less by the progress of the general Sinn Féin campaign than by individual incidents. It was one such incident at the end of March 1919 that awakened Northern interest and prompted the first realisation of what was happening in the rest of the country. On 29 March J.C. Milling, a Resident Magistrate in Westport, Co. Mayo, was sitting in his drawing room with his wife in their house in the town. At 11 p.m. he got up to go into the dining room to adjust the clock there to British Summer Time, taking with him a lamp to light the way. A shot, fired through the window, hit him and he later died.[6]

As a Resident Magistrate, Milling was even more a symbol of lawful authority than an RIC constable. Moreover he had been shot and killed, not while in uniform on escort duty, but in his own home in the presence of his wife. Coincidence again was important, for while Westport is a long way from Belfast and though Milling had grown up there, he was well known in Ulster. He had been an RIC officer until his appointment as a magistrate, serving as District Inspector in Belfast. He had also served in Ballymena, Co. Antrim, and in Co. Fermanagh. He was a member of the Protestant sect, the Plymouth Brethren. His murder brought the violence much closer to Belfast and to the Protestant readers of the *News-Letter*. On 1 April it reported the Milling murder and also, under the heading 'Murder and Terrorism', commented on Sinn Féin activities in the rest of the country:

> In many parts of the South and West the methods of intimidation which they [Sinn Féin] are adopting are proving successful, and multitudes of people who have little sympathy with them are joining them because they believe they are stronger than the Government.

This threat of intimidation, of violence against those who did not support Sinn Féin, became a Northern preoccupation. On 21 May the *News-Letter* declared that lawlessness and terrorism prevailed over a large part of the south and west, where Sinn Féin was trying to make impossible the administration of the law:

> There are districts in which it is no exaggeration to say that the lives of loyal subjects of the King are unsafe, while the right to differ publicly from the Sinn Feiners is denied by them, and its exercise treated as an offence.

In June the General Assembly of the Presbyterian Church passed a resolution viewing with 'profound apprehension the violent outburst of disloyalty, sedition and murder which has characterised the operation of the Sinn Feiners' and recorded its conviction that the putting into operation of Home Rule would be an open and gross betrayal of the loyal and peace-abiding community in Ireland.[7] In mid-1919 that community was largely, though not exclusively, Protestant. The dilemma for that community in the south and west had already been spelled out in stark terms by the Tipperary Brigade of the IRA after the proclamation of the county as a military area after Soloheadbeg. An IRA counter-proclamation said that every person found within the South Riding of Tipperary after a certain date, who was an upholder of the foreign Government, would be held to have forfeited his life.[8] This threat had few or no immediate results. In mid-August the Chief Secretary, giving details of outrages in Ireland, reported only seven people killed since the beginning of the year – all of them policemen apart from Milling.

But perhaps a more significant figure was that forty-six dwellings had been attacked in the same period. Most of these involved raids for arms, and as the 'big houses' likely to have arms were largely Protestant-owned, the perceived pattern of the war as one against Loyalists and Protestants, who were Irish, rather than against English power, was emphasised.[9] Some of the raids for arms had been in Ulster. Ballyedmond Castle, near Rostrevor in Co. Down, had been raided in May. An impressive force of 100 men was reported to have carried out the raid. The house had been the home of Major O.S.W. Nugent, the UVF leader who had died in 1914, and had some significance for many Ulstermen. Drumkilly House in Armagh was also raided in early August.

On 7 September 1919, the IRA carried the war directly to the British military. But once again, by coincidence or not, the incident had special meaning for the Ulster Protestants. On that day a squad of British soldiers on church parade to Fermoy Methodist Church in Co. Cork was fired on. One soldier was shot dead, and three wounded. The event was given splash treatment in the Belfast papers. On 9 September the *News-Letter* reported how the fifteen soldiers had been forming up outside the church when a number of men rushed at them from a car, shooting with revolvers, while another party attacked from the rear. Horror was added by the report that a corporal who went seeking a doctor in the town, twice had doors shut in his face.

There was genuine shock in the North that an attack should be carried out at a church door as worship was about to begin. The Methodist community in Ireland, and Protestants generally, also felt it was an attack upon them. The Vice-President of the Methodist Church sent a telegram to the minister in Fermoy expressing the horror and indignation of the church at 'the cowardly and murderous assault made on the soldiers who were quietly proceeding to divine worship'.[10] The secretary of the Methodist Conference sent a succinct telegram: 'Greatly shocked at yesterday's dastardly outrage on Methodist soldiers.'[11] Although there was as yet no general condemnation in the North of the IRA campaign as a sectarian one against Protestants, incidents such as that in Fermoy helped make such an interpretation inevitable.

On the political front the constant criticism of the Catholic

Church for supporting Sinn Féin and for, in the Unionist view, failing to condemn the violence, continued and intensified. On 26 June the *News-Letter* stated bluntly that the Catholic bishops supported the rebels. (This was in the wake of the shooting of a District Inspector in Thurles.) It did, however, report on 12 August the Bishop of Galway denouncing the murders as grievous sins and saying no amount of Government provocation could justify such deeds. But on 3 November it returned to what it called the 'silence of the priests over assassination', and claimed that a recent meeting of the Catholic hierarchy in Maynooth had not condemned the killings.

In October 1919 the Belfast newspapers had reported an incident in starkly sectarian terms for the first time. A house near Skibbereen, Co. Cork, had been bombed, allegedly because the owner was friendly with a Protestant who had opposed the campaign against conscription in 1918. The friend's crime, perhaps, was not that he was Protestant, but that he had refused to subscribe to funds for the fight against conscription. But on 10 October 1919 the *News-Letter*'s treatment of the story, with the heading 'Farmer's House Burned Because He Was Friendly With A Protestant', is an indication of how the sectarian element, incidental or not to the actual event, assumed paramount importance in the North.

There was the widespread belief among northern Protestants that the whole Sinn Féin rebellion and the demand for independence was being backed by the Catholic Church for its own ends, if not indeed invented and originated by that church. On 20 November 1919 the *News-Letter* laid the blame for the violence squarely at the feet of the church:

> It is the bigotry of this Church and its constant efforts, open and secret, to increase its power, which have brought a large part of Ireland to the state of lawlessness which is disgracing it today.

As the Sinn Féin rebellion progressed into 1920, the authority of the Dáil and of the IRA extended across ever larger areas of the south and west of the country. On 1 May the *Irish Times* reported that the Government was fighting a losing battle, and the forces of the Crown were being driven back on Dublin. The King's Government had virtually ceased to exist south of the Boyne and west of the Shannon. In these circumstances the Unionists or Protestants, scattered across those areas, found themselves in a parlous position. It was this aspect of the situation that caught the attention of the Belfast newspapers. On 4 March 1920 the *News-Letter* commented that it was difficult in the North to realise the conditions in which many loyal and law-abiding citizens in the south and west had to live. In May 1920 Carson launched a Defence Fund for Southern Unionists. This was not a political fund to fight Home Rule, he said, but rather to make known the plight of Loyalists threatened by the revolutionary movement in the south and west, and to give assistance in all cases of oppression.[12] On 10 May 1920 the *News-Letter* spoke of the spread of cattle-driving and the wholesale publication of threatening notices to herdsmen and employees of Unionist farmers.

When the General Synod of the Church of Ireland met in Dublin in May, the Archbishop of Dublin Dr Charles Frederick D'Arcy, declared that they could not fail to realise that they were threatened with complete anarchy.[13] There were two great burdens on the church: one was the state of the country, the other the depressed level of clerical stipends. In the event the synod debated long the matter of stipends but spent little or no time on the state of the country.

About this time 'incendiarism' became a major feature of the IRA campaign. The Northern papers carried reports of two such incidents so labelled in June 1920: the burning of Oakgrove House in Cork, and the home of Captain Smith in Co. Meath.[14] In June the General Assembly of the Presbyterian Church, meeting in Belfast, passed a resolution of sympathy 'with all loyal citizens who reside in those parts of Ireland where they are exposed to terror and outrage'.[15] Like their Church of Ireland brethren, however, the Presbyterians in mid-1920 spent more time on ministers' salaries than on the state of the country, although there was debate on the plight of the Protestants in the south and west. The Moderator, the Revd H.P. Glenn of Bray, Co. Wicklow, said the fair name of Ireland, once the 'Island of Saints', was now the synonym for 'cowardly assassination, cruelty to the dumb beast, and such disregard to all the rights of private property as to make them the scorn of all civilised nations'.[16]

The assembly was concerned with the 'Partition Bill', or the Bill for the Better Government of Ireland, which was then going through

Westminster and proposing separate parliaments for North and South. The Revd J.B. Armour, the veteran Presbyterian Home Ruler, argued strongly against the Bill. The six-county Northern parliament would mean that they and other Protestant churches had sacrificed the Protestants of the other parts of Ireland, handed them over to the lions in order to save themselves. Armour himself had been overtaken by history. He was a Home Ruler, not a separatist. At that assembly in 1920 he declared: 'In my opinion an Irish Republic is an impossibility, and can never come into existence.'[17]

In reply, the Revd William Corkey said the loyal men of the south and west were already being devoured by the lions. Scores had been murdered in the past few months. He went on to say that it was not all David Lloyd George's fault and that the hierarchy had to share the blame. He quoted an example of what children were being taught in Catholic schools on the presence of 'the British, or Protestants' in Ireland:

> Pause not till each dun and tower, planted by the stranger's hand,
> Blazes like a Viking's beacon, guiding them out of the land,
> Till the last of the pirates to their galleys shall have fled,
> Shuddering at the dire destruction, as the trump that wakes the dead.[18]

The Home Mission Report, presented to that same assembly in 1920, said there were few districts anywhere in Ireland where the Presbyterian population was declining. The situation was a great trial to members, but the Home Mission had not heard of any counsels of surrender or flight. Men who, by property and occupation, had a stake in the country, the report stated, did not easily uproot themselves. The disposition was to endure and stay. But there were places, it continued, from which there had been withdrawals; it was not easy to say how much of what had taken place had its explanation in the civil commotion.[19] While not reporting any significant withdrawal of Presbyterians from the south and west, the report's authors clearly had no doubt that pressure was being put on Protestants to get out. The Revd Corkey's speech put that very plainly. His reference to Lloyd George is also significant as it indicates that there was a readiness to blame London for the plight of the Southern Loyalists.

By mid-1920 the Northern Unionist view of what was happening in the rest of the country was that it was descending into anarchy. Protestants were at risk, and some had already been subjected to violence. There was widespread use of terror to divert allegiance from legitimate authority. This, rather than an account of a self-declared parliament and government asserting its authority in remarkable and largely unprecedented circumstances, was the picture presented by the Northern newspapers, and perceived by politicians and public.

It was not the whole picture and certainly conflicted with accounts given elsewhere. For instance, a correspondent of the London *Daily News*, writing on 5 July 1920, saw things quite differently:

> Sinn Fein has accomplished an amazing work in producing law and order in those parts of Ireland in which it is in power. Sinn Fein law has a sanction behind it such as no other law in Ireland has had for generations. One hears that it has put the fear of God into the criminal classes. The courts are stern to those who slight them. . . Ireland is taking pleasure in law and order for the first time within the memory of man. It is because of this enthusiasm for law and order perhaps that it is able to remain unexpectedly calm. . . That is the one great hope in the situation. Even Unionists are astonished and pleased by it.

But even if the Northern view in mid-1920 was an incomplete one, it was not without foundation and it was to be confirmed rather than modified over the following twelve months. But also by mid-1920 the Unionists of the north-east had come into confrontation with Sinn Féin in their own area. On 24 February 1920 the *News-Letter* reported that the 'operations of the Sinn Feiners' were extended to the north of Ireland when the centre of the 'loyal County of Down' was the scene of an outrage – in this instance an attack on the police barracks in Ballynahinch. In May 200 Sinn Féiners were reported besieging the barracks at Newtownhamilton and the *News-Letter* on 10 and 14 May was talking of a Sinn Féin campaign in the North as barracks were attacked and shots fired in Downpatrick and Belfast.

The first really serious trouble in the North began in Derry in April. The capture of the city council by a nationalist majority in the January elections had led to heightened tension in the city. The majority in the corporation now refused to fly the Union Jack or attend Government functions. In the same month IRA prisoners were brought to the city's jail in Bishop Street and that became the focal point for sectarian disorder among crowds of demonstrators. The IRA went into action and attacked the police barracks in the Bogside. Desmond Murphy, in a detailed history of the Derry area, records that the IRA took the initiative and caught the Protestant working class unprepared to fight back.[20] Serious violence continued in Derry in May, when the first deaths occurred, and into June. On 20 June five people were killed in the city. Murphy estimates that this local civil war claimed forty lives in little over a month. However the blame is apportioned for events in Derry from April to June, it is clear, and was clear then, that the IRA was organised and active in the city. Also in April and May IRA units attacked tax offices and police barracks in about ten Northern towns.[21]

As the July Orange marching season approached, Unionist anger against Sinn Féin was mounting. So was the identification, in the Unionist mind, of the Catholic population with Sinn Féin. The local elections and the combination of Sinn Féin members with other nationalists to control local authorities and, in many cases, to declare allegiance to Dáil Éireann were taken as evidence of this. Statements by the Catholic hierarchy were assumed to confirm Catholic identification with Sinn Féin. In particular, a statement in January 1920 by the Catholic bishops which blamed the confusion and disorder in Ireland on 'the principle of disregarding national feeling and national rights, and carrying everything with the high hand over the heads of the people' was taken in the North as open church-backing for Sinn Féin. On 29 January 1920 the *News-Letter* commented at the time that 'the Roman Catholic Bishops have issued a manifesto which will encourage the rebels and it must be assumed that that is what they intended'.

In its editorial comment on the Twelfth celebration, the *News-Letter*, on 13 July 1920, returned to the attack on the Catholic Church. Sinn Féin was her tool: 'The Hierarchy had stirred up and led the campaign against the partition agreement in 1916. Why? Because that would have safeguarded the Protestantism of Ulster against the domination of the Hierarchy.' At the Twelfth Field at Finaghy, near Belfast, Carson had delivered a speech of 1912 vintage, threatening, in effect, to reorganise the UVF. His message was to the Government in London, that if they could not protect

Ulster from the machinations of Sinn Féin, then Ulstermen would take the matter into their own hands and defend themselves.[22] The speech may well have constituted incitement but its content and its vehemence also indicate the extent to which his listeners felt threatened by Sinn Féin.

That same week letters appeared in the *News-Letter* that linked the Sinn Féin threat to the person of the ordinary Catholic in Ulster. One, on 16 July, spoke of the 'insidious system of peaceful penetration of Ulster by Catholics', of a new plantation, and of the well-intentioned but foolish policy of employing Catholics. Another talked of Sinn Féiners pouring into Ulster, getting situations in offices and shipyards. This bogey of peaceful penetration had arisen towards the end of the war, when it was alleged that Catholics from the South were moving into the North to take the jobs of those who had volunteered for the war service. It was particularly explosive in the contexts of employment and of local elections; with the onset of the postwar recession, unemployment was already soaring in Belfast. Nationalist victories in the local elections, particularly in Counties Tyrone and Fermanagh, were ascribed by Unionists to the effect of 'peaceful penetration' during the war years.

The letters to the *News-Letter* were probably as much a reflection of how working-class Unionists were thinking, as they were an incitement to action. However, the specific mention of the shipyards was ominous. But the actual spark that lit the fires in Belfast in July 1920 was struck in Cork. On 17 July Colonel G.F.S. Smyth, Divisional Commander of Police for Munster, was shot dead by the IRA at the County Club in Cork. Colonel Smyth had a distinguished war record, but more relevant in this context, he was from Banbridge, Co. Down. His murder, so soon after the Twelfth, caused intense anger in the North, heightened by problems in bringing his body North for burial in his home town. The driver and fireman refused to work the engine on the train from Cork.[23]

Anger over the Smyth affair helped ignite the already considerable anti-Sinn Féin and anti-Catholic feelings, particularly among the Protestant working class in Belfast and other Northern towns. On the day of his funeral, 21 July, Catholic workers were expelled from the shipyards in Belfast and serious sectarian rioting and sniping began. In three days, eighteen people were killed;

trouble spread also to Banbridge, Dromore, Bangor, Lisburn, Newtownards and Ballymena, with attacks on Catholic business premises and homes.

In Belfast the rioting was far from one-sided: IRA snipers were in action and both Catholic and Protestant areas suffered. But the expulsion of Catholics from their places of work was on a large scale. The Catholic Protection Committee set up by Dr Joseph MacRory, Bishop of Down and Connor, claimed a total of 11,000 Catholics were put out.[24] Official figures for the two shipyards were a total of 2,250 expelled.[25] Whatever the exact figure, the expulsions constituted a major, deliberate, concerted attack on the Catholic community as such, and became a keystone in nationalist attitudes towards the Unionist community.

A similar event was to happen a month later. On 22 August District Inspector Oswald Swanzy of the RIC was murdered in the centre of Lisburn. He was shot on a street corner at lunch time on a Sunday, just across from the cathedral as service was ending. He himself was on his way home to his mother's house from another Church of Ireland service in the town. Swanzy had been in Cork at the time of the killing of Tomás MacCurtain in March 1920, and had been charged by a coroner's jury with the wilful murder of the Lord Mayor. Shortly afterwards he was transferred to Lisburn. On the Sunday afternoon following his murder devastating reprisals were taken against Lisburn's small Catholic minority. Only one person died, but all shops, public and private houses occupied by people supposed to be connected with Sinn Féin activities or sympathies were systematically attacked, and many Catholics fled the town.[26]

Northern Catholics found themselves in a similar position to Protestants in the south and west. Because they were Catholic they were assumed to be, and in many cases were, sympathetic to the general aims of Sinn Féin. Backing Sinn Féin was taken to mean backing the actions of the Sinn Féin army, and helping financially or practically. As the actions of Sinn Féin included the murders of Smyth and Swanzy – and similar actions that preceded these – Ulster Protestant anger was readily directed against any Catholic, and particularly against those who gave any indication of overt Sinn Féin attachment. Just as elsewhere in Ireland any Protestant was seen as a potential informer and traitor because it was assumed, usually correctly, that his sympathies lay with the British administration and the forces of the Crown.

The sectarian violence of mid-1920 had one other immediate result – the imposition of the economic boycott of Belfast and other Northern towns. Officially instigated by Dáil Éireann in August 1920, the Belfast Boycott, as it was generally called, was not formally ended until early 1922 and continued unofficially beyond that.[27] Dáil Éireann's move, in August 1920, was specifically a counter-measure to the expulsion of Catholic workers from employment in Belfast and other Northern towns in July and August. It was adopted in response to a petition from Belfast members of the Dáil, led by Seán MacEntee. On 6 August MacEntee and others drew the Dáil's attention to what they called a 'war of extermination' against Catholics in Belfast and urged the Dáil to fight this by means of a commercial boycott, making special mention of the banks with headquarters in Belfast.[28] Five days later the Dáil ministry agreed on a boycott of banks and insurance companies with headquarters in Belfast. This was to be implemented through the General Council of County Councils, already under Sinn Féin control, and through Sinn Féin itself. Almost immediately the boycott was extended to include goods manufactured or distributed from Belfast.[29] The reason given was the alleged imposition of religious tests on workmen in Belfast and the forcible expulsion from work of those who refused to submit to them. The boycotted area was defined to include also Lisburn, Newtownards, Banbridge and Dromore.

A Belfast committee was set up to help make the boycott effective, and financial support for it was voted by the Dáil. In September the Dáil appointed a member, Michael Staines, to have overall organisation of the boycott.[30] The following year this had developed into a Department of the Boycott with a minister in charge, Joseph MacDonagh, and substantial funds voted to support it.[31]

In the many parts of the country where Sinn Féin authority could be enforced, firms breaking the boycott were warned and then fined. But there was also a great deal of direct enforcement of the boycott through the interception and destruction of goods from or to Belfast. The Northern papers for a period of two years carried regular reports of raids on trains from Belfast, with bread, newspapers and other items taken and burned, and whiskey stolen.[32] The IRA was the agent of enforcement. A résumé of the boycott among the Dáil papers, dated 20 January 1921, speaks of a vigorous effort by Belfast merchants to circumvent the boycott and adds: 'We have warned our committees to be specially alert just now, instructions have also been issued from GHQ to the officers of the Republican Army. . . to counter this push.'[33]

If the course of 1920 saw violence and conflict engulf the North, it also saw the constitutional path ahead for Northern Unionists becoming much clearer. In February 1920 Lloyd George presented his new Government of Ireland Bill at Westminster. In March the Ulster Unionist Council effectively decided not to oppose it – it was ready to settle for two Home Rule parliaments in Ireland. The Bill was flatly rejected by Sinn Féin whose efforts from then on were directed at defeating the 'Partition Bill', as it was known, and preventing the North from having its own parliament. Local elections in January and June of 1920 gave Sinn Féin, and nationalists in general, a chance to express political opposition to London's new proposals. In January Derry city was won by a combination of Nationalists and Sinn Féin. In June Fermanagh and Tyrone county councils were in nationalist hands, and twenty-three other urban and rural councils also were under nationalist control. A number of these, but not all, declared their allegiance to Dáil Éireann. In any event, the fact that nationalists controlled the local government of the second city of the area, plus two of the six counties, was a serious argument against the Unionists' right to the Home Rule parliament promised in the new Bill.

Sinn Féin's determination to resist any partition settlement had been enunciated by de Valera at the Sinn Féin convention in Dublin in April 1919. Any minority difficulties, he said, they could settle, because they had the will to settle them and would soon have the way if the English army of occupation was removed. This was taken in the North as a clear threat of force. But despite Sinn Féin's rejection and the continuing violence throughout 1920, the Government of Ireland Act became law in December 1920 and partition, with a devolved parliament and administration in Belfast, became an immediate prospect.

This political activity did nothing to lessen the violence. In November Michael Collins directed the Bloody Sunday operation in Dublin against British intelligence officers, in the course of which twenty-four people died. Cork was sacked and a pattern of reprisal and counter-reprisal developed, within which sectarian violence in Belfast against Catholics was linked to the boycott and to IRA actions elsewhere in the island.

The widespread depiction in the South of the events of the summer of 1920 in Belfast as a pogrom against Catholics did nothing to ease the position of Southern Protestants, already caught between loyalty to the existing legal Government, and the claims and real powers of Sinn Féin and the IRA. From early in the new year of 1921 the plight of Southern Protestants became an important feature of Northern reporting of the Sinn Féin rebellion. Under the heading 'War on Protestants' the *News-Letter* reported, on 26 January 1921, that Thomas Bradfield, a Protestant farmer, had been shot dead near Bandon the previous Sunday. A note pinned to his body said he had been shot after a court martial which found he 'intended' to inform the enemy of the presence and movement of 'Republican troops'. The report added that more than one recent account of murders and other outrages in the South had suggested that Protestants had been the victims of rebel vengeance.

The following day, the paper's Cork correspondent wrote about the difficult position of Loyalists in the martial-law area if they obeyed General E.P. Strickland's proclamation of 3 January, which ordered all citizens to refuse aid, comfort, food and shelter to the IRA volunteers, and to report to the authorities any person suspected of being in possession of arms. Anyone failing to obey was liable to court martial and the proclamation declared that an attitude of neutrality was inconsistent with loyalty and would render a person liable under the order.

A week later two more Protestants were murdered: a JP was shot dead at his home at Dunlavin in Co. Wicklow, and another man died at Maryborough in Queen's County (now Co. Laois). On 3 February the *News-Letter* combined these with the death of Bradfield under the headings 'Three More Murders', 'Protestants Killed', 'Cork Farmer's Awful Fate'. On 11 February, under the heading 'The Cork Horror', the *News-Letter* reported the death of Alfred B. Reilly JP, murdered at Douglas, near Cork, on 9 February by Sinn Féiners:

The crime has created consternation among Southern Protestants, for Mr Reilly was a leading member of the Methodist Church in Ireland, and while taking no part in politics, was prominent in the municipal and commercial life of Cork.

Three similar murders were reported on 15 and 16 February, and on 18 February came news of an outrage that was to have a deep impact on Protestant opinion. Mrs J. W. Lindsay, an elderly Protestant woman, was kidnapped along with her chauffeur while driving near her home in Coachford in Co. Cork. The tragic saga of Mrs Lindsay was not fully revealed for another five months, and in that period a considerable number of Protestants not connected with the armed forces died in the south and west, particularly in Co. Cork.

The 'War on Protestants' heading on the report of the Bradfield killing on 26 January, in the *News-Letter*, had been the first real indication to Northern readers that Protestants in the South, that is civilian resident Protestants, were not just at risk or being harassed, but were actually being killed. The list of *News-Letter* reports after Mrs Lindsay's kidnapping in mid-February is an indication of the picture such readers were receiving of events in the South:

21 February: 'Awful Fate of Two Protestant Farmers in Co. Cork': William Connel and Matthew Sweetman murdered at Skibbereen.

28 February: 'Protestant Murdered': Alfred Cotter, baker, shot at Bandon.

15 March: 'War on Protestants': Leemount House, the home of the kidnapped Mrs Lindsay, burned down.

30 March: Forty armed men attack farm of William Flemming, a Protestant, in Co. Monaghan. House burned and father and son taken out on road and shot, son dead. TCD student William Good, a former army captain, shot dead at Ballycotton, Co. Cork. His father, John Good, shot dead earlier in the month.

31 March: William Flemming dies. His mother, eighty-six, dies of shock in the workhouse (later reported alive).

1 April: Spaight family mansion mansion burned at Union Hall, Cork, William Latimer, Protestant, murdered at his farm at Mohill, Co. Leitrim.

13 April: George Johnston, Protestant farmer of Bayling, Athlone, taken from his home by thirty-seven armed men, shot as a spy.

15 April: Sir Arthur Vicars, former Ulster King of Arms, murdered at his home at Listowel, Co. Kerry. Taken out in his dressing gown by thirty armed men and shot. House destroyed. Note left 'Traitors beware, we never forget, the IRA.' Protestant postman, Hugh Duffy, shot, on 1 April, near Rockcorry, Co. Cavan.

22 April: 'War on Protestants': house of Harry Mills, Protestant, burned at Ennis, Co. Clare.

23 April: John Harrison, Protestant farmer of Ballinamore, Co. Leitrim, shot.

25 April: 'Sinn Fein Huns': desecration of parish church at Meenglass, Co. Donegal. Doors broken open, provisions taken.

30 April: Twenty-four cows and thirty-two young cattle taken from home of Elizabeth Good at Timoleague, Co. Cork (widow of Protestant shot earlier).

In May Lloyd George was asked in the House of Commons about attacks on Protestants. He replied:

I am aware that there have been a number of murders of Protestant farmers in the South of Ireland. The circumstances of these crimes are still under investigation.

Lieutenant Colonel Henry Croft asked if, in the last three months, murders of these farmers, in no way connected with the Crown forces, numbered something like forty. Lloyd George replied, 'Yes, there have been a considerable number of them.'[34]

On 13 June the *News-Letter* reported the particularly shocking killing of Dean John Finlay, at Bawnboy in Co. Cavan. The eighty-year-old Church of Ireland clergyman was dragged from his home and the house burned. He was battered to death. On 16 June a Protestant farmer in Tipperary was found dead, and a note left saying 'spy'. On 21 June the Earl of Bandon was kidnapped. On 12 July the *News-Letter* had a headline 'Appalling Orgy of Murder in Southern Ireland: Prominent Loyalist's Fate'. Major G.B. O'Connor JP of Rochestown, Co. Cork, had been shot. He was over seventy years of age.

The Truce of 11 July 1921 between the Crown forces and the IRA brought respite. Mrs Lindsay's fate became known. The Northern papers reported that her sister had received a letter from Dáil Éireann's Department of Defence, informing her that Mrs Lindsay had been shot some months ago as a spy. It came out that

Mrs Lindsay, on setting out for a drive, had seen an ambush in preparation and had warned the police. As a result, several IRA men were arrested and convicted and sentenced to death.[35] Dorothy Macardle says Mrs Lindsay was held as a convicted informer, as hostage for the lives of the condemned men and was shot when they were executed.[36] On 3 August the *News-Letter* reacted with horror to the story of an elderly woman being held in terror and eventually shot. It quoted Dr Miller, Bishop of Cashel, as saying that the murder was worse than the tragedy of Nurse Cavell, shot by the Germans in Belgium during the First World War. The chauffeur had also been shot and the *News-Letter* noted that the Dáil statement made no reference to any charge against him. He was shot, the paper declared, because he was a Protestant.

Several factors added to Northern outrage over Mrs Lindsay. One was that news of her fate came in a public announcement by the man who accepted responsibility for her death – Cathal Brugha, the Dáil's Minister of Defence. Not only because of the Truce was no action taken against him but the British Government was now in active negotiation with the Dáil leaders. On 4 August London's *Morning Post* asked:

Who in their hearts dare blame the people of Ulster [for rejecting new proposals for a settlement] for being more fastidious than His Majesty's Ministers and refusing to shake bloody, black-hearted murder by the hand?

What sense of unity can self-respecting Ulstermen feel with the savages who did Mrs Lindsay to death, as they had previously done to death Dean Finlay?

The catalogue of murders of Southern Protestants presented in the Belfast papers in the first half of 1921 dominated coverage of the Sinn Féin campaign as it affected the rest of the country. It came, no doubt, as confirmation of what Unionists already believed – that Sinn Féin's strength was based on terror and intimidation and that it was anti-Unionist and anti-Protestant. While there was certainly under-reporting of the positive side of the rebellion, of the extension of Sinn Féin authority, the operation of its courts and so on, the reporting of violence was not exaggerated. Both the *Whig* and the *News-Letter* referred occasionally to a 'reign of terror' in the south and west, but many incidents went unreported. By 1926 the Compensation (Ireland) Commission had made awards of £7 million to those who had suffered damage to property in the period from January 1919 to July 1921.[37]

Alleged excesses and reprisals by the Crown forces in the South were major news items in the Dublin papers. In Belfast the incidents that gave rise to these claims were often reported in detail, but the allegations themselves were recorded only when made in official forums such as parliament or a coroner's court. In reporting such incidents the Unionist papers, as in the sacking of Cork, carefully followed any official indications. Thus on 22 November 1920 the *Belfast Telegraph*'s report of Bloody Sunday and the reprisals at Croke Park, said the police believed the assassins had come to Dublin using the Croke Park match as cover, and had therefore planned a raid on the match. The report said armed pickets placed around the ground had opened fire first and that police had then exchanged shots with armed spectators.

When the Lord Mayor of Cork, Tomás MacCurtain, was shot in March 1920, the *News-Letter*, on 22 March, stated that it was not the work of the police or army, but of Sinn Féiners. Two months later, even after a Cork jury had found against the Government, the RIC and District Inspector Swanzy, the *News-Letter*, on 10 May, was still insisting that he had been killed by Sinn Féin.

Towards the end of 1920 it was no longer possible to deny that reprisals were taking place. On 21 October an editorial in the *Telegraph* noted that for twenty long months the police and military had borne outrage and assassination without the slightest retaliation. No assassins had been brought to justice, the public was afraid or unwilling to give evidence, juries were afraid to convict: 'There is a limit to human endurance, and is it to be wondered, that, in some cases, the police and military saw red?' According to the *Telegraph*, these reprisals had been few and far between compared with the amount of provocation and had, in practically every instance, been directed against known Sinn Féiners.

A *Whig* editorial of 2 May 1921, coinciding with the opening of the campaign for the first elections under the Government of Ireland Act, summarised the Northern Protestant view of what was happening in the rest of Ireland:

The arch-coercionists in Ireland today are neither the Government, the Royal Irish Constabulary, the soldiers of the regular army, nor the Auxiliaries. They are the murderous ruffians of the so-called Irish Republican Army and the utterly unscrupulous men who direct their operations. In the name of freedom they are terrorising the bulk of the population in the South, and a certain proportion in the North. . . The Sinn Feiners are not leading the population of Ireland, they are driving them.

It went on to make a comparison with Russia after the revolution:

There also a determined, fanatical minority of extremists make quite unjustifiable claims to speak in the name of the whole nation, and maintain their authority by methods which violate every moral precept.

Two days later the *Whig* took up de Valera's statement that the policies of Sinn Féin remained unchanged, but noted some change in methods:

There has for some time been a steady descent towards crude savagery. The kidnapping of Mrs Lindsay, the butchery of English officers in the presence of their wives, the hideous murder of poor Kitty Carroll and the bestial behaviour of the filthy scoundrels who defiled a Protestant church, are all typical episodes in the 'Republican' crusade for the liberation of oppressed Ireland.

We are asked to believe that if the whole country were placed at the mercy of the criminals and degenerates who commit these abominations, they would suddenly be converted into humane, kindly, law-abiding citizens, overflowing with charity and goodwill towards their Protestant and Loyalist fellow-citizens.

The Protestant churches, particularly the Church of Ireland, were caught in the violence. Archbishop D'Arcy, opening the General Synod on 10 May 1921, said:

For many months past we have been horrified – horrified until we have almost lost our capacity for horror – at the tragedies that have stained our land. Violence and bloodshed – deeds that shock and bewilder – have blackened every page in the daily record of our history, and the horror of it comes very close to us today.

He was referring to two members of the synod recently murdered. He continued:

Members of our church, and others in several parts of the country –

quiet, defenceless farmers for the most part – have been most cruelly killed. We do not know for what reason, and can but conjecture that it was because it was believed their political opinions were not acceptable. Yet being a small minority with no means of defence, their very inability to protect themselves should have kept them safe. Further, I cannot omit to mention the shocking outrage at Meenglass. The shameful desecration of one of our churches is, I believe, an event which stands alone in our history. It is hard to believe that Irishmen were guilty of this profanation. . . Many of us have been earnestly hoping and praying that nothing might happen which would add the heat of religious antagonism to the flame of political excitement.[38]

The churches were understandably reluctant to cry religious war, for they stood to lose in such a situation. The outgoing Moderator of the General Assembly, Dr H.P. Glenn, told the Presbyterian gathering in Belfast in June 1921 that wherever he had gone in the south and west, he had heard his people say that as yet there was no trace of a religious war manifesting itself. Another minister, the Revd B. Young from Galway, said his district covered half a county, but he had never seen an armed Sinn Féiner, nor a trenched road, nor met with the slightest discourtesy in the course of his work. He believed that any interference that took place was not for religious reasons. There might be those who occupied farms coveted by their neighbours, or those who, because they were Loyalists, came under the ban of the IRA.

Northern Presbyterians had no such doubts. Hugh M. Pollock, just elected to the Belfast parliament, and to be a member of the new Northern Government, told the General Assembly there was

. . . overwhelming evidence that there had been many cases of persecution of Protestants in the South. It is well known that this is going on and that one of the objects of the rebels is to drive the Protestants from their districts.[39]

The Northern papers did not ignore Protestant violence against Catholics in the North: expulsions from work were reported, as were sectarian attacks on Catholic areas. Indeed the *Whig,* in particular, frequently and vehemently denounced resort to violence as a means of retaliation. But such violence was invariably reported as the unfortunate consequence of the Sinn Féin rebellion and of IRA intervention in the North.

As the election of 24 May 1921 approached, when North and

South were due, under the Government of Ireland Act, to elect their respective parliaments, the Northern Unionists could see themselves as the constitutionalists in Ireland, the supporters of British Government policy, as opposed to the nationalists, now rejecting and fighting against that policy. The events of the First World War had in broad terms transformed the Unionists into Loyalists and the nationalists into rebels – a reversal of the position in 1912. It was Unionist acceptance of the Government of Ireland Bill, in March 1920, that completed the transformation, even though Carson, in his Twelfth speech in July 1920, was still sounding as if it were 1912 and even though units of the old UVF were beginning to rearm in the summer of 1920. By November the Special Constabulary (B Specials) was legally constituted and recruitment had begun; in December the Government of Ireland Act became law. The North was accepting Britain's solution, and was determined to make it work; the South had rejected it, and was determined to continue with violence and chaos.

While Unionists themselves firmly believed in the rightness and righteousness of their cause, they were concerned that some in Britain could still not see the real state of affairs in Ireland. On 4 May 1921 the *Whig* complained about 'bored and weak-kneed British Unionists' who found the Irish question an awful bore and wondered if Sinn Féin might not be quite so stiff-necked as the Ulster people made out, and who thought the Ulster Unionists could just be a bit bigoted. Surely, the *Whig* felt, the 'steady descent towards crude savagery' on the part of Sinn Féin would help even those people see things correctly.

4
THE SHUTTLECOCK COMES TO REST

The election on Empire Day, 24 May 1921, for the new parliament of Northern Ireland was a momentous event for the Unionists of the north-east. The intense violence of the war between Sinn Féin and the British Government forces had been concentrated in the south and west, leaving Belfast comparatively quiet after the upheavals of mid-1920.

From January 1921 onward, Unionist attention had been focused on the implementation of the Government of Ireland Act and the creation of a Northern parliament and administration. In January the Ulster Unionist Council formally invited Sir Edward Carson to submit himself for appointment as the Prime Minister of Northern Ireland, though it was known he would refuse on the grounds of health and age. At the end of January the obvious alternative, Sir James Craig, was approached and he agreed. On 4 February the Ulster Unionist Council formally named him as their leader at a meeting at the Assembly Hall in Belfast.

Craig left his Government post in London – he was Parliamentary Secretary to the Admiralty – towards the end of March and returned to Belfast to set about preparing both for the election and for the creation of a new administration. The contrast between the positive work of politics inside the designated six counties, and the rampant disorder elsewhere, rapidly strengthened Unionist attachment to the Government of Ireland Act settlement they had accepted originally with little enthusiasm.

A letter from a J.V. Bates, printed in the *Northern Whig* on 2 May, was anxious to ensure that the *Whig*'s readers fully appreciated the significance of the coming election.

> Question today is, do we in Ulster fully realise that we are now masters of our own fate? Do we realise that Great Britain has acknowledged to the full our oft-attested claim to be regarded as a free and independent people, under the Union Jack, and within the British Empire. And do we truly realise that henceforth we are to be held solely responsible for our own actions?

From Gladstone's conversion to Home Rule in 1886, the fate of Ulster had been very much a matter of British politics. Of paramount importance had been the strengthening of Unionism as a British political force, and the presentation of the Ulster – or Irish – Unionist cause in Britain. Now the issue depended also on the vote within the six counties, so the absolute premium was on maximising that vote. J.V. Bates finished his letter with the cry: 'United we stand, divided we fall, and our fall will be great.'

A year earlier, in March 1920, Captain Charles Craig, brother of Sir James, told the House of Commons why Unionists now wanted their own parliament, even though they would much prefer to remain part and parcel of the United Kingdom. Profound distrust of the Labour Party and of the Liberal leader Asquith, he said, made Unionists believe that if either of those parties were in power again, Unionist chances of remaining in the United Kingdom would be very small indeed:

> We see our safety, therefore, in having a Parliament of our own, for
> we believe that once a Parliament is set up and working well. . . we
> should fear no one, and we feel that we would then be in a position
> of absolute security.[1]

It is often asserted that Sir James Craig himself saw partition as only a temporary solution. This was scarcely true in May 1921 when, at the start of his election campaign in Banbridge, Co. Down, he declared that the fate of all Loyalists inside the six counties, and many outside, would be settled on 24 May 'for many years to come'. On election day itself he said the 'shuttle-cock had come to rest'; people would have to come to terms with the new situation in which concessions from Ulster would no longer be the natural escape from every Irish deadlock.[2]

The road that led eventually to Stormont was paved with good intentions. Despite the circumstances of appalling violence in Ireland at the time, the Unionist leadership, and, as far as can be seen, the Protestants of the North generally, approached the choosing of their new parliament in Belfast with enthusiasm, even some euphoria. There were protestations of generosity. In February 1921, Craig spoke at a Reform Club lunch in Belfast and looked forward to partition and the new parliament. They were not putting a paling around Ulster, he said, and he urged the other three provinces to take the opportunity to take their own government into their hands and show they themselves could be just as good as Ulster:

So far as I am concerned, that sort of competition, that sort of rivalry will always be most acceptable, because, after all, if we rival one another in our legislation for the welfare of the people, for the prosperity of our industries, agricultural or otherwise, surely that is a business competition that will appeal to all classes and all creeds in this province of Ulster. We are very much bound up in the rest of Ireland, and therefore do sincerely hope that in the heat of the coming contests no word will be said which would alienate the sympathy of those desirous of having, as Sir Edward Carson said the other day, peace throughout the whole of our land. We must hope not only for a brilliant prospect for Ulster, but a brilliant future for Ireland.

Remember that a Parliament and an executive established in Ulster means that we have to govern not you and me, but the whole people of this province. Remember that the rights of the minority must be sacred to the majority, and that it will only be by broad views, tolerant ideas and a real desire for liberty of conscience that we here can make an ideal of the Parliament and the executive.[3]

In his Banbridge speech in May, Craig again spoke of fair government inside Northern Ireland, as it was to be, and of relations with the South. Ulstermen, who never asked for Home Rule, fought against it and even today disliked it intensely, were prepared to operate it and to do what they could to manage the six counties, not in a one-sided way, but with the full responsibility that rested on any executive to govern all the people within the ambit of its responsibility.[4] Even the *Whig* caught the spirit. In an editorial on 30 May it said nothing would be easier than to preach a vendetta against their political enemies. Instead, it quoted Abraham Lincoln's rule – with malice towards none, with charity for all. 'We hold out to them [Sinn Féiners] the right hand of friendship and we ask them to work with us for the good of Ulster.'

On 13 July that year the *Belfast News-Letter* delved into history and condemned the Penal Laws as a direct violation of the Treaty of Limerick, 1691, and indefensible. Even when repealed, their evil traces remained and the hatred they inspired was not yet dead:

Today Ulster has the opportunity not only of proving what it stands for among the young nationalities, but also of showing the rest of Ireland how minorities can exist and flourish without oppression.

The churches joined in. Preaching at a service of intercession for the new parliament on 5 June, the Church of Ireland Archbishop of Armagh, Dr D'Arcy, said if there was partition it was not of their doing. Meanwhile, they should remember they had duties to the whole of Ireland:

> If due regard is given to the welfare of all the people of this province of every creed and class, of minority as well as majority, it must have in the long run, a very great effect. Righteousness exalteth a people.[5]

In the same week the Moderator of the General Assembly of the Presbyterian Church, Dr William Lowe, declared that partition would not interfere with church unity. He said Ulstermen were accused of being narrow, bigoted and intolerant, but he hazarded the belief that the doings of the Northern Ireland Parliament would give an undeniable refutation to these mischievous and misleading representations.[6]

Several times in the course of the election campaign Craig said he would welcome a Sinn Féin or Nationalist opposition in the new Northern parliament.[7] He also publicly, and with seeming enthusiasm, committed his party and Government to operating the clause in the Government of Ireland Act which envisaged a Council of Ireland, with both Northern and Southern representation on it. He declared that he himself would lead the Northern delegation to it, and he hoped that de Valera would do the same for the Southern side.[8] One of the first acts of the new parliament was indeed to nominate members of the Council of Ireland, with Craig at their head.[9]

In September 1921 he told the Northern House of Commons:

> We are prepared to work for the betterment of the people of Ireland, not to quarrel – not to continue political strife. We here. . . are prepared to work in friendly rivalry with our countrymen of the South and West, to vie with them in the government of the people, to vie with them in the markets of the world. We are prepared to do our part – every line and every letter – not alone in the letter, but in the spirit of the Act with which we have been entrusted.[10]

It was not all just words. In early May Craig had gone to Dublin for a secret meeting with de Valera – a remarkable action for the new Unionist leader who had just embarked on his election campaign. Certainly he did it at the behest of Dublin Castle and the

British Government, and presumably in the hope, however remote, that it might help in persuading de Valera to work the Government of Ireland Act. His own justification for going was that it was an attempt to do something to stop the killings.[11]

Early appointments by the new Belfast administration included a Catholic Lord Chief Justice, Sir Denis Henry, and a Catholic, Bonaparte Wyse, to a senior post in the Education Ministry. Sir Denis was a Unionist MP at Westminster for South Derry and Attorney General for Ireland, and Wyse was a Southerner who had transferred North at partition, having already achieved a senior level in the Civil Service. Neither was representative of the Northern Catholic community, but their appointments would have been unthinkable ten years later.

Yet the Council of Ireland was to become anathema to Northern Unionists, and their main concern was soon to be the minimising of all relations between North and South. As to fair play within Northern Ireland, Craig's party had, within a year of the 1921 election, drafted and presented in parliament the Local Government Act (Northern Ireland) which was to end proportional representation in local elections and set in motion the gerrymandering of local government constituencies which rapidly became the focal point of Catholic grievances.

Craig himself, who in 1921 had said that 'the rights of the minority must be sacred to the majority', and who had preached 'broad views, tolerant ideas and a real desire for liberty of conscience',[12] was to declare eleven years later from an Orange platform 'ours is a Protestant Government and I am an Orangeman',[13] and in 1934 was to tell the House of Commons in Belfast that he was an Orangeman first and a politician and an MP afterwards, 'all I boast is that we are a Protestant Parliament and a Protestant State'.[14]

The gulf between the sentiments expressed by Craig and others in 1921 and those of later years is obvious. Were the protestations of fairness and readiness to co-operate with the South therefore insincere? Certainly it is easy to see tactical reasons for many of the progressive or flexible actions and statements of the period. From early in 1921 it was presumably clear to Craig that some sort of negotiation between London and Sinn Féin was inevitable.[15] In these circumstances, Unionist policy had one primary aim – to ensure that whatever settlement was reached between London and Dublin did not disturb the Government of Ireland Act arrangements that had just brought Northern Ireland into existence, and which, in Captain Craig's phrase, constituted Unionists' 'absolute security'.[16] Ideally, Sinn Féin would accept the Government of Ireland Act. This was what Craig, by his own account, tried to persuade de Valera to do when they met in Dublin in May 1921. It was also, clearly, the reason for Craig's positive references to the Council of Ireland, and for the Northern parliament's prompt action in naming its representatives to that council. On 6 August the *News-Letter* commented:

> If they [Sinn Féin] bring the Southern Parliament into existence, establish a just system of administration and legislate reasonably, they will go far to gain the confidence of the people of the North, and may within a reasonable time, gain it altogether. In that case, the Government of Ireland Act provides the means of establishing Irish unity. But they refuse because they think they know better. They are still under the delusion that Ulster can be intimidated or coerced, directly or indirectly.

As late as the end of November 1921, Craig was again pushing the Council of Ireland as a bait towards Dublin. He told the Northern House of Commons that he wanted a settlement:

> Even at this late hour we renew the offer we made to them before, that through the machinery of the Council of Ireland we are prepared to meet them, to talk round a table, to discuss these matters which are of vital interest to the whole prosperity of our common land. . . We will be only too happy to come to some common settlement with regard to maintaining the good name of our common land.[17]

Even if the hope of persuading de Valera to accept the Government of Ireland Act must have been forlorn, the aim of Unionism was to keep the British Government firmly attached to the Act and the settlement under it. Ulster Unionism, ever careful of its image with the British public, could in 1921 present itself as the dutiful, even enthusiastic, backer of British Government policy. If a settlement in Ireland was still elusive, then it could not be the fault of the Unionists, busily implementing the Government of Ireland Act, and ready to co-operate, through its provisions, with a sister government and parliament in Dublin.

Apart from the Unionists' assessment of the tactics most likely to suit their own interests, the British Government was constantly pressurising Craig towards flexibility. As Lloyd George told Craig in July 1921, when urging him to come to a meeting with de Valera, it would be a very bad thing 'to break' on a refusal by Ulster to meet representatives from the South.[18] There seems little doubt that, in his references to the Council of Ireland, Craig was frequently tailoring his remarks to both London and Dublin. His real opinion of the council was probably closer to what he told the Belfast parliament in September 1921. He was listing what he called four vital functions of the Northern Government held up by the delay in transferring various powers and services to the new administration in Belfast. Of the four, he put power over the police first and the setting up of the Council of Ireland last:

> The Council of Ireland deals only with minor matters, and really the North here is very little affected whether the Council ever comes into operation or not.[19]

The delay in transferring the services was caused by the South's rejection of the Government of Ireland Act. In theory, until both devolved parliaments were operating and both administrations, North and South, were in existence, the full terms of the Act could not be implemented. This was one of several factors evident from the very beginnings of the Northern Ireland Parliament that gave the Unionists real cause for fear that the shuttlecock had not come to rest, that they were not masters of their own fate and that a parliament in Belfast did not, after all, give them absolute security.

In June 1921 Lloyd George had opened negotiations with de Valera, officially described by the British as the chosen leader of the great majority in the South; in July a truce was declared halting army and police operations against the IRA, but in July IRA violence resumed; and throughout the period the economic boycott of Belfast and other Northern towns, decreed by Dáil Éireann the previous summer, continued. Nationalist-controlled local authorities pledged allegiance to Dáil Éireann and refused to co-operate with the new Northern administration.

The violence and boycott were seen by Unionists as direct Sinn Féin assaults on the new Northern parliament and Government, and on the whole Government of Ireland Act settlement. The London–Dublin negotiations, and the delay in transferring full services to the new Belfast administration were seen as evidence that the settlement was not yet considered firmly cemented in place by London, and as real threats to the terms of that settlement.

The suddenness with which the ground began to shift under the Unionists was dramatic. On 22 June 1921 George V formally opened the new parliament in Belfast's City Hall, with pomp and splendour. The royal visit was 'nothing but one huge success from first to last', according to Lady Craig's diary.[20] Yet only two days later, Lloyd George was inviting de Valera and Craig to talks in London. This decision to negotiate had been preceded by some preliminary contacts, but an open invitation to a man who had been regarded as one of the leaders of a murder gang to come to London as the legitimate leader of his people was a thunderbolt. Winston Churchill later commented that no British Government in modern times had ever appeared to make so sudden and complete a reversal of policy.[21]

Earlier in June, at the opening of the first meeting of the Northern Ireland Parliament, the Lord Lieutenant, Lord FitzAlan, had caused a flurry when, in his speech, he had said the Government of Ireland Act was not perfect: 'It needs amending, and I should not be surprised if it were amended in the near future.'[22] But opening negotiations with the men denounced as assassins and terrorists, and against whom the Government had been waging pretty terrible war, was much more than shifting ground. Inescapably what was to be negotiated, or renegotiated, was the Government of Ireland Act. The fact of such negotiations being offered, and eventually commencing, was a severe blow to Unionist confidence and morale. But the circumstances in which the negotiations took place added still further to Unionist frustration and anger.

The Truce, signed in Dublin on Saturday 9 July by General Sir Nevil Macready, head of the British forces in Ireland, and by Chief of Staff of the IRA, Richard Mulcahy, should have meant the end of violence in all Ireland when it came into force at noon on 11 July. But during the intervening weekend, violence broke out in Belfast: an RIC man was shot dead, severe rioting followed and fourteen people died on the Sunday. By the end of the week a total of twenty-three had died in the city. One member of the new Northern parliament, William Grant, had been wounded by sniper fire. By 15 July the *News-Letter* was calling for the Truce restrictions on the security forces to be lifted. Under the Truce, the IRA had agreed to cease attacks on Crown forces and civilians, and to stop interference with Government or private property. The British Army agreed there would be 'no pursuit of Irish officers or men or war material or military stores', in fact, no action against IRA men. Yet in Belfast it was public knowledge that IRA snipers and others were in action during the riots. Could no action be taken against them because of the Truce?

Serious rioting broke out again in Belfast at the end of August. On 31 August the *News-Letter* reported six dead overnight in rioting and sniping. The following day it reported seven killed in sniping, with lawlessness rampant in Sinn Féin areas. An editorial commented:

> There is a 'truce' between the Government and Sinn Fein and it looks as if the Government was indifferent as to whether or not the truce was kept by Sinn Fein in Belfast, so long as it was observed in Dublin and in the Twenty Six Counties.

Violence continued in September, when bomb throwing by both sides was added to burning and sniping. It reached new levels in November, coinciding with the transfer of authority for law and order to the new Belfast administration on 21 November. The following day the *News-Letter* reported three dead in Belfast from sniping and on 23 November it declaimed: 'Belfast's Day of Terror, ten killed, over fifty wounded'. An editorial said Sinn Féin had opened war on the Loyalists of Belfast as a rebel reply to the transfer of powers for the maintenance of law and order to Belfast. Its news report of the day said Sinn Féin gunmen and bombers had spread terror throughout certain areas of Belfast, their attacks being chiefly directed at workers passing to and from their various places of employment.

> Concealed at vantage points, the snipers kept up systematic firing from early morning, and by curfew time last night the casualty poll was appalling. . . About six o'clock a dastardly and cowardly bombing attack was made on a tramcar crowded with shipyard workers in Corporation Street.

Two died in the tram bombing. The following day another tram was attacked in Royal Avenue in the centre of the city, a bomb was thrown into the crowded car and four people were killed. Shooting and rioting continued up to Christmas. On 21 December the *News-Letter* was still headlining a reign of terror.

Much of the violence in Belfast between June and December 1921 was of a sectarian, communal nature, with attacks on identifiable Catholic or Protestant areas by hostile mobs, snipers and bombers. Nationalist accounts presented it as a pogrom against the Catholics; the Unionists saw it as an organised Sinn Féin–IRA onslaught on the new Northern administration. The IRA activity was not confined to a purely defensive role protecting Catholic areas from mob attack. Individual policemen were shot; the bomb attacks on crowded trams were not acts of defence, though an element of retaliation may have been involved against shipyard workers.

The IRA did use the Truce to reorganise itself in the six counties, and officers and men were moved North from the now quiet South.[23] The *News-Letter* particularly noted a speech by General Eoin O'Duffy, then a senior IRA officer with responsibility for the north-east and a Dáil member, that he had ordered action to be taken to protect Belfast Catholics from the Orange mob, and placed IRA men at vantage points in the city. It was evident, said the *News-Letter* on 2 September 1921, that the evil of the past few days – the intense violence of late August, early September – was the work of Sinn Féin.

Later that week O'Duffy, along with Michael Collins, was in Armagh to address a Sinn Féin meeting. Referring to the violence he remarked that 'Sandy Row had got its eyes open', and went on, according to the *News-Letter*'s report of 5 September:

> They [Sinn Féiners] were told it was not right to use force against the people of the North. That was so. They did not like to use force against them. . . but they should not be allowed to stand in the march of a nation. They were acting as the bridgehead of the British Government in this country. So far as the people were concerned, they would get an opportunity very soon of deciding whether they were for Ireland or the British Empire. . . if they decided that they were against Ireland and against their fellow countrymen, they would have to take action. They would have to put on the screw – the boycott. They would have to tighten that screw, and, if necessary, they would have to use the lead against them.

The speech was much noted in the North, particularly the threat to 'use the lead', and was taken as explicit proof that Sinn Féin was out to coerce the North, and that economic boycotts and killings were not, as was generally claimed, retaliatory measures to protect Catholics in the North from victimisation, but direct action to bring down Northern Ireland.

Later O'Duffy himself, during the Treaty debates in Dáil Éireann, tried to explain his threat to use the lead:

> I did not then, nor do I now recommend the lead for the purpose of bringing Ulster in with the rest of Ireland. What I said was that if the Orangemen were to murder our people in cold blood, as they had done in the past, then they should get the lead.[24]

O'Duffy's explanation is hardly consistent with reports of his speech. It was taken as a clear threat that the war against Northern Ireland would be stepped up again if the Unionists remained obdurate during the London negotiations. It was widely believed too that Sinn Féin units were moving into Belfast and other Northern areas in preparation for such an attack.

The simplistic nature of O'Duffy's views on the Northern problem was shown in the report of the private session of the Dáil in August 1921. Speaking as an Ulsterman on the North, as he invariably did, he told the Dáil that they in Ulster thought force should be used against Ulster. There were enough volunteers in Belfast to hold it for Ireland. The Ulster people had very little force themselves if unaided by British armed forces. So far as Ulster was concerned, they could not meet them by concession. He had dealt with them by force in Monaghan, Fermanagh and Tyrone, and those people were now silent.[25]

The previous month the *News-Letter* had dismissed de Valera's assurance, given in the new Dáil, that he and his colleagues did not contemplate the use of force against Ulster. This, said a *News-Letter* editorial on 17 August, was altogether untrue:

> What have they been doing for two years? They have sent their flying columns throughout Ulster murdering loyal citizens and burning property, robbing Post Offices and cutting telegraph and phone wires, and committing other outrages – all of them ordered by de Valera and his ministers. Yet these are the men who say they do not contemplate the use of force. Let no one in Ulster trust them. They fully intend to do all the damage they can.

Also in August, Lady Spender (then Mrs Spender, wife of the Secretary to the Northern Ireland Cabinet) had written in her diary that it was an open secret that the Sinn Féiners were not keeping the Truce, but were using it to intensify the trade boycott, to levy funds and to drill their forces. It was a question of 'how long the people can be kept in hand under such circumstances'.[26]

Many Unionists anticipated a stamping out of violence within the new six-county area even before the Truce was announced. In early June one newly elected MP, Samuel McGuffin, said they would not tolerate this lawlessness and outrage in the six counties. If they could not achieve this through the Imperial Parliament, they would assume control of affairs themselves and by the organisation of a special force they would drive Sinn Féin, 'bag and baggage', out of the six counties.[27] Another Belfast Unionist MP, William Grant, spoke at the same time of the priority that had to be given to law and order. If the Sinn Féiners would not come under their law, they would have to take steps to expel them from the six counties.[28]

Craig, in his Twelfth speech in July 1921, had mixed the promise of peace with resentment against Sinn Féin, and with the threat of toughness:

How can we ever forget what has been done to our kith and kin in the South of Ireland? It is a hard thing, but I say this on behalf of the whole Ulster people that we are prepared now and today to say 'No Republic, no tampering with Ulster, never.' And then you can have peace and God be with you. Peace throughout Ulster does not rest with us, but peace in Northern Ireland rests with me, and we are going to have peace in Northern Ireland. We are going to enforce peace if it does not come naturally.[29]

But the Truce and the delay in transferring control of the police to Belfast meant that Craig and his Government had no means of enforcing peace and, in particular, no means of acting against the IRA. Looking back later, the Minister of Home Affairs Dawson Bates told the Belfast House of Commons that at the Truce all operations by the Crown forces against the IRA ceased, as did prosecutions under the Restoration of Order Act. Recruiting for the RUC and the B Specials ceased. The B Specials were ordered not to function, but from July down to 22 November

. . . the IRA proceeded to re-arm, re-equip and re-organise their forces. Arms and ammunition were carried into Belfast, drilling with arms was carried on, rifle and revolver practice was indulged in, and all in the presence of the police, who, under orders from the Imperial Government, were unable to interfere.[30]

The anger and frustration of the Northern Unionists was understandable. It led, in the summer and autumn of 1921, to moves to re-form the UVF, and undoubtedly to action by *ad hoc* Loyalist forces against not just the IRA but Catholics in general. Nor was it frustration only at the operation of the Truce; there was growing alarm at what might emerge from the spasmodic negotiations in London. On 21 September the *News-Letter* voiced the mounting impatience:

> Naturally there has been created throughout Northern Ireland a feeling of irritation, unrest and anxiety as to the intention of the Imperial Government in these negotiations with Sinn Fein, a feeling made the more acute by the results of the 'Truce' in Ulster, through the growing menace of Sinn Fein and by the understanding that the negotiations are being used by the rebel leaders to launch an attack on the existence of the Northern Parliament.

Control over law and order had just been transferred to Belfast, and that to the accompaniment of the late-November violence in the city, when the details of the Treaty settlement emerged. On 9 December the *News-Letter* denounced the Treaty as a betrayal and a disgrace – its sole aim being to force Ulster into the Free State. Unionist objections were threefold: to the principle of the Treaty, which theoretically included Northern Ireland in the Free State with the option of leaving; to the financial provisions which were thought likely to lead to high taxation and a tariff border, all to the detriment of Northern Ireland; and above all else, to the proposed Boundary Commission to look again at the North's territorial limits.

Lady Craig's diary records that 'J was very suspicious of the Boundary Clause and the financial arrangements' when he first received his copy of the Treaty agreement, sent by special train and steamer to Belfast. He immediately went to London to tell Lloyd George that on no account would he agree to 'tracts of Ulster being given up'. According to the diary, Lloyd George assured him that

> . . . mere rectifications of the Boundary are involved, with give and take on both sides, that is to say if one entirely Nationalist area close to the Border was put into the South, so correspondingly Unionist areas just over our Border would be put into Ulster.[31]

The impact of the Treaty on Unionist opinion is well conveyed by another diarist, Lady Spender. After recording initially that her husband Sir Wilfrid Spender had said the terms were 'a trifle better than he expected as far as Ulster is concerned', she admitted that she herself hated and loathed the whole thing.[32] A week later she wrote in her diary, addressed to her family in England:

> I think the past week since the publication of the Treaty has been the most depressing I have ever known over here. Up to the last I don't think we ever really believed England would do this thing – would reward murder and treachery, treason and crime of all kinds, and penalise loyalty. . . And now we know that worse is to come, and further pledges are to be broken, for two of the six counties may be taken from us. Tyrone and Fermanagh. It is this that took W and Sir J across to London last night. Sir J's last remnant of faith in Lloyd George has gone – why it lingered so long I cannot imagine.[33]

For Ulster Unionists their brief period of strict constitutional orthodoxy was coming to an end. It had lasted, essentially, from their acceptance of the Government of Ireland Bill proposals in March 1920. In that period Unionists found themselves in the unusual position of espousing and implementing British Government policy in Northern Ireland. But Northern Ireland was no sooner in being than British policy began to change; with the Treaty the Unionists were again the rock in the road, the obstacle to harmony between London and Dublin. Instead of implementing British policy in Ireland, they were once again denouncing it, and preparing to resist it by refusing to co-operate with the Boundary Commission. The events of June to December 1921 had confirmed Unionist views of Irish nationalism, which they had perceived to be attacking Northern Ireland militarily through the IRA, economically through the Belfast Boycott, and politically in the negotiations in London. But the impact of the short period on relations between Unionism and British authority was more dramatic. First World War loyalty and dutiful, if reluctant, acceptance of British policy in Ireland had been betrayed; treachery and murder had been accommodated. The settlement that had meant so much to Unionists in June 1921 had been reopened in December by 'that traitorous little Welshman', as Unionists now regarded the Imperial Prime Minister.[34]

5
THE WAR UPON ULSTER

Northern fears as to the extent to which the Anglo-Irish Treaty could mean a complete overthrow of the Government of Ireland Act settlement were somewhat assuaged by Lloyd George's reassurances to Craig on the Boundary Clause. Initially there was greater indignation at the fact that the British Government had actually come to terms with Sinn Féin – the most abject surrender to crime the world had ever seen, setting an example to Egypt and India, according to the *Northern Whig* on 3 January 1922. The *Belfast News-Letter* on 5 January 1922 saw the Treaty as 'an agreement extorted from a pusillanimous government by a campaign of murder and terrorism unprecedented in the history of even the most lawless political agitation'.

Northern Unionists watched in fascination, and with some delight, as the Dáil debated the Treaty into January 1922. 'Why on earth are these people making such a ridiculous exhibition of themselves?' asked the *Whig* on 6 January. And the *News-Letter* on 4 January noted: 'the notorious "Countess" Markevitch' being violent, vulgar and abusive, and making an outrageously insulting reference to Princess Mary. Rumour had it that Lord Lascelles's engagement to the royal Princess had been broken off, and she was to marry Michael Collins instead. But there were hopes too that acceptance of the Treaty might mean an end to disorder.

On 7 January the Dáil approved the Treaty by sixty-four votes to fifty-seven, and Michael Collins became the head of a Provisional Government that took over immediate responsibility for the country, pending the establishment of the Irish Free State. As the British administration withdrew from Dublin Castle, Collins and his Government were left as the legitimate authority in Dublin, with whom Craig and his Government would have to deal. The two leaders met with little delay on 21 January 1922 in London, the encounter being arranged by Churchill at the Colonial Office, with Craig seemingly anxious to reach some sort of understanding that would take pressure off the Northern state. An agreement was arrived at, the first Craig–Collins Pact. Under it the Belfast Boycott was officially called off, and the Boundary Clause was defused to the extent that the commission would now consist only of representatives of Belfast and Dublin, and Craig and Collins would have to agree their recommendations.

On 23 January the *News-Letter* saw the agreement as a document of far-reaching importance:

> If we can take it as evidence that the Provisional Government of Southern Ireland is prepared to adopt an attitude of goodwill towards the Government of Northern Ireland over these matters of government and administration in which both are now involved, then we say with certainty that the agreement is a source of gratification and is likely to turn out a blessing to the whole of Ireland.

But the writer was still nervous about the altered arrangements for the Boundary Commission, and assumed that what was being talked about was a 'frontier adjustment', nothing more.

But within two weeks all optimism was shattered. On 2 February a meeting in Dublin between Craig and Collins confirmed that fundamental differences existed over the Boundary Commission, and that it was still very much a threat to the North. On 3 February reports were published in the *News-Letter* of the Provisional Government's plans to do all in its power to obstruct and disrupt the workings of the Northern parliament and administration. Moreover the boycott was still in operation, with Belfast commercial travellers being driven out of Cork. Michael Collins, the *News-Letter* reported on 4 February, had now changed his friendly attitude to one of hostility.

There now followed a period of five months up to the outbreak of civil war in the South at the end of June 1922, of the severest pressure on the Unionists. IRA activity increased substantially, both inside the North and in border areas, mass kidnapping of prominent Unionists occurred, the North's territory was invaded in force from the South, assassination of prominent individuals began, incendiarism in Belfast and attacks on 'big houses' formed part of the assault. The Provisional Government proceeded with its plan to try to disrupt the North administratively, and initially at least, encouraged and financed Northern nationalists' noncooperation with the Belfast administration. In addition there was the threat of the Boundary Commission and the possible dismemberment of the six counties. Unionist awareness was growing that London was more concerned with the fate of the Provisional Government in Dublin than with Unionist worries and sensitivities.

Two of the most spectacular incidents, the mass kidnapping of early February and the occupation of the Belleek–Pettigo salient in June are little mentioned in accounts of the period and where they are, they are generally dismissed as peripheral, and even amusing or faintly ridiculous. But to the Unionists in 1922 they were deadly serious assaults on the territorial integrity of Northern Ireland, especially significant in the light of possible boundary revision.

The major kidnapping took place on the night of 7–8 February 1922, when gangs of armed IRA men crossed into Fermanagh and Tyrone and took prisoner a substantial number of prominent Loyalists, carrying them captive across the border. There was confusion as to the actual number taken, but newspaper accounts referred to a figure of 200, and this was generally taken to be correct at the time. The actual figure turned out to be closer to forty. The news was presented dramatically to the readers of the Belfast papers on 9 February. 'War on Ulster' was the heading in the *News-Letter,* while the *Londonderry Sentinel* of the same day declared 'War on Irish Loyalists' and talked of 'wholesale seizures in Northern counties', highlighting a figure of 200 kidnapped. On 10 February the *Tyrone Constitution* announced the news with twelve headlines before the details:

> Onslaught on Northern Loyalists; Dreadful Happenings on Frontier Border; Rebel Outrages on Extensive Scale; Violation of Truce and Treaty; Murders, Woundings and Wholesale Kidnappings; Tyrone, Fermanagh and Donegal Loyalist Victims; Imported Assassins from Cavan, Leitrim, Longford; Wild Night in Clogher Valley; Monaghan Moonlighters Busy; Desperadoes Captured at Enniskillen; Unionist MP's House Attacked; Tyrone Grand Master Seized.

The story to support such extraordinary presentation stated bluntly: 'Two hundred prominent Protestants, Orangemen and Special Police were kidnapped and taken across the border.' The Grand Master referred to in the heading was Anketell Moutray, aged eighty, of Favor Royal in Tyrone, Orange County Grand Master in Tyrone, and President of the South Tyrone Unionist

Association. Accounts of his captivity tell how his response to IRA questioning was to sing 'God Save the King', or metrical psalms – one reason why the whole affair has tended to be dismissed as an amusing anecdote.[1] It was far from it at the time. The numbers seized, and the people they were, meant that the affair was seen as a concerted attack on the Unionist establishment which sent a thrill of horror across the state. It was also clearly an act of war against the territory of Northern Ireland, something much more sinister than just another 'outrage'. On 9 February the *Whig*'s comment on the kidnapping was headed 'The Invasion of Ulster', and questioned what was the assumed reason for the seizures – the intention of the IRA to take hostages as a means of securing the release or the reprieve of IRA men under sentence of death in Derry. Whether this was true or not, said the writer, it was impossible to forget the recent threats to force Ulster to surrender the disputed areas.

On the same day the *News-Letter* commented:

> It is difficult to express in terms of restraint the indignation which every Loyalist in Northern Ireland feels at the audacious act of war committed by armed Sinn Fein Bands all along the Ulster Frontier from the Clogher Valley in the East to the Donegal–Fermanagh line in the West. . . [these] constitute an act of war against the British Crown of the most offensive and heinous sort, an act which, if perpetrated by an alien people, would be visited with retaliatory violence.

Details of the kidnappings emerged over the following days, and while the numbers declined – by 10 February the *News-Letter* was talking of 'seventy or more' Loyalists being held prisoner in the *garda* barracks in Ballybay, Co. Monaghan – the sense of outrage was increased by statements from Collins and O'Duffy in Dublin and by the seeming readiness of the London Government and the London press to take a soft line on the kidnappings.

O'Duffy, now Chief of Staff of the IRA, had said that it was not surprising that there should have been 'spontaneous and determined action in Ulster', resulting from 'the continual raids, arrest and torture inflicted on them [Northern nationalists] by the agents of the Northern Government'.[2] And he referred specifically to the arrest inside the North of a party of Gaelic Athletic Association footballers, alleged to be IRA men on their way to Derry to rescue the IRA prisoners there under sentence of death. The Derry prisoners were, in fact, reprieved but it seems clear that the kidnap raids had been arranged before this was known. The *News-Letter*'s interpretation of O'Duffy's remarks, however, was that he was justifying the raids. 'Kidnappers Have His Full Approval', read the headline on 10 February.

A Press Association report from London on 10 February gave what was probably the official view there, that the raids were the work of small bands reluctant to accept the Treaty, and that the occurrence was as much regretted by Michael Collins and Arthur Griffith as it was by the British Government. But the failure to release the victims promptly was taken in the North as proof of quite the reverse. The only conclusion, wrote the *News-Letter* on 10 February, was that either the Provisional Government was not acting in good faith, or it did not have the power to maintain law and order in the Free State. It added that some of the raiders who had been captured during the operation were in the uniforms of the Provisional Government. Was this a deliberate attempt to smash the Treaty? Clearly it was carefully planned and skilfully executed.

The following day the *News-Letter* firmly placed the kidnappings in a wider context:

On the day on which Sir James Craig and Mr Collins were unable to agree, it was semi-officially announced that the Provisional Government had made far-reaching plans for rendering the Government of Northern Ireland untenable. Was this wholesale kidnapping one of them?

As further evidence of a concerted move against Northern Ireland, the *Freeman's Journal* was quoted as saying that on the night of the raids thousands of armed men had been concentrated in east Donegal, with the intention of marching on Derry, where the executions of the IRA men were to have taken place.

Before the kidnap victims had been released, their fate became mixed up with that of a number of B Specials, held at Clones, Co. Monaghan, after a shooting incident on 11 February in which four of their colleagues died along with the local IRA commandant.[3]

Ten days after the raids, the *News-Letter* was reporting that seventeen Loyalists were still being held, having been taken as far as Trim, Co. Meath. On 24 February Churchill was able to tell the

House of Commons in Westminster that all those taken on 7–8 February had been released.

Other less spectacular kidnappings followed, and two men from Clady, Co. Tyrone were not released until mid-March.[4] On 30 March the *News-Letter* carried the headlines 'Border Again Violated', 'Murders and Kidnappings', 'Series of Sinn Fein Outrages'. The main incident referred to was an attack on the police barracks at Belcoo, Co. Fermanagh, when all arms and ammunition were stolen, and sixteen or seventeen of the occupants of the barracks taken prisoner across the border. Houses of Unionists in the village were also raided and four civilians taken and held for a short time.

Another agreement between Craig and Collins was reached in London at the end of March and should, in theory, have ended the border war and all IRA activity in the six counties. But violence throughout the North continued, as did tension along the border, culminating in the seizure of the two villages of Pettigo and Belleek in Co. Fermanagh by Republican forces at the end of May. 'Invasion of Ulster', said the *News-Letter* headline on 30 May, over a report that thousands of Protestants were fleeing into Enniskillen from the occupied villages and the triangle of territory between them and the border. Readers of the paper were told:

> Northern territory was invaded by huge forces of IRA men on Sunday, and according to the latest news to hand, a considerable portion of a triangular part of County Fermanagh lying below Pettigo and Belleek, jutting into County Donegal, is now in the hands of the IRA.

The paper said the invasion could not be considered the work of Irregulars, the anti-Treaty faction of Sinn Féin, as the forces who made the attack included Collins's men.[5]

Collins was actually in London in conference with the British Government when the invasion occurred. According to Churchill, both Collins and Griffith, who was with him, made a prompt unqualified repudiation of the raiders and their conduct, saying the forces were not theirs, and disclaiming any responsibility for them.[6] (In correspondence with Collins, Churchill referred to information received that 'armed Republican forces had invaded Northern Ireland',[7] but later, addressing the House of Commons, he sought to play down the incident, saying that he did not think

76

'anything in the nature of an invasion' had taken place.[8])

On 31 May the *News-Letter* reported that the IRA were advancing and that Protestants were being driven in front of the IRA gunmen. Twelve rebels, it said, had been shot dead. That same day, addressing the Northern Ireland House of Commons, Craig spoke of the incursion and the holding of Northern territory. Anywhere else in the Empire, he said, such an act would be considered a declaration of war.[9] While he spoke, he said, a portion of Ulster was actually occupied and he raised the fear of a boundary revision by force, linking the IRA action with the dominant preoccupation of the Unionists since the Treaty – the threat to the existence of Northern Ireland posed by the promised boundary revision.

In the end Churchill and the Government in London had to treat the incursion as 'war', and despatch artillery from Enniskillen to retake the village of Pettigo on 4 June, though a triangle of Northern territory still remained in Southern hands. On 8 June 200 men of the Manchester Regiment advanced on Belleek from Enniskillen, with artillery, and retook the village, shelling the old fort across the border in Southern territory. In fact, British troops continued to occupy the fort until 25 August 1924, a bone of contention between London and Dublin. Following the Belleek–Pettigo incursion, a neutral zone along the border, under British military control, was set up.

Full-scale civil war in the South eventually ended the major threat along the border, but not before further outrages inside Northern Ireland, seen by Northern Unionists as a continuation of the 'Border War'. On 19 June the *News-Letter* reported: 'Massacre Near Newry'. On the morning of Saturday 17 June, in an operation lasting just an hour, four houses occupied by Presbyterians in Altnaveigh and Lisdrumlisha, just west of Newry, were burned and six of their occupants shot dead in the roadway as the families were lined up. The reports said the raid was the work of an IRA gang from Dundalk. It was taken as further indication of an attempt to force a boundary revision by violence – terrorising Protestant families out of an area likely to be claimed by the South in any border revision.

On 17 April a writer in the *News-Letter* had described a tour of the border area, and added this comment:

The tactics of the Sinn Fein gunmen are perfectly plain. They are designed to paralyse the administration of law and order in the Six Counties and so force the Northern area under the Dublin Parliament. . . . There is not the slightest doubt that the gunmen believed that they would be able to spread such terrorism along the border and through the interior of Fermanagh and Tyrone, that the Loyalists of those counties would, for the sake of peace, agree to inclusion in Southern Ireland. This would render the position of the other four counties precarious, if not untenable, and would be a long step in the direction of a united Ireland.

But kidnappings and other border outrages were only part of a pattern of violence at an unprecedented level inside Northern Ireland that continued from late 1921 until the outbreak of the Civil War in the South in the summer of 1922. In the six months from the beginning of December 1921, when the control of law and order was at last passed to the Northern administration, 236 people died in the North, most of them in Belfast.[10] This new wave of violence coincided with the transfer of control at the end of November and was seen in the North as the deliberate response of the IRA to that development.

But even worse violence followed the February kidnappings, and the Clones massacre, as it was termed in the Belfast press. The day after the Clones incident 11 people were reported killed in Belfast, the following day 10 more, and 9 the day after that. Between 1 January 1922 and mid-March, 83 people were killed in Belfast and 157 wounded. The second Craig–Collins Pact of 30 March 1922 promised peace, but was followed by another weekend of horror in Belfast, with 7 deaths.[11] The violence reached yet higher levels in late May and early June.

A chart in the Cabinet files in Belfast shows the incidence of all outrages in Northern Ireland from November 1921 on. From January the total rises to a first peak in March and then to a second, higher one in May and June, when a monthly total of more than 600 outrages was recorded.[12] A note on the chart says the attacks of Sinn Féin against Ulster, 'which reached their height in May' account for the increased number of outrages. Another chart in the same file records the weekly totals of those killed and wounded by 'Sinn Féin aggression', that is excluding those caught in cross-fire or shot by the security forces. A peak was reached in the week ending 20 May, when 32 people died. The following week saw a record total of almost 60 wounded by Sinn Féin activity. The preparation of statistics listing those killed and wounded 'as a result of Sinn Féin aggression' stemmed from a Cabinet decision to try to counter what was seen as virulent anti-Unionist propaganda, particularly in Britain, which attributed the state of affairs in Belfast to Orange persecution of Catholics.[13]

The conduct of the Special Constabulary was a constant source of concern to the British Government, and indeed to the Army commanders in Belfast. There seems little doubt that at least some of the violent incidents commenced with B Specials' indiscipline, or Orange mob attacks on Catholics. Neither Craig and his Government nor the Unionist newspapers denied that mob and sniper attacks were taking place on Catholic districts. The Government denounced these, and the newspapers both reported and condemned them. But the general Unionist view was that the blame for the overall situation lay with Sinn Féin and the IRA, whatever the details of individual incidents. On 21 March 1922 the *News-Letter* commented:

> The existence of a hostile military organisation in Northern Ireland is the crux of the whole problem, it is the root of all the disorder and violence in Belfast; it is the cause of the dangerous condition along our frontier.

On 1 June the paper declared that it was an

> ... undoubted fact that the blame for the deplorable state of the city rests exclusively on Sinn Feiners. They are trying to overthrow our Government by murder and fire-raising, and they are responsible for all the violent deaths, whether they are perpetrated by themselves, or provoked by them.

Something like sectarian warfare was raging in Belfast. At least since the previous summer the *Whig* and the *News-Letter* had been warning of the dangers of Protestant retaliation against Catholics in the wake of IRA actions.[14] These warnings were also acknowledgements that retaliation was taking place. In March 1922 Lord Londonderry, Craig's Minister of Education, referred specifically to Loyalist outrages, 'as reprehensible as those committed by Sinn Fein', which were placing the Belfast Government in an impossible situation. When negotiating with British ministers, he said, he should like to have clean hands; that was by no means the case.[15]

But, basically, in the Unionist view the violence in Belfast was caused by the Sinn Féin rebellion, and specifically since the Truce of July 1921, by deliberate IRA activity in the six counties. On 27 March 1922 the *News-Letter* commented:

> When the British Government made their truce with the rebel leaders, it left them free to increase their activities in Ulster. Arms, ammunition and gunmen were poured into it for the purpose of making administration impossible. One of the leaders has publicly admitted, or boasted, that he posted gunmen at strategic points in the streets of Belfast.

At the meeting in London between Collins and Craig in March that led to the second Craig–Collins Pact, Collins, according to Lady Spender, was in 'very truculent and boastful mood and did not attempt to deny responsibility for outrages in Ulster and Belfast – indeed he boasted of them'.[16] He went on to say that he could stop the trouble on the border at any minute and he 'openly admitted that certain of the Belfast murders were done by his men'.[17]

In March R.D. Megaw, Junior Minister of Home Affairs, had told the Northern Ireland Parliament:

> We have captured documents that show the IRA never became really active in Ulster until they could carry on their operations in security under the protection of the so-called Truce. In one district. . . a battalion was raised and equipped between September last and December. We have had this growth of sinister activities detailed from day to day under the command of the commandant of the battalion itself. In other districts the enforced cessation of police activities resulted in the importation of very large quantities of arms and ammunition. . . very much greater than at any previous time.
>
> It is clear that the so-called Truce was used as an instrument to organise in our area a hostile army for the overthrow of the Northern Government; its intention was to make our work impossible. It has aided powerfully the conspiracy that is directed against our very existence.[18]

The Sinn Féin leadership was, of course, undivided at the time of the Truce in July 1921; after the Treaty split and the creation of the Provisional Government, London tended to blame the Republican faction for IRA activity on the border or in the North, but the Unionists did not agree. In late March 1922, Craig spoke in the

House of Commons in Belfast about the part pro-Treaty leaders were playing in encouraging IRA violence in the North. He referred again to the 'use the lead' speech by O'Duffy, and then to two statements in the immediate past. According to Craig, General Seán McKeown, speaking at Mullingar on 24 March, had told hecklers at a pro-Treaty march that if they wanted to fight he knew a young officer getting up a flying column to fight in Belfast and if they gave their names he would send them to the proper quarters, or if they liked he would lead them himself. Craig also mentioned a speech by Joseph McGrath, Minister for Labour in the Provisional Government, who had told hecklers at a meeting on 27 March that they could show their sincerity as Republicans and concern for what was happening in Belfast by handing in their names as volunteers for fighting on the Northern border.[19]

On 11 April the *Whig* reported the discovery of IRA plans to burn the main commercial areas of the city. The month of May saw a succession of major fires in the city, with damage put at half a million pounds.[20] On the weekend of 20–22 May, a weekend of exceptional sectarian violence in Belfast, the arson campaign was extended to the 'big houses' of Ulster. Under the heading 'Sinn Fein War Against Ulster', the *News-Letter* reported on 22 May, 'Campaign launched in Antrim and Down: Many beautiful residences destroyed: Barracks attacked: A Policeman Murdered'. In an editorial headed 'War' the *News-Letter* commented:

> The Loyalists of Ulster must now brace themselves for war, for the long threatened attack by the forces of Sinn Fein has begun. The wholesale eruption of incendiarism in Belfast on Friday morning was the signal for action. It was instantly taken up all over the Six Counties.

The paper went on to note the boast of Sinn Féin leaders that they had 30,000 IRA men enrolled in Northern Ireland. The most that could be looked for from the Provisional Government, in the paper's view, was 'malevolent neutrality'.

Among the houses destroyed that weekend was the O'Neill family home at Shane's Castle, on the shores of Lough Neagh. Old Court, near Strangford, was burned, so too were Crebilly Castle, near Ballymena, and Glenmona House at Cushendun. A few nights later the Londonderry residence at Garron Tower, on the Antrim coast road, was destroyed, along with Kilclief House at

Strangford, and Hawethorne Hill, Armagh. As well as taking IRA action into parts of Ulster where it had hitherto been almost unknown, the destruction of these 'big houses' hit hard at the heart of Unionism. Northern Protestants had long tended to look to the 'big houses' for leadership, to the nobility such as the O'Neills and the Londonderrys, and to the wealthy gentry, like Craig himself or the Brookes in Fermanagh. The attack on Shane's Castle was a particular affront to Unionism. Lord O'Neill, aged eighty-two, had been ordered out of his home at gunpoint, along with Lady O'Neill. Apart from being the head of one of the most eminent Unionist families, he was also father of Sir Hugh O'Neill, Speaker of the new Northern House of Commons.

On the Monday morning after the burnings at Shane's Castle and elsewhere, W.J. Twaddell, Unionist MP in the Northern Ireland Parliament for West Belfast, was shot dead in the centre of Belfast. Despite the high level of fatalities in the city since the summer of 1921, no prominent Unionist politician had been killed. The murder of Twaddell, a draper and long-standing Unionist in local government in Belfast, was clearly a deliberate assassination, and brought the reality of IRA violence very close to his thirty-nine Unionist colleagues who made up the Northern parliament.

Exactly a month later, on 22 June, Field Marshall Sir Henry Wilson was shot on the doorstep of his house in London. This assassination was of even greater significance, for Sir Henry, a hero of the First World War, was also the Unionist MP at Westminster for North Down, having taken the seat vacated by Craig himself and had been, since mid-March, official adviser to the Belfast Government on security.

The news of his killing could hardly have been treated more dramatically. No story since the Armistice of 1918 had such a prominent presentation. On 27 June 1922 the *News-Letter* commented:

> He was ours. . . ours by blood, ours by sympathy and ours by service. He died as a martyr to the cause of the freedom and liberties of Northern Ireland. . . The assassination of Sir Henry Wilson is an epochal crime; it stands out stark in its fiendishness, marking for all time the criminality of the Sinn Fein movement.

On the news of the assassination, Lady Spender wrote in her diary:

We are stricken to the heart by the murder of Sir Henry Wilson. Is this the 'piercing pain, the killing sin' that is driven into the dead heart of the British Government 'to stab its spirit broad awake'. If not, if more is yet needed, God help us all.[21]

The Unionist view of the events of the first half of 1922 clearly contrasts starkly with the general nationalist belief, held particularly by Collins himself, that essentially what was happening in the North was a pogrom against Catholics. It is true that more Catholics than Protestants died in the period, but the casualty figures indicate that the violence was far from one-sided. Of the 236 people killed in Northern Ireland between December 1921 and the end of May 1922, 147 were Catholics and 89 Protestants or members of the security forces.[22] The presence of IRA gunmen in Catholic areas meant much greater use of firearms by the Crown forces in those areas, and therefore the likelihood of a greater civilian casualty toll. The totals for both wounded and killed in the period are much closer still, 313 Catholics and 269 Protestants or Crown forces – figures which are hardly consistent with a pogrom conducted by armed Orange mobs and B Specials, and which certainly indicate a high degree of IRA activity. Moreover many of the actions of the IRA in the period were far from defensive – the bombing of tram-cars of civilians in the centre of Belfast, the assassination of Twaddell, the campaign of burning of commercial premises in Belfast and of 'big houses'. The occupation of the Fermanagh triangle in June was a spectacular offensive, as were the mass kidnappings of early February, even though they may in part have been aimed tactically at securing the lives of condemned IRA men in Derry jail.

The Unionist belief that Northern Ireland was under concerted attack by forces aiming at its destruction can therefore be seen as not unreasonable. Moreover, it is now known that Collins was actively encouraging a build-up of IRA strength in the North and that he aided the supply of arms to the IRA in the North, agreeing to the exchange of British-supplied rifles in the hands of the Provisional Government for non-British weapons in the possession of anti-Treaty factions in the South. These weapons could then be sent North without fear of the British authorities identifying them as having been supplied by Dublin.[23] In April and May 1922 he was, according to Florence O'Donoghue, who became Adjutant

General of the Republican forces in April, working with Liam Lynch, one of the leaders of the Irregulars, 'in a spirit of harmony reminiscent of the Tan War days' on a new joint pro- and anti-Treaty aggressive policy on the North.[24] O'Donoghue comments that in the face of that policy, and coterminous with it, it was not a little surprising to find Collins signing an agreement with Craig on 30 March which included a provision that all IRA activity in the North should cease.[25]

The minutes of the North East Advisory Committee, which Collins set up in April 1922, supply further evidence of Collins's close links with the IRA in Belfast and his sympathy with their activity there. He included on the committee the IRA commanding officer in Belfast, Joe McKelvey, and other IRA officers. In April Dr Russell McNabb, a leading Belfast nationalist, complained in the committee that the Pact, the Craig–Collins agreement of 30 March, had apparently meant the suspension of the campaign of arson:

> We were getting along famously when the Pact came. There were beautiful fires in Belfast each night and it was getting uncomfortable for the other side. . . I think this burning campaign, if they had some arms in addition, would bring them to heel.

On which Collins's immediate comment was:

> I know for a good many months we did as much as we could to get property destroyed. I know that if a great deal more property were destroyed. . . I know they think a great deal more of property than of human life.[26]

In the first half of 1922 the Unionists certainly knew they were under comprehensive attack from the forces of Irish nationalism – diplomatically through the threat of boundary revision, politically through the campaign of non-recognition and non-co-operation, economically through the boycott, and physically through IRA violence both inside Northern Ireland and from across the border. The Provisional Government in Dublin was overtly backing some of these moves and was either unwilling or unable to block others. Until the Civil War actually commenced in mid-1922, the breach in Sinn Féin between pro- and anti-Treaty factions was incomplete, and was frequently discounted by Unionists. To the beleagured Northerners, the source of all these assaults was the authorities in Dublin and the new Irish nationalist state.

The Belfast Boycott, to which Dáil Éireann attached such importance, and to which it devoted so much energy and resources, was demonstrably a failure as regards its stated objective – the reinstatement of the Catholic workers expelled from their jobs in Belfast in 1921. It did have an impact on particular sectors – banks, distilleries, bakeries, tobacco and other goods which had Belfast as a distributive centre. But its overall impact on the economy of the North was slight. It was, however, greatly resented by the Unionists and perceived as yet another attempt by Sinn Féin to destroy the North. It was decreed, said the *News-Letter* on 2 February 1921, with the object of penalising the Ulster Unionists for their opposition to Home Rule. It was, said the *Whig* on 2 May 1921, an attempt to frighten Unionists into abandoning the Government of Ireland Act settlement.

There is ample evidence that the boycott was generally seen by the Sinn Féin side as a broad weapon to use against the North. This was particularly true after June 1921, when the separate Northern administration came into being with the opening of the new Belfast parliament. In the Dáil, on 18 August, Deputy John O'Mahony said some of the appointed organisers had placed an embargo on the whole six counties – he cited Limerick. Deputy Collivet said the people of Limerick had decided to exclude the goods of all the six counties and he thought it would be a good thing to have this adopted generally. Limerick was perfectly justified in doing what it had done. Arthur Griffith said when the boycott was decided on the ministry had discussed excluding the whole six counties, but had opted to confine it to 'those areas that drove out the Nationalist population'. Limerick's action was absolutely indefensible. But Collivet came back to ask if the Dáil was now going to tell them they had to buy from the six counties – 'The thing had been going for six or seven months and the Dail had never pointed out that it was wrong.'[27]

De Valera himself had contemplated the use of economic measures against the North as a means of forcing the Unionists to come to terms. In an interview with the Associated Press in March 1921, he had said the coming elections for the new Northern parliament would show that industrial Ulster was not so blind to its own interests as to court being cut off from its markets in the south and west. He continued:

The boycott of Belfast goods which is now operating is but the opening stage of what will become a complete and absolute exclusion of Belfast goods if the Partition Act is put into effect.[28]

In January 1922, Eoin O'Duffy was also talking of the boycott in similar terms:

I know the businessmen of Ulster don't want separation because they fear economic pressure – the boycott has given them a taste of that. In the *Gazette* every week at least two or three of the principal men in Belfast appeared there for bankruptcy. With bankruptcy staring numbers of others in the face they will see that the Northern Parliament comes to terms with the rest of Ireland.[29]

The continuation of the boycott after the Truce of 11 July 1921 caused particular annoyance to Ulster Unionists. With the Northern administration in place, there was frustration that nothing could be done either in the North or South, the South still being, theoretically at least, under United Kingdom administration, to halt it. Dáil Éireann continued to levy fines, and to encourage enforcement through armed hold-ups of trains and lorries, and by physical intimidation of shopkeepers and others. All these activities were illegal, as were the publication in newspapers of boycott notices, and the printing of posters and handbills advocating the boycott. But the British Government had already made up its mind, long before the Truce, that legal action against printers and publishers was not practical.

The attempts to enforce the boycott inside Northern Ireland caused particular resentment. On 4 October 1921 the *News-Letter* reprinted a notice sent to Loyalist shopkeepers in Armagh from the 'Belfast Boycott Committee, Sinn Fein Rooms, Armagh'. The notice said it had come to the knowledge of the committee that they were doing business with Belfast and ordered them to cease such trading at once – otherwise they themselves would be blacklisted 'and further drastic steps taken to enforce the boycott'.

In the twenty-six-county area many of those directly hit by the boycott were Unionist, or Protestant, shopkeepers, often reluctant to obey the Dáil decree and therefore subject to threat and intimidation. Both they and the general public in the North often saw the Belfast Boycott as a continuation of the general campaign of intimidation that had been waged by Sinn Féin.

The Provisional Government in Dublin formally directed that

the boycott be discontinued on 24 January 1922, following the Craig–Collins Pact in London, and the machinery for implementing it was dismantled. (Not without some opposition from the Bishop of Down and Connor, Dr MacRory.[31]) Michael Collins, who had never seemed an enthusiastic supporter of the boycott, remarked in Cabinet that it had been 'comparatively ineffective' and that if it became necessary to fight the Northern Ireland Parliament, they could set up an effective tariff barrier in its stead.

The Provisional Government did consider reimposing the boycott and met a delegation from Ulster on 21 March 1922 to discuss it. At that time several local councils in the South were demanding such a reimposition in view of what they called atrocities in Belfast. No decision was taken, and the dismantling of the boycott department went ahead, with complaints of ill-treatment from the eighteen staff made redundant. But the boycott was partially revived unofficially by the Republican side in the growing split in the South. In April the Provisional Government had to supply a guard to the Royal Hibernian Academy after that body had been ordered to withdraw Northern pictures from its exhibition. Shops in Dublin complained they were still being ordered to pay fines to the 'Director of the Belfast Boycott', even though the post was abolished.[32]

Eventually the inevitable happened, and what had been threatened by Belfast merchants and Northern politicians came to pass – a retaliatory boycott was launched from Belfast. The Ulster Traders' Defence Association surfaced in May 1922, with large advertisements in the Belfast papers calling for a boycott of Southern goods.[33] A letter from A.J. Dudley, General Secretary, with an address in the Scottish Temperance Buildings in the centre of Belfast, dated 17 May, went out to traders starting the counter-boycott.[34] It said the Belfast Boycott, although officially discontinued, was at present being carried on more bitterly than ever. It urged that so long as this continued no goods of any kind should be accepted by Northern traders from any part of Ireland outside the six counties.

Certainly the newspaper reports of the preceding months of early 1922 suggested that the boycott was being enforced more energetically by the de Valera faction than it had been by the Provisional Government. The IRA convention that met in the

Mansion House on 26 March decided 'drastically to enforce the Belfast Boycott' and to extend it to the six counties, reported the *News-Letter* on 27 March 1922. On 3 April the *News-Letter* also reported that a boycott of Belfast goods was now in full swing in the South, goods being confiscated by armed men and destroyed or stolen. On 7 April the *News-Letter* said the Provisional Government was either incompetent or unwilling to prevent the boycott

> . . .which was being so rigorously enforced by the de Valera section of the IRA in the South.
>
> Every day large consignments of Ulster goods are burned or destroyed and yesterday was no exception. Almost hourly reports of burnings from Dundalk. Dublin wholesalers 'fined' for accepting Belfast goods.

That same day saw one of the most spectacular episodes of the boycott. One hundred IRA men raided bonded stores in Dublin and seized Northern spirits – casks were smashed in the cellars and 500,000 gallons of whiskey spilled. Dunvilles later said they lost 992 butts, 697 hogsheads and 7 quarters, worth £50,000.

Ironically it was yet another action enforcing the boycott by Republican troops that triggered off the eventual conflict between the Free State authorities and the anti-Treaty faction. It was the Civil War, in turn, that meant the end of the boycott. On 26 June a party of Republicans from the Four Courts garrison raided the Belfast-owned Harry Ferguson's garage in Baggot Street in Dublin, and seized fifteen cars. The raid was led by Leo Henderson, then designated director of the boycott in the garrison. He was captured by Free State troops. In return, the Deputy Chief of Staff of the Free State Army was kidnapped. The Government issued an ultimatum, following which the attack on the Fourt Courts began in the early morning of 28 June 1922.

For almost two years the boycott's status as an official policy of Dáil Éireann, funded and administered by it, heightened Unionist perceptions of the Dáil and the whole Sinn Féin movement as an enemy of the Unionist community, determined to wreck the Government of Ireland Act settlement and to inflict hardship on people already suffering economic decline and unemployment. It was additionally divisive in that it led to a counter-boycott and because it spawned numerous local sectarian boycotts – of

Catholics by Protestants and Protestants by Catholics – in towns and villages in both parts of Ireland. It also contributed to the destruction of one aspect of Irish unity – the commercial unity of the country based on the importance of Belfast as a distributing centre for most of Ireland. In 1924 exports from the six to the twenty-six counties were half the level of 1920.[35] The boycott also contributed to the deterioration in relations between Belfast and London. Anxious to reach a settlement with Dublin, the British Government was not prepared to take action to stop the boycott after the July 1921 Truce – or even before it. The fact that the boycott was still being enforced in the second half of 1921 by the same Sinn Féin leaders who were being welcomed in London as negotiators, did nothing to encourage Unionist confidence in the British Government.

6
THE USUAL LITTLE GANG

It was against this extraordinary background that the political entity of Northern Ireland came into existence and, in the year from mid-1921 onwards, that the pattern of politics within it began to take shape. The creation of the Belfast-based institutions under the Government of Ireland Act placed Unionism in a radically new context. Hitherto, the main end of Unionism had been to ensure that British Governments did not capitulate entirely to the arguments of Irish nationalism. Now there was a Belfast focus for Unionist activity in the new framework, which gave Unionist politicians the task of administering substantial sectors of life in the state.

The Act, in theory, settled the question of the Union by giving the power of decision on entering, or not, an all-Ireland parliament to the Belfast assembly. (Subsequently the Treaty gave it the power to opt out of the Free State.) So it was inevitable that the basic constitutional question of 'the Union' would be the dominant one in electing the first Northern Ireland Parliament in May 1921. But the Northern boundary had been so drawn as to ensure that the new Northern parliament would have a Unionist majority. That was the whole point of partition. Consequently, the Northern parliament started off with an unshakeable majority in favour of the Union, one which it was impossible to see overturned in the short or medium range. Once the parliament had performed the fundamental function accorded it under the Treaty arrangements and voted itself out of the Free State as it did on 7 December 1922, it was, in theory at least, by no means inevitable that politics within the new entity would be dominated by the basic constitutional issue.

As Craig himself had said in May 1921, the 'shuttlecock' had come to rest, and the constitutional issue settled for many years to come. Now the new parliament could, again in theory, devote its energies to the internal administration of the state: to social and economic problems, to relations with the Catholic minority. It was here that the context for Unionism was radically changed, for until that time Ulster Unionism had only one political objective, only one policy – the maintenance of the Union. It was in no way equipped as a political movement to present coherent policies on the areas of administration and government now being allocated to the devolved administration and parliament.

Dawson Bates, then Secretary of the Ulster Unionist Council, had written to Carson in June 1919:

> The two principal Unionist organisations which exist at the present time in Ulster are the Parliamentary Constituency associations and the Orange Institution. Having regard to the fact that members of both these organisations comprise all classes, it is obvious that it is a practical impossibility that matters outside the question of the Union should be the subject of discussion and action. Therefore no subjects except those directly affecting the Union are discussed.[1]

In short Unionism had only one policy – the preservation of the Union. Yet the movement did indeed comprise all classes, and the Unionist community in Northern Ireland, while united on the Union, was potentially divided, and indeed actually divided, on many other issues of more daily concern. These included denominational rivalry, the temperance question, the division between east and west in Ulster, and divisions related to class and economy, in the countryside as well as between industrial worker and employer.

Tensions within Unionism had, of course, existed before 1921. Dawson Bates's letter to Carson was about the recently founded Ulster Unionist Labour Association, created at Carson's urging in 1918 to try to tie the industrial working classes more closely into Unionism, and specifically to try to ensure that working-class candidates could win nominations for election. A split along class lines with a breaking of sectarian barriers was the most obvious possibility; to an extent it had happened in the first decade of the century in Belfast. Postwar, the Labour movement in Britain was already a force. In 1920 non-Unionist Labour candidates inflicted defeats on Ulster Unionist Labour Association men in the local elections in Belfast, and even in the 1921 election to the Northern Ireland Parliament Unionists had been opposed, albeit unsuccessfully, by five Labour Party candidates.

But these potential divisions were all submerged under the

91

pressure of the extraordinary circumstances of 1921 and 1922. The settlement of 1921 almost immediately turned out not to be a settlement at all, and the constitutional question was kept dangerously open, from the Unionist viewpoint, by the negotiations between London and Dublin and by the various assaults, physical and economic, being maintained with renewed vigour by the forces of nationalism against the new Northern state.

One element in this campaign had particular impact on the new political institutions in Northern Ireland. This was the boycott of these institutions by nationalists, the non-recognition of the existence and functions of the new devolved administration, and the counter-recognition, by nationalists, of Dáil Éireann and its claims to be the legitimate authority for all of the island. When the new Northern House of Commons assembled in Belfast City Hall for the formal opening by George V on 22 June 1921, only the forty Unionists attended. The twelve Sinn Féin and Nationalist members boycotted the parliament and continued to do so. Cardinal Logue, the Catholic Archbishop of Armagh, declined an invitation to attend the royal ceremony. Later in 1921 he refused to co-operate with the work of the Belfast Government's new Lynn Committee on Education.[2]

Nationalist-controlled local authorities within the Northern area refused to co-operate with the Belfast authorities. In all twenty-one such councils were dissolved for non-cooperation under legislation adopted by the Northern Ireland Parliament at the end of 1921.[3] Such councils looked to Dublin instead. Even before the creation of Northern Ireland several nationalist-controlled councils in the Northern area had declared allegiance to Dáil Éireann. There was general agreement between the Dáil leadership and Northern nationalists that non-recognition was essential, and this was confirmed after the ratification of the Treaty by the Provisional Government under Michael Collins.[4] At a meeting of the Provisional Government in Dublin on 30 January 1922, attended by Bishop MacRory representing Northern nationalists, Collins insisted that non-recognition was essential, and he promised to support local authorities in the North who refused recognition.[5] He also pledged financial support for schools and schoolteachers in the North who followed a similar policy, including refusal to accept salaries from the Belfast authorities. By

May 1922 teachers in more than one third of the North's 740 Catholic schools were refusing payment from Belfast. And by the end of September the Dublin Government had paid out more than £170,000 in wages to some 800 Northern Catholic teachers.[6] (This costly policy was not popular with all the members of the Provisional Government, but Collins was still pressing it in August 1922. After his death in that month, however, it was rapidly abandoned by Dublin.)

The strategy by the nationalist and Catholic community of non-recognition and non-participation left politics within the new institutions of Northern Ireland to begin on a completely artificial basis. In a parliament without an opposition, it was inevitable that some form of critical, even dissident, group would form within the Unionist ranks. Those Unionists who had sat at Westminster were well accustomed to seeing their role in parliament as essentially that of keeping a suspicious eye on the activities of Government, and they brought such habits with them to Belfast. So from the outset the spectrum of political debate within Northern Ireland was Unionist – Government against backbench, moderate against extremist – but not Unionist against nationalist. The whole centre of gravity of Northern politics was thus set from the start far into the ranks of the majority community. Various factors helped ensure the 'opposition' to the Government came from the Orange extreme, not from any moderate centre.

Craig's first administration, including Cabinet, Parliamentary Secretaries and the Attorney General, totalled fourteen, all but two of them in the House of Commons. The Speaker and the Deputy Speaker removed two more from the backbenches, so out of the forty members in the first Commons, fourteen were office-holders of one sort or another.[7] Little effort was made to ensure any geographical spread in the distribution of offices. Of the fourteen jobs available, twelve went to MPs from Belfast, Down or Antrim. The only exceptions were Edward Archdale, Minister of Agriculture and Commerce, who sat for Fermanagh–Tyrone, and Richard Best, the Attorney General, who sat for Armagh. Even the two members of the nobility in the Government, who sat in the Senate, Lord Londonderry, Minister of Education, and Lord Massereene and Ferrard, Parliamentary Secretary in the Prime Minister's department, had their family seats in east Ulster.

To an extent this preponderance of office-holders from east Ulster reflected the all-Unionist membership of the house. With the four Queen's University members included, thirty-one out of the total forty represented Antrim, Down or Belfast. Eight of the missing twelve non-Unionists came from the west of the state. Consequently, the administration was heavily weighted in favour of the east or, more specifically, the non-border constituencies. There was therefore inbuilt the possibility, even the probability, of a political divide between east and west, or between border and non-border.

In a stable Northern Ireland, threatened neither by armed violence nor by political extinction through negotiation in London, or through dismemberment by boundary revision, such a divide might never have acquired much significance. But security was overwhelmingly the dominant issue in the first year of Northern Ireland's existence, and from November 1921 responsibility for law and order rested with the Craig Government. Inevitably too, the responsibility for ensuring that Ulster was not in any way betrayed or weakened by London, or by London's dealings with Dublin, was seen to rest with Craig and his Government.

Unionists from the border counties felt particularly threatened in 1922 by physical violence in view of the cross-border kidnappings and armed actions, and also by the seemingly real possibility that boundary revision would see whole counties incorporated into the Free State. One other group of Unionists also felt particularly threatened by violence in 1921 and 1922: these were the Protestant working class of Belfast, inclined by history towards sectarianism, and very much in the front-line as regards IRA activity. So not surprisingly the sharpest critics of the Craig Government in the first Northern Ireland Parliament were the representatives of the border constituencies, and those who sat for the more rabidly Orange constituencies in Belfast.

The real opposition in the first parliament came from what Craig called, according to Lady Craig's diary, 'the usual little gang, of Coote, Lynn and McGuffin'. On that occasion, 4 April 1922, Sir James reported back to Lady Craig that 'Cooper was also violent'.[8] William Coote and James Cooper represented the key border counties of Tyrone and Fermanagh; Robert John Lynn and Samuel McGuffin sat for West Belfast, with their main bases in the intensely Orange Woodvale and Shankill areas. Three of the four, not Cooper, were also members of the Imperial Parliament at Westminster. In 1923 a writer in the *Northern Whig* added the name of Thompson Donald to those of Coote and McGuffin as 'the three severest critics of the Government'.[9] Donald sat for East Belfast, representing the shipyard workers of what was also an intensely Orange part of the city.

In 1921 Lynn had been a journalist on the *Whig* for eighteen years, and editor and managing director for ten. Coote, originally from Co. Cavan, had a woollen business in Clogher, Co. Tyrone. An energetic Presbyterian, he was representative of the intensely Protestant strain in Unionism, and an early articulator of Protestant fears of Catholic infiltration into jobs, and votes, in Northern Ireland. Cooper was an Enniskillen solicitor and a leading Fermanagh Orangeman.

Much of Coote's criticism was directed towards the cost of the Belfast administration, and what he saw as unnecessarily extravagant expenditure. Lynn had a similar preoccupation, which was reflected in the editorials of the *Whig* from the very first days of the new parliament. But from the start Coote, in particular, showed his strong opposition to any dealings with Sinn Féin, his suspicion of London, and his readiness to hold Craig and his Government responsible for ensuring that London was kept in line on law and order and on dealings with Sinn Féin. In his first speech in the Belfast Commons, in June 1921, he said:

I would like very simply to ask you how you can expect life and property to be safe either in these six counties or in any other part of Ireland while the leaders of all this murder gang, leaders who are known to His Majesty's Government, remain at large.[10]

In September he was persistent on the subject of law and order – not yet a responsibility of the Northern administration. And he was explicitly critical of Craig and the Cabinet over the Truce:

We are out to assist His Majesty's Government in upholding law and order and we have no right to suffer from the effects of this lamentable truce. I hold it has been – I was going to say criminal but I won't use so strong a word – but it has been remiss on the part of the Cabinet of Northern Ireland that they allowed such instructions to be given to the police and the military to cease taking active steps to protect the lives and property of the loyal people of the Province, irrespective of creed.[11]

In the same speech he asks what Craig has done, and comes close to blaming him for recent deaths in Belfast:

> We had peace until this truce began, and until gunmen came down in pairs and dozens – they are in the city today. We know they are there. There is a camp at Ballykinlar, about four hundred strong, with the Sinn Fein flag flying there. Is the Prime Minister aware of this? Has he made any protest to the Dublin authorities? I charge the Government with weakness. I charge the Government with over-confidence in the British Government. I believe we are being made the catspaw of the British Government.[12]

In March 1922 Lynn took up the theme of the Northern Ireland Government's failure to deal with violence. There were good grounds for dissatisfaction with it, he told the Commons in Belfast. He said there had been eighty-three murders since January and no one had been brought to justice. Every loyal man and woman should rally round the Government, but the Government should be doing more.[13] This dissatisfaction with the Belfast Government over its handling of security was one of the aspects of the 'extremism' illustrated in the public statements of Coote, Lynn, Cooper, McGuffin and others in the first year of the Northern parliament. It manifested itself particularly in criticism of any suggestion of leniency in dealing with those arrested for subversive crimes in the North. Coote was especially sharp in his attack on Craig over the clause in the London agreement with Collins (at the end of March 1922) about the release of 'political' prisoners. There was criticism too over the reprieve of the Derry prisoners in February 1922.[14]

Two other elements in 'extremism' emerge from public statements of Coote and others in this first year. One was criticism of the Government for its alleged weakness in dealing with the Imperial Government in London, or in allowing London to talk it into compromising positions *vis-à-vis* Dublin. In April 1922 Coote was critical of Craig's 30 March agreement with Collins on the grounds that it implied that the B Specials in Northern Ireland had been breaking the law. He was critical of it because it made no reference to the plight of Protestants and Loyalists in the South, and was extremely sharp over the clause on the release of 'political' prisoners.[15] Later in 1922 McGuffin talked of the Government's lack of policy on relations with the Imperial Government. They all, he said, had ideas or suspicions that something very serious was taking place, because of the frequent visits of the Prime Minister to London.[16] There was criticism too of Craig over ambiguity on the boundary question, stemming partly, perhaps, from Craig's lingering fondness for the idea of minor revisions that would bring in more Loyalists and exclude some Republicans.

A third element in the 'extremism' of these Unionists was their attitude towards their Catholic–nationalist fellow Northerners. Public utterances in this regard were generally very cautious, particularly in parliamentary debates, but there is a clear distinction between Craig's continued conciliatory references and remarks by Coote, Lynn and McGuffin. Certainly 'extremism' in Unionist terms included a more than customary preoccupation with the threat of Rome Rule, and perhaps more significantly, a greater readiness to talk about it bluntly in public. In November 1921 Lynn said, in the Commons in Belfast, that it was asked why would Ulster not go into a Dublin parliament, keeping the powers they now had, but allowing an all-Ireland parliament manage the reserved services. His answer, he said, was in the words of Lord Birkenhead: 'We are a Protestant Community and we will not be governed by a Roman Catholic Parliament.'[17] This question of subservience to the Vatican, he said, was one the average Englishman was afraid to face. He was afraid of being called a religious bigot, 'yet we know this is a religious question. There are two peoples in Ireland, one industrious, law-abiding and God-fearing, and the other slothful, murderous and disloyal.'[18]

In the same debate Coote treated the Commons to a lecture on sacerdotalism. This was the great dominating factor in the south of Ireland:

> When sacerdotal authority over-rides the civil law in any country, there must be trouble. That is the source of trouble in Ireland. It is the ecclesiastical authority, especially in the South of Ireland, trying to dictate to the Government of the day what they do and what they should not do. This will always be the case so long as the ecclesiastical authority has a grip on the minds of the people of Ireland.[19]

Such views would have been held by many Unionists, but tended to be expressed by the Cootes and Lynns rather than by the Craigs and Andrewses. These former were also more ready to explore the implications within Northern Ireland of a close link between Catholicism and Sinn Féinism.

In a speech to Orangemen in Belfast on 30 November 1921 Coote spoke about strengthening the hands of the Loyalist people.[20] They would try to hold the farms, the businesses and the employment for the Protestant working people. They were going to insist that the employers of Ulster would clear out the black-guards who were trying to make trouble in their midst. They used to be told that they could hold nine counties; if they did not look to their laurels, they would soon lose the six counties. The Sinn Féiners were coming over the border, they were burrowing in like rabbits, they would accept work at any price, they would even blacken boots in order to get in and get the power and then would give the Loyalists sauce, he said. Going on to speak about the Belfast Boycott, he indicated his equation of Sinn Féin with Catholics. If the boycott went on much longer, he said, they would have to take it in hand. They should resolve to have nothing to do with Roman Catholic pubs, they should boycott charities that helped Catholics.

On 23 May in the Commons in Belfast Lynn raised the emotive imagery of 1641. Not since that date, he said, had Ulster been confronted with such a serious difficulty:

> And the spirit that underlay the attack made on the Protestants of Ulster in 1641 is the spirit that animates the attack that is being made on Ulster today.[21]

And he went on, with protestations of fairness, to implicate all Northern Catholics in this 1641-type attack:

> There is no Member of this House, and no man or woman whose view is worth having, who wants to see crime and disorder or anything done to our Roman Catholic fellow countrymen that we do not want to see done to ourselves. We want to hold the scales evenly and fairly and justly so far as each one is concerned, but we have ample proof, proof in the papers today, that these people are out to render the Northern Government impotent.[22]

In March McGuffin made a speech that has turned out to be remarkably perceptive in its analysis of the long-term problems of governing Northern Ireland. Dismissing the then current split in the South between Free Staters and Republicans as a distinction

98

without a difference, he noted that the South had a largely homogeneous population:

> There is a unanimity of ideas and policy that does not exist in the North and to my mind can never exist in the North. In the North you have a population which is far from homogeneous, which is divided and is divided in such a proportion as always to make it a menace to those who govern in this area. . . What I fail to see is how we can be sure except under the most extraordinary pressure by the Government of anything like a safe and satisfactory peace. Something must be done. I am not here to suggest what it will be. . . the conditions are permanent. We cannot alter them. We have been trying to control law and order. Up to the moment we have failed and I do not know whether the policy that is in prospect by the Prime Minister is going to produce the necessary desirable results. You have the border difficulties. You have in the first instance the area in which we live infested by those we call our enemies.[23]

It was in their response to the problem outlined by McGuffin that the extremists took issue with Craig, and it was this tension that dominated Unionism and held it together for half a century.

In parliamentary terms, the opposition was hardly a matter of great concern to the new Government. There was never any chance of a parliamentary reverse. In four years of the first parliament Coote himself only voted nine times against the Government. The biggest anti-administration vote was eleven, on the question of ministerial salaries. That was not a token stand against salaries to denote no-confidence in Craig and his ministers, but a reflection of the widely held view, strongly voiced by Coote, that there was too much extravagance in the new Northern administration – too many posts, too high salaries. But even with eleven voting against him, in a House of Commons of forty, Craig was left with a comfortable majority of more than two-to-one.[24]

Clearly the significance of the 'usual little gang' was far greater than their number. At crucial moments their arguments appealed to a substantial segment of Unionism, including many members of the Commons and possibly some members of the Government. At the end of March 1922 Craig certainly did not underestimate the threat from them. Writing in her diary on 31 March on the terms of the controversial Craig–Collins Pact of the day before, Lady Craig commented:

I feel sure every decent person will approve of them, and if Ulster does not want moderation and fairness, she may expect J to resign and make way for the extremists, and then they would jolly well stew. The Orangemen who stand for civil and religious liberty can hardly object.[25]

A few days later on 4 April she had more to say:

What makes me so raging is the lack of guts of them all: none of the people who heartily approve of his action [Craig's Pact with Collins] have the courage to get up and say so, and just let this noisy trio have things all their own way. It makes one wonder whether they are worth someone slaving oneself almost to death for. How I wish sometimes he had stayed in England, where he is so much appreciated, of course I know all the people themselves adore him.[26]

Craig did not, however, resign, nor did he abandon the Pact with Collins, but there was a clear reluctance to proceed with the release of prisoners as had been agreed in the Pact. The reason, presumably, was the strength of the opposition voiced by Coote and others, but shared by many more, including some within the Cabinet.

If that was probable over the Craig–Collins Pact, and the release of prisoners, it was certainly true over the question of a judicial inquiry into the violence in Belfast in May and June 1922 – an inquiry demanded by Collins and the Provisional Government, and desired by the Government in London. Craig acquiesced in the idea of an inquiry, but only on condition that the request for it came from him, and that it was not seen as something imposed on the North by London. But at a meeting in London in June 1922, with Bonar Law, Churchill and others on one side, and himself and Lord Londonderry on the other, Craig had to tell the British Government that his colleagues would not consent to ask for a public inquiry. He himself now took grave exception to the idea of an inquiry appointed by the British Government into the affairs of Ulster.[27]

Dawson Bates, now Minister of Home Affairs, had argued in a letter to Craig that it was impossible to agree to Churchill's suggestion 'without gravely weakening the authority of the Government of Northern Ireland'.[28] Considerable pressure had been put on Craig by Churchill, who had pointed out that London had shown its readiness to defend Ulster with force – as had just happened at Pettigo. But the pressure from his own Unionist colleagues was clearly stronger. They had not liked the Pact with Collins at all. Stephen George Tallents, the British civil servant sent over to report on the North in place of the judicial inquiry, wrote, in a confidential note on 4 July 1922, that aspects of the agreement had exasperated Craig's supporters:

> He had a cold reception when he returned to Belfast with the agreement, and at least one of his Ministers seems to have shown little enthusiasm in forwarding the work either of the conciliation committee or of the police committee.[29]

On 30 May Churchill had told the Cabinet in London that Craig had made a great effort to help on the Pact but that after the de Valera–Collins electoral agreement in the South, 'he had gone over to the other side'. Initially, said Churchill, Craig had been willing 'to go to great lengths'.[30] 'The other side' in this sense was clearly not just Coote, Lynn and McGuffin, but a majority of the Cabinet, particularly Bates and the Attorney General, Richard Best, and probably too the majority of the Ulster Unionist Council. The driving force of this 'extremism' was a combination of border Unionism, as represented by Coote, and the virulently anti-Catholic, Orange working-class districts of Belfast. Lynn and McGuffin represented such constituencies.

The circumstances of 1921–2 greatly strengthened the forces working against any form of moderation. The high level of IRA activity in Belfast and the accompanying descent into disorder meant ever-more strident calls, notably from Lynn and the *Whig*, for vigorous enforcement of law and order, and no 'softness' on Sinn Féin. In the border counties Unionist insecurity had already been heightened by the final abandoning of the additional three counties in the acceptance of the Government of Ireland Act – if it could happen to Cavan, Monaghan and Donegal, it could happen to Tyrone and Fermanagh. The Sinn Féin–Nationalist victories in both counties in the 1920 local elections were serious blows to the Unionists.

Against that background the Boundary Clause of the Treaty, and the nationalist claims based on it, became a dire and almost immediate threat to the Unionists of all border areas. The preponderance of Belfast, Down and Antrim Unionism in Craig's first administration did nothing to ease the insecurity. Writing in December 1922, after a visit to Pettigo, Tallents had this to say:

It is interesting to note the difference between the Tyrone and Fermanagh, and the Belfast points of view. The people living near the Western frontier are apt to regard 'the Belfast crowd' as inspired solely by their own material interests. This, no doubt, is partly a reflection of the old decision which excluded Donegal, Cavan and Monaghan from Northern Ireland.[31]

Some recognition of the problem was implied in Craig's regular border tours – one after the kidnappings of February 1922, another just before Tallent's comment of December. Tallents also hoped the appointment of the Duke of Abercorn with his seat in west Tyrone, as Governor of Northern Ireland, would offer some reassurance.

It was pressure from border Unionism that helped push Craig into early action to abandon proportional representation for Northern local government elections, and thus open the way for the rigging of sensitive constituencies in the resulting distribution. The ending of PR had been agreed Unionist policy in the election campaign of 1921, but the pledge had been to move against it within three years. In the event, the Local Government Bill was going through parliament within one year. Craig told the Commons that his Government had been pressed by fifty-nine local authorities to bring the Bill forward as quickly as possible.[32] One factor in the urgency was undoubtedly the Boundary Commission, and the use that nationalist spokesmen were making of their control of Tyrone and Fermanagh county councils. An end to PR would mean a redrawing of constituency boundaries, and the chance to maximise Unionist control along the border.

The Government in London for a long time blocked the Royal Assent to the Bill and contemplated, at the urging of the Provisional Government in Dublin, vetoing it. However, in the face of a resignation threat from Craig and his Cabinet, the Bill was allowed the Royal Assent. This threat by Craig, in late July 1922, in order to force London's acceptance of the Local Government Bill, was an indication of how strongly he was now ready to go along with the 'extremists', and was in marked contrast to earlier talk of his resignation rather than accept the dictates of that same element.

The whole episode of local government reorganisation, which made possible the degree of discrimination against Catholic voters that was to be taken for years as an indication of all that was worst about Unionist rule in Northern Ireland, was also in stark contrast to the sentiments expressed by Craig in 1921 over the need to treat the minority with absolute fairness. So too was the implementation of the Special Powers Act, under which several hundred suspected IRA supporters were interned in May 1922, and the refusal of Craig to allow proper investigation into allegations of atrocities by the B Specials.[33]

It was principally on these two factors – the fear of boundary revision and security – that any hope of a conciliatory attitude towards the Catholic minority foundered. In both areas the attitudes and actions of the Northern Catholics themselves, of the Provisional Government in Dublin, and of the Imperial Government in London stengthened the extremist argument among Unionists.

The Boundary Commission was seen by neither side as a legitimate exercise in rationalising the division between North and South. Collins's Provisional Government and Northern nationalists saw it as a means of undermining Northern Ireland and ending partition. Craig and the Unionists – while open to minor adjustments by agreement, for their own convenience – saw it as a trick, as something basically unfair, if not illegal. Their argument was that it was agreed in a negotiation between Sinn Féin and London, in which Northern Ireland, though in existence with its own Government, was not involved. And that it conflicted with what was already on the statute book – the Government of Ireland Act.

There was also the feeling that any major boundary revision was illogical: partition had been devised as a means of giving Northern Unionists the chance to opt out of Irish self-government, thereby opening the way to a solution between Dublin and London. After much heart-searching, the Unionists had agreed on the six counties as the unit likely to give the desired result, that is, an area sufficiently large to function with reasonable economic efficiency, yet containing within it a guaranteed and comfortable Unionist majority.

In 1922 the Unionists were correct in seeing any major boundary revision as a threat to the whole settlement they had accepted in the 1920 Act, and it was a threat brought about by a change of the rules since they had accepted that Act. When Northern Ireland came into existence, it was a known fact that both Fermanagh and Tyrone had Catholic, or nationalist, majorities in terms of population, and that both county councils had been won by nationalists. In 1921 that had been no barrier to both counties being within Northern Ireland; suddenly, at the beginning of 1922, it became very much a possibility that it would be grounds for taking them out of Northern Ireland, thereby, it was generally assumed, terminating Northern Ireland's existence.

Hence the obsession with local government representation, and the urgency to end PR and ensure, by any means, Unionist control of the maximum number of local authorities. An added incentive was the unfounded belief that the small nationalist majorities in Tyrone and Fermanagh were 'artificial', in so far as they emerged during the First World War when, in the words of the *Whig* on 6 February 1922, the Loyalists volunteered and fought for Britain, while the rebels stayed at home and did what they could for Germany. A similar belief, that Southern or rural Catholics had flooded into Belfast for work during the war, was a factor used in stirring up anti-Catholic feeling among the Protestant working class in the city, and undoubtedly contributed to the mentality that allowed the expulsion of Catholic shipyard workers from their jobs in July 1920.

This question of Catholic infiltration into the North was to rise again periodically over the next thirty years. It appears to have been widely believed, though the evidence for it is slight. According to the 1926 census there were 64,000 people resident in Northern Ireland who had been born in the area then the Free State. This figure was an increase of about 8,000 over the corresponding figure for the six counties in the 1911 census. In percentage terms the increase was from 4.5 per cent of the North's population in 1911 to 5.1 per cent in 1926. Given the upheaval at the time of partition, the increase is hardly significant, particularly as numbers of Protestants would have moved North. Belfast had 22,606 Southern-born citizens in 1926.[34] But in the turbulent atmosphere of 1921–2, with the promised boundary revision threatening to destroy Northern Ireland, it was an added argument turning Unionists against all nationalist or Catholic voters – 'those we call our enemies', in the words of McGuffin. With boundary revision pending, the ordinary Catholic voter was now a threat to the existence of Northern Ireland.

The open, and quite general, Catholic identification with the Provisional Government in Dublin and parallel rejection of the new institutions in Belfast, reinforced the view of many Unionists that Northern Catholics, as a community, were part of the on-slaught on Ulster – if not actually involved in IRA violence, then supporting the systematic Sinn Féin attempt to make impossible the functioning of Northern Ireland.

There were indications that not all Catholics were of such a mind. Leading Catholic businessmen contacted Craig and went to meet Churchill in London. On 2 June 1922 a three-man deputation told Churchill that

> ... the Catholic businessmen of Belfast, excluding Republicans and the professional men, would be ready to recognise the Northern Government, but for the rest of the Catholic population, the idea of religious persecution dominated their political preferences.[35]

During the discussion Churchill suggested four kinds of Catholic in Belfast – followers of de Valera, of Collins, of MacRory, and of Devlin. The Catholic businessmen drew no distinction between followers of Collins and Bishop MacRory, but thought the fol-lowers of de Valera very few, and those of Devlin were numerous. Joe Devlin, member of both the Belfast and Westminster Parlia-ments, was the leader of the non-Sinn Féin Nationalists.

At that meeting Churchill declared that 'the brushing aside of Mr Devlin had been one of the worst disasters of the situation'.[36] Yet it was the London Government that did most to brush him aside, when it formally recognised Collins as the representative of Northern Catholics and asked him, under the Pact of 30 March, to nominate Catholic members of the two Belfast committees set up under that agreement. Tallents, writing on 4 July, saw this quite clearly:

> It is worth noting for future consideration that the system employed in that agreement of inviting Mr Collins to act as the representative of a minority in the territory of another government both encouraged the Catholics in their policy of non-recognition of the Northern Government and exasperated Sir James Craig's sup-porters. . . For practical purposes the Catholics of Belfast, outside the gunmen and a few such irreconcilables, seem to be divided into the followers of Mr Devlin and the followers of Mr Collins.[37]

In his formal report, dated two days later, Tallents wrote that several prominent Catholics he met in Belfast were anxious that the Catholic community in the six counties

> . . . should now recognise the Northern Government. I should infer from their attitude that Mr Devlin would not be averse to this. On the other hand, Bishop MacRory, who is in close touch with Mr Collins, and evidently has great influence among the Catholics in Belfast, said that he would 'not be willing to recognise the Northern Government, unless it 'co-operated for large purposes with the Southern Government'.[38]

The extent of such desired co-operation is not explained, but would no doubt have gone far beyond anything Craig could have offered. Tallents then returned to the question of Collins and the Northern Catholics:

> The present system by which the Belfast Catholics appeal direct to Mr Collins, who then passes on their complaints to London, naturally irritates the Northern Government. I venture to doubt whether it will be found in future wise to allow Mr Collins to act as their representative to the extent to which he so acted in the Agreement of March 30.[39]

In March 1922 Collins had set up his own advisory committee in connection with the whole six-county question.[40] In letters of invitation sent out on 8 March he explained that the Provisional Government wanted advice and assistance on the boundary question, on the Belfast pogrom and the possible re-imposition of the economic boycott, and on 'all governmental functions as affected by or affecting the Belfast Parliament'.[41] More than forty invitations went out, fourteen to Catholic clerics including two Northern bishops, and also to Eoin O'Duffy, IRA Chief of Staff, and Joe McKelvey, IRA officer commanding in Belfast. On 5 April telegrams were sent to twenty-two people, inviting them to the first meeting on 11 April, by which time the Craig–Collins Pact had been published and was already in serious trouble.

Even though Tallents was undoubtedly correct in seeing the fact of the Collins–Belfast–Catholic link as encouraging the Northern nationalists to withhold recognition from Craig's Government, in discussions within the advisory committee it was the Provisional Government that was the moderate element. Cosgrave told the 11 April meeting of the committee that he was against continuing refusal to recognise the Belfast administration. It was not practical and had no chance of success – there was no chance of money from Dublin. A 'headline' had been agreed, he said, with regard to local government not to recognise the Northern parliament, but no regular policy had been inaugurated. A 'local government war for the Six Counties' was not a proposition that would commend itself to anybody who looked towards success.[42] To which Cahir Healy, the Fermanagh Nationalist, replied that the nationalist councils had been put out of existence for recognising the Dáil, and today they heard the Dáil recommending a policy of surrender.[43] Kevin O'Higgins told the same meeting that it was inconsistent to stand on the Treaty and 'say you do not recognise the Northern Parliament'.[44]

On 15 May a sub-committee meeting in Belfast agreed to a policy of obstruction, proposed by Cahir Healy with the comment: 'At the moment it would be hard to say where passive resistance should end and other activities begin.'[45] The meeting formally recommended

> . . . an active destructive policy inside the Six County area apart from the Border; the destruction of roads, bridges etc., and all other ways in which we can make Government impossible in the Six County area.[46]

The chairman of the Belfast sub-committee was Frank Crommie, who had told the meeting that there were two ways

> . . . of dealing with these people in Belfast – one way is to hope they will come in later on and the other way is to kick and trample on them. . . I am very much inclined to the second method.[47]

Crommie was one of Collins's nominees for the two committees set up under the 30 March Pact with Craig. He was later arrested under the Special Powers Act.

Not that the Provisional Government was over-impressed by the committee's ideas: a confidential memo addressed to the chairman of the Sinn Féin Standing Committee dated 26 May 1922 refers to a long list of 'very exquisite resolutions sent in by the [North East Advisory] Committee, none of which were at all practical'. The resolutions were sent back to the committee with the recommendation that they should 'outline their general plan for rendering null and void the functioning of the Northern Government'.[48]

But while Dublin regarded the Belfast suggestions as 'exquisite' and impractical, the Provisional Government policy on the North throughout this period was based on the assumption that the North could not survive, and was directed towards achieving its downfall. As Richard Mulcahy, the Dáil's Minister of Defence, told the committee at its meeting in Dublin on 11 April:

I take it that under the terms of the Treaty we recognise that [the northern] Parliament in order to destroy it and I think it is just obvious from the circumstances of the case to take all this Treaty and to carry out all its terms will ultimately unify the country and destroy the Northern Parliament.[49]

Michael Collins's approach was much more direct. Defending the Treaty, he told Northern IRA leaders in 1922 that although the Treaty seemed to be an expression of partition, the Government had plans whereby they would make it impossible and that partition would never be recognised even though it might mean the smashing of the Treaty.[50] O'Duffy had also assured the Northern IRA that it was the intention of the pro-Treaty Dáil members and the IRA headquarters' staff 'to work to try to overcome the Treaty position with regard to Ulster'.[51]

When non-recognition, support for the Northern IRA, and whatever additional plans Collins had in mind early in 1922 failed to bring down the Northern administration, there remained the great hope of the Boundary Commission. The expectation then was that the commission would be set up as soon as possible, and that its recommendations would inevitably mean such loss of territory by the North that partition would not survive. Such an attitude meant that neither the Provisional Government nor the Northern nationalists with whom they were dealing had any interest in the concept of eventual unity by way of partition. This concept had been enshrined in the Government of Ireland Act and had, theoretically at least, been accepted by Craig, Carson and the Unionists. Partition was the only way to accommodate the irreconcilable claims of Unionism and nationalism, and achieve the better government of Ireland. It was to be the means of defusing the impasse over Irish self-government in the short-term, while leaving the way open to eventual unity through the Council of Ireland.

That approach was firmly rejected by Sinn Féin in 1920–21, and while both partition and the Council of Ireland were accepted in the Treaty, it was an acceptance bought by the Boundary Clause, which was taken to be a guarantee that partition would not last. Even the pro-Treaty side in 1922 was still committed to achieving unity by ending partition and dismantling Northern Ireland, rather than by accepting one and working the other.

Even when the Provisional Government realised in the second half of 1922, particularly after Collins's death, that they had no option but to work the Treaty arrangements and abandon the campaign of non-recognition, their hopes remained pinned to the Boundary Commission. Already by that time they had helped frame the pattern of politics inside Northern Ireland, leaving the Catholics there firmly established in Unionist eyes as 'those we call our enemies'. In all this both Dublin and Northern nationalists failed to grasp the reality of Unionist intransigence, or if they did, to come to grips with it in a rational fashion. There are numerous examples of leaders in Dublin assuming a readiness on the part of sections of Unionism to accept, or be forced into acceptance of some form of unity. During the Treaty debates, both Ernest Blythe and O'Duffy, claiming to know the North, argued that economic boycott, or 'suitable propaganda' would soon convert the Loyalists.

Northern nationalists were usually more aware of the diffi-culties involved in persuading Unionists into Irish unity. Most comments from Northerners recorded in the North East Advisory Committee's minutes indicate that the Northern nationalists believed force was the only answer – burning, trampling, kicking or, possibly, expelling. It is significant that in Dáil Éireann corres-pondence with Belfast on the subject of the economic boycott in 1921, reports from the Belfast organisers of the boycott tended to use the terms 'the garrison' or 'anti-Irish' to refer to the Unionist community or Protestants, and to speak of Catholics as the 'Irish community' in Belfast.[52]

Northern Unionists in the first half of 1922 were well aware of these attitudes, and painfully conscious of the general nationalist determination to encompass the downfall of Northern Ireland. Some responded by direct and brutal action against Catholics. Others brought increasing pressure upon Craig to enforce law and order, and take new powers to do so, and also to move to ensure that the dangers of boundary revision be at least lessened, by abolishing proportional representation and revising electoral districts. Craig in turn was under the utmost pressure from London to curb Orange extremists, to reach an accommodation with the Provisional Government, and to put his own house in order as regards allegations against the B Specials.

The dilemma that Craig thus found himself in crystallised in the few days or weeks following the Pact with Collins of 30 March 1922. Under it he was supposed to release political prisoners, to give Catholics an equal share in policing in mixed districts, to accept a Catholic Advisory Committee to help select Catholic recruits to the B Specials, to accept a half-and-half conciliation committee to hear complaints on intimidation and outrages, and to agree to one further meeting with Collins, after the Free State's Constitution had been confirmed, to discuss 'whether means can be devised to secure the unity of Ireland'.[53] In return, he was promised an end to IRA activity in the six counties.

No doubt Craig accepted this remarkable package under extreme urging from Churchill. He put a brave face on it presenting it to parliament in Belfast, and envisaging a Northern Ireland in which Catholics would play their proper role. Many had expressed a desire to help with law and order, he said. He was not without hope that before the year was out, Catholic representatives would come and take their seats in parliament 'and relieve us of the awkward position of having, as it were, to deal behind their backs which to me is an unfortunate way of doing business and one which I most heartily detest'.[54] But Coote, reflecting Unionist feeling more accurately, saw the Pact as the result of intrigue in London, and had many points of criticism.

In the event the IRA violence did not cease, the economic boycott continued and was, if anything, intensified, Collins delayed making his nominations to the two committees, and finally buried the Pact, where Craig was concerned, by his own electoral Pact of 20 May with de Valera and the Republicans. Tallents, in a note on a conversation with 'B', possibly the Catholic businessman Raymond Burke, remarks that Collins was very slow to nominate to the committees, and that when he did give names 'their bearers proved to be impossible people who must have been nominated by Collins in the desire that the machinery should not work'.[55]

On 23 May 1922, after a weekend of intense sectarian violence in Belfast and widespread IRA activity, Craig delivered a speech to the Northern Commons that probably marked the end of any hopes he had, or efforts he was prepared to make, for an amicable settlement with the South and an opening towards the Catholic community in the North. Talking about the 'war upon Ulster', he denounced first the incendiary campaign against the 'big houses', including Shane's Castle, and crimes and outrage across Down, Antrim and Belfast.[56] But the most serious factor was the de Valera–Collins Pact agreed the previous Saturday, 20 May.[57] He quoted Collins as saying the Treaty was a step towards a Republic, and said Ulster was now faced with a government in Dublin that was half-Republican.

He then proceeded, finally and categorically, to reject the Boundary Commission:

> We, as a united Cabinet, now state that we will not have any Boundary Commission under any circumstances whatever. . . We have to look back with concern, and in my case with the very greatest regret, that there was not a more reasonable spirit shown towards us, and that the upholder of the Treaty in the South had not got the courage to stick to his guns and carry out what he had promised he would do, and to see that settled government was provided in the South and West. The first result of that pact is to allow me to make that statement to the House and to the whole of the Six Counties, that they may understand there is a complete washout, and that we will hear no more about a Commission. . .
>
> The second immediate result of that pact was to make us search our hearts as to whether some immediate action should not be taken against those in our midst, not so much the tools, not so much the lower down class who carry out the outrages, schemes of all sorts against our people, but those who are responsible for thinking out those schemes and orders.[58]

He went on to announce 'drastic steps': the IRA was proscribed and more than 500 people arrested and interned.

On both law and order, and on local government reform and maximising Unionist control, Craig had gone a long way to satisfy the 'extremist' demands of the border Unionists and the Orange working class of Belfast. In part, he was forced into these measures by the continued IRA violence and the attitude and actions of both factions in the South. In part, probably with the 'very greatest regret' he professed, he was going along with the tide of Unionism that had no time for conciliation or negotiation, and saw no point in trying to please those who would not be pleased.

Craig's position in the early years of Northern Ireland was an unusual one for a Prime Minister. He had come back to Northern Ireland to take up that role at the express invitation of the Ulster Unionist Council, and had done so under persuasion, with some regrets and some misgivings. His selection was obvious once it was clear that Carson's health would not permit him to lead Unionism inside Northern Ireland. But his position as the obvious choice rested on his leadership and organisational ability in the dramatic crisis of 1912–14. In 1921 the Ulster Unionist Council looked to him again as an organisational leader, even a figure-head. But the Unionist members elected in 1921 to the Belfast parliament, and the party at large in the state, particularly on the border and in industrial Belfast, were not his creation. They, it was, who brought him back to do a job for them.

This almost contractual relationship between organised Unionism and Craig is seen in the editorials of the *Whig* in the first half of 1922, most of them presumably the work of Lynn. Behind the repeated eulogies of Craig there is a hint of the schoolmaster surveying the pupil's work, or the employer keeping an eye on the new man. There is repeated concern over the security situation in Belfast. First the *Whig* suggests, on 3 January 1922, that the citizens of the city have been too passive, have not protested enough, have had too much confidence in the authorities. It was not for the *Whig* to prescribe the means the authorities should adopt, but that was the business of the Government.

The following week, on 7 January, the *Whig* was noting 'criticism from a good many quarters of the Northern Government' over the continuing violence. On 10 March, the *Whig* saw 'unmistakable signs that the capacity of Belfast's citizens to endure scandalous conditions has reached its limit'. The authorities, the *Whig* felt sure, would take note of manifestations of public indignation – 'They certainly cannot afford to ignore them.'

The *Whig* was also keeping a watchful eye on Craig's dealings with London and Dublin. It did not like the initial Pact with Collins in January, though it warmed to it just before it collapsed. When it did break down, the *Whig* commented on 4 February, 'that Sir James Craig was misled is certain'. It was an arguable proposition that he had been mistaken in accepting the British assurances.

By mid-March, before the second Craig–Collins Pact of 30 March, the *Whig* was plainly disappointed in Craig's failure to take exceptional measures against the IRA in Belfast, and was unhappy with his handling of London. Citing lessons to be learned from the actions of the Imperial Government, the *Whig*, on 10 March, added:

> We are convinced that the ultimate judgement of Ulster on the work of Sir James Craig will mainly depend on the extent to which the moral of these ideas is assimilated.

Craig was still on probation.

On 10 May 1921 Craig, in a speech in the Ulster Hall, had replied to criticism of his meeting with de Valera. It was the business of a leader to lead, and not to crawl behind, he said. A year later, while not crawling behind, he had settled for leading his fervent Unionist band in the direction it, rather than he, wanted to go.

7
A GRIEVOUSLY WOUNDED MINORITY

The first six months of 1922, which saw increased violence in the North, was also a period of danger and suffering for Southern Unionists, or rather for those who had been Southern Unionists but were now largely identifiable as Protestants. The violence against this minority in the south and west of Ireland between 1919 and the Truce of July 1921 could be seen, to some extent, as the incidental concomitant of a war between Sinn Féin nationalism and British authority. But after the Truce, and particularly after the withdrawal of the British and the handover to the Provisional Government, such violence continued, even intensified, and assumed much more undeniably the character of persecution – certainly to the victims of it, and to their co-religionists in the new Northern Ireland.

But the term 'persecution' was also used by others. In a sermon in May 1923, sixteen months after the Provisional Government had assumed power, the Most Revd Dr Fogarty, Catholic Bishop of Killaloe, declared that while he regretted having to say it, their 'Protestant fellow-countrymen had been persecuted and dealt with in a cruel and coarse manner'.[1]

It was in the post-Treaty factionalism and the descent to civil war in early and mid-1922 that the Protestants suffered most. Again, some were the indiscriminate victims of the general breakdown of law and order. Others suffered because they presented a strategic or emotional 'big house' target. But in some areas at least, there appear to have been deliberate campaigns against the Protestant community as such.

Throughout the period from 1919 to the Treaty, the Protestants, or Unionists, of the South had indeed been loyal supporters of the British authorities and therefore the enemies, active or passive, of Sinn Féin. They were, as a group, so designated by at least one Dáil speaker during the Treaty debates. Deputy Art O'Connor described the Southern Unionists as professed enemies who stood in the way every time the people tried to make a little advance.[2]

In fact, representative Southern Protestants had already declared their acceptance of, and allegiance to, the Free State envisaged in the Treaty. The Archbishop of Dublin, Dr Gregg, in a statement on 11 December 1921, said it concerned all in Ireland that they should have a strong, capable and wise government:

> And therefore it concerns us all to offer to the Irish Free State so shortly to be constituted our loyalty and our good will. I believe there is a genuine disposition on the part of those from whom we have so differed in political outlook to make room for us and to welcome our co-operation. And we should be wrong, politically and religiously, to reject their advances. The new Constitution will claim our allegiance with the same solemn authority as the one that is now being constitutionally annulled.[3]

Dr Gregg also supported a meeting of prominent Southern Unionists held in Dublin on 19 January 1922, which formally 'recognised' the Provisional Goverment.[4]

Nevertheless on 14 February the *Belfast News-Letter* reported a Protestant blacksmith, Thomas Saddler, murdered at Butlersbridge, Co. Cavan, and less than two weeks later, Samuel Herbert Burns, also a Protestant, shot at Milford, Co. Donegal. During this period violence was at a considerable height in Belfast, with upwards of thirty people dying in two weeks. The *News-Letter*'s report, on 2 March, of Burns's funeral was headed 'Loyalists in the Free State – Safe neither in the open or in their houses'. It said many hundreds assembled to show their sympathy with the family, 'which has lately been suffering the lot of Loyalists in the Free State'.

March was a particularly bloody month in Belfast, with the murder of five members of the Catholic McMahon family on the morning of 24 March, followed by a weekend of violence. On 27 March the *News-Letter* reported the eviction of three Unionists from Clones, ordered to leave by the IRA. The men, a postman, a driver and a bakery representative, were all ex-soldiers. They were taken before IRA officers and told to get out of the Free State by 10 a.m. the next morning 'or abide the consequences'.

The following day under the heading 'Donegal Protestants' Plight', the *News-Letter* reported that all Orangemen had been ordered to leave the town of Buncrana as a reprisal for the McMahon murders. The same issue of the paper, 28 March, reported a Protestant ex-RIC man murdered in Cork, and a notice posted in Dundalk threatening 'all non-Catholics of Louth' with reprisals. The notice said that no resolution of sympathy with the McMahons had been passed by any non-Catholic body in Louth:

> We take their silence and indifference as aiding and abetting murder. We now inform them and compel them to act in this very serious matter. Failing to do this we are determined to use the same methods as they used in Belfast on our fellow Catholics.

The threat to Southern Protestants was, by early April, serious enough to alarm the British Government. Churchill, in a memorandum to the Cabinet on 5 April, dealing with the danger that the Republican side in the Treaty split might seize power from the Provisional Government, spoke of the question of refugees. There were, he wrote, 300,000 Unionists living in the twenty-six counties: 'Their position may become very grave. Veiled threats have already been directed at them at recent Republican meetings. They may be compelled to fly to Dublin or the sea.'[5]

April saw the realisation of Churchill's fears. On 7 April the *News-Letter* reported the murders of five disbanded RIC men. The following day it carried a letter from a provisional committee of Southern Protestants which was clearly an attempt to head off the mounting sectarian violence. The writers, Edward Culverwell and Charles Jacob, urged all Southern Protestants to sign a declaration of abhorrence at sectional bitterness and violence. They also put on record their view that the south of Ireland had been notably free from sectarian violence and that 'it is only by the maintenance of friendly relations between members of the different religious bodies that the future prosperity and happiness of our country can be achieved'.

But in the last week of April the growing animosity against Protestants spilled over into a murderous attack on the small Protestant community in west Cork. 'Protestants Slain' was the stark heading on the *News-Letter*'s report of the first killings in its issue of 28 April. Three men, a seventy-two-year-old solicitor and an eighty-three-year-old draper among them, had been shot. In the Dublin area Orange and Masonic halls were seized by armed men. The following day the heading in the *News-Letter* was 'Massacre of Protestants', with eight dead in Co. Cork. Recounting the 'ghastly crimes of the night', the *News-Letter* continued:

An appalling state of affairs exists in the South and West of County Cork, where a general massacre of Protestants appears to be in progress, eight murders being already reported. The victims in some cases were elderly men, others, mere boys.

The killing had begun on a Wednesday night, when the first three victims had been shot in Dunmanway. Other Protestant men had fled into the fields, including the Church of Ireland rector and the Methodist minister. The following night five more Protestants were murdered in the area of Clonakilty. The *Northern Whig*'s treatment of the story was equally dramatic. On successive days, 28 and 29 April, it reported: 'A terrible story of massacre of Protestants comes from West County Cork', and 'Cork massacre continues'.

The folk memories that were easily awakened by such attacks on small isolated Protestant communities were indicated by the *Whig* in its comment, on 1 May, on the statement issued in Dublin by the Sinn Féin leaders of both sides, assembled in the unsuccessful conciliation conference called by Dublin's Lord Mayor and the Catholic Archbishop. All participants had signed a statement on the Cork killings saying that these murders were 'unprecedented, and totally alien to the Irish character'. This was a curious statement, said the *Whig,* 'for it is a matter of notoriety that the murders, far from being unprecedented, are only the last in a long series which began as far back as 1641'.

Dorothy Macardle suggests the killings were reprisals for the shooting of an IRA man called O'Neill, near Bandon, on 25 April, and for the murders of Catholics in Belfast. She adds that the local IRA then ordered all arms 'to be called under control and all citizens protected'.[6] But the immediate result was a flight of Protestants from west Cork. Another Protestant was killed in the area over the weekend of 29–30 April, and on Monday morning the *Whig* reported:

> During Friday and Saturday over one hundred persons from Dunmanway, Ballineen and Bandon left and travelled to Cork, leaving in most cases their female relatives to look after their homes in what they hope will be their temporary absence. Most of the refugees boarded the Rosslare train. . . en route for various destinations across the Channel, and so hurried was their flight that some of them had neither a handbag or an overcoat.

117

The *News-Letter* of the same day also reported 'The Flight from Cork', with accounts of 'terrified Protestants' crossing to England.

The west Cork incident was the most dramatic, but far from the only case of Protestants coming under attack. On 1 May a question was asked at Westminster about the forcible ejection of large numbers of Protestants from Queen's County (now Co. Laois).[7] On 4 May the *News-Letter*, under the heading 'The Continued Persecution of Southern Protestants', said Protestants in south Donegal had received notices ordering them to clear out. Those threatened included a Church of Ireland rector, farmers and householders. Further south, in Clonmel, Co. Tipperary, the Presbyterian minister, the Revd J.T. Montgomery, had left town 'in consequence of threats'.

On 8 May fifty refugees from the south of Ireland turned up at the House of Commons in London. Reporting this on 9 May the *News-Letter* hoped that every effort would be made to bring to the understanding of the British people

> . . . the systematic persecution of Protestants which is going on all over the South and West of Ireland. . . Never since the rebellion of 1641 have the minority been in greater danger. They are living in constant fear of murder. . . During the last few days the campaign of terrorism has been intensified, and thousands of men and women are in imminent danger.

At Westminster the refugees had some success. The Lord Privy Seal, Austen Chamberlain, who reported to the Cabinet on 10 May on a meeting with MPs on the distressed conditions of the refugees, said it had been decided that 'while every effort should be made to discourage any general exodus of Southern Unionists from Ireland, special assistance might be necessary in certain individual cases'.[8] The sum of £10,000 was to be given to a committee – the Irish Distress Committee under Sir Samuel Hoare – but 'it was most desirable that the existence of this special relief should not be advertised'.[9]

On 9 May, in Dublin, the General Synod of the Church of Ireland met in emergency session to consider what had become an alarming crisis. After the first news of the west Cork killings, the Archbishop of Dublin, Dr Gregg, had called publicly on the Government

... to take necessary steps to protect a grievously wounded minority, and to defend the Protestants of West Cork from a repetition of these atrocities and to save the Protestants there, and in other parts of the South, from threatened violence and expulsion from their homes.[10]

He spoke of 'these horrible events' and of the 'savage blood lust they disclosed' of 'this organised massacre'. Early in May, Dr Gregg expressed his deep private concern in his diary:

A week of great anxiety as to the Church's future. News of evictions, ejections and intimidations everywhere. Where is it all to lead to? Is it the beginning or end, or a short storm? Prol. Govt. so far seems powerless to intervene.[11]

On 9 May the synod decided on a direct approach to the Government. Dr Gregg was to head a delegation of himself, Dr Miller, Bishop of Cashel, and Sir William Goulding, and their mission was

... to ask advice as to the best way in which the fears of Church people can be allayed, and to assure the authorities that the best efforts of the bishops, clergy and laity are enlisted in support of law and order.[12]

The delegation met Collins and Cosgrave on 12 May, and according to statements issued afterwards, 'they asked for assurances that the Government was desirous of retaining them, or whether, in the alternative, it was desired that they should leave the country'.[13] Behind the archaic phraseology lies an indication of the extent to which a real feeling of persecution existed among the Protestant community in May 1922.

The British Government was considerably alarmed at the possibility of a flood of refugees from the south of Ireland. On 16 May Churchill told the Cabinet in London that the flow of refugees was not yet large in volume, 'but might be a large stream into this country'. They might have to establish a pale around Dublin, with camps in it for refugees.[14]

The assurances given by Collins to the Church of Ireland delegation on 12 May did not stop the attacks, partly at least because many of these were in areas dominated by anti-Treaty elements. In its issue of 29 April the *Londonderry Sentinel* reported that Irregulars in Donegal were commandeering the goods of Protestant shopkeepers. In Raphoe the houses of Loyalists had been forcibly possessed. In mid-May the *Sentinel* commented:

The persecution of Loyalists in Co. Donegal and other parts of Southern Ireland is becoming so terrible that Protestant families are finding it absolutely necessary to forsake their homes and seek refuge in Londonderry and elsewhere in Northern Ireland.

The plight of the Protestant people is pitiable; their homes are raided, their property commandeered, and they are made act as slaves to gunmen. One lady of gentle birth, in whose residence fifteen armed rebels billeted themselves last Wednesday, and whose servants fled with the advent of the gunmen, has been acting as cook to these ruffians ever since.

The previous day, according to the *Sentinel,* a number of refugees from Donegal had arrived in Derry, and many more were expected. It also reported that several Protestant families had been ordered to leave their mansions, and two Wexford farmers had also been ordered out.

In the following weeks the *Sentinel* reported more evictions from Donegal – from Raphoe, Buncrana and Letterkenny. In Letterkenny three Protestant shops in the main street were wrecked by bombs, and a farmhouse was burned. In some cases those being evicted were told their houses were needed for Catholics from Belfast.

On 13 May the *News-Letter* reported that the Masonic Order had suspended all lodge meetings in the Free State because of continued attacks on Masonic halls and individual members. Elsewhere, it said, there had been extensive cattle drives on land held by Protestants in Kildare and Mayo. Threatening notices had been posted and Protestant property seized at Belmullet and Ballycastle, Co. Mayo.

A *News-Letter* report on 29 May conveys the intensity with which the news of these events was presented to Northern readers. Under the headings 'Donegal Huns' and 'Persecution Campaign Against Protestants and Loyalists' it said:

The plight of Protestants and Loyalists in Co. Donegal grows worse and worse every day. The rebels on the run from Northern Ireland are intensifying the campaign of persecution, and life has become unendurable for the abandoned Loyalists. Thousands have fled to Londonderry, Belfast and other places in Northern Ireland, leaving their belongings behind. They state that a reign of terror has been instituted. The Republican and Free State forces are now joined in the work of murder, robbery and incendiarism.

On 2 June the *Whig* reported 'a considerable number of refugees', mainly from Castlefin in Co. Donegal, arriving in Castlederg, Co. Tyrone.

There was a substantial Presbyterian population in east Donegal and not surprisingly, their welfare was of concern to the General Assembly meeting in Belfast in early June. It was agreed that an approach would be made to the Imperial Government 'with regard to the painful situation in which many Presbyterian people find themselves in County Donegal and other districts'.[15] That assembly was also concerned about the rapid decline in the Presbyterian population of the South. Its Home Mission Report said that in almost every part of the country where Protestants were in a minority, there had been a serious shrinking of the Protestant population. Since 1915 there had been a reduction of 45 per cent in the number of families in Cork presbytery, excluding Cork city, of 44 per cent in Munster presbytery, of 36 per cent in Connacht and 30 per cent in Athlone. The decline in Dublin, outside the city, had been 16 per cent.[16] The Moderator, Dr Strahan, said he did not suggest for one moment that all those who had left had been driven out, but there had been many 'instances of terror'.

Even while the assembly was in session in Belfast, reports were appearing of more trouble in Donegal. On 12 June the *News-Letter,* in 'Plight of Donegal Protestants', quoted a refugee in Derry as saying that since the 'Rorys of the Hills' had been deprived of petrol, they were seizing Protestant horses, cattle, and goods from Protestant shops. The following week serious trouble was reported from Leitrim and from Louth. On 17 June the *Whig* carried a story headed 'Hunting Leitrim Protestants'. It said:

> The persecution and driving out of Protestants from North Leitrim particularly in the Manorhamilton area continues, and on Thursday another family of well-to-do Protestant farmers had to flee to Enniskillen to save their lives, leaving behind all their goods and stock.

Similar expulsions were reported from Monaghan in the same issue. On 22 June the *News-Letter* had a story on an attack on railway workers living in Dundalk:

> For the past few months the Protestants of the town have been receiving notices warning them to leave Southern Ireland. Many refugees have arrived in Belfast and other parts of Ulster, and the

attack on these railway workers and their families was another step in the plan of extermination and eviction.

Much of the blame for the plight of Southern Protestants was, in the North, placed on the Provisional Government. The brief de Valera–Collins Pact of late May confirmed the Northern view that there was little difference between the two sides in the South, and that the Provisional Government was more interested in an accommodation with the Republicans than in asserting its authority. In addition, the Provisional Government was accused of putting Protestants at risk by talking of anti-Catholic pogroms in Belfast. On 24 June the *News-Letter* quoted with approval a *Daily Telegraph* editorial saying the Provisional Government 'by its lying propaganda' had poisoned the minds of the south of Ireland against Belfast. It had represented the conflict there as a purely Protestant pogrom in which Catholics were the only victims, 'and the consequence of that most wicked falsehood is seen in the brutal persecution of Protestants which for the first time in history has broken out in the South and West'.

At that time Griffith and Collins were placing great emphasis on the treatment of Catholics in Belfast. In his report back to Cabinet on his London meeting with them at the end of May, Lloyd George said they were more anxious about the north-east than about anything else:

> They talked of the extermination of Catholics. . . we could get Mr Collins to talk of nothing else, and when we were at last able to point out that there had been thirty-seven murders in the South, he replied that this was due to the excited state of feelings provoked by Belfast.[17]

The figure of thirty-seven murders used by Lloyd George, relating to a period of less than six months, shows the intensity of the violence against Protestants in the new Irish state.

There is no doubt that the periodic outbreaks of violence against Catholics in the North, particularly in Belfast, which had begun in the middle of 1920 with the expulsions from the shipyards, had a major impact on opinions and attitudes in the South, and contributed considerably towards the plight of the Southern Protestants. The attacks recommenced in the summer of 1921, and were part of the severe communal violence that flared up again in November 1921, and continued for the first half of 1922. Particularly savage incidents, like the murders of the Catholic McMahon family in March 1922, caused general outrage, heightened by the belief that members of the security forces were involved.

The official view in Dublin of the situation confronting Southern Unionists was put in a letter, dated 18 May 1922, from the Provisional Government Secretary to the Cabinet Committee in London dealing with the Provisional Government. In reply to a British note informing Dublin of the creation of the committee to aid refugees from the south of Ireland, and asking Dublin to admit financial liability and responsibility for compensation for damage and for restoring refugees to their homes, it said:

> My Government regrets that a certain small number of law abiding citizens have recently been obliged to flee from their homes in this country under threat of violence, and they are aware that some of these people have left for England.[18]

The letter thanked the British Government for its prompt action on their behalf and said the Provisional Government had no hesitation in accepting liability. The letter continued:

> The Provisional Government, however, are aware that, apart from cases where people have left Ireland owing to intimidation or violence, there is an organised movement amongst a certain element of the population in both countries which has for its purpose and political object the discrediting of the Provisional Government in Ireland and of His Majesty's Government in Great Britain, and it is a matter of common knowledge that, in accordance with the settled policy of that movement, a considerable number of people have left Ireland on the plea of compulsion without any justification whatever for that plea.[19]

The letter went on to say that the Provisional Government anticipated that normal conditions would be re-established in Ireland 'in the course of the next two months' and that any refugees could then return. It repeated the assurance given by Collins to the Church of Ireland delegation on 12 May that the Government would protect its citizens, ensure civil and religious liberty, and restore homes and property to any who had been deprived of them.

The letter concluded by mentioning the 'organised campaign of violence and intimidation' pursued for many months against Catholics in Belfast, with the result that a very large number had been forced to flee from Northern Ireland, and 'it had fallen upon the people all over the rest of Ireland to provide relief for the starving and destitute sufferers'.[20] The Provisional Government wanted London to accept financial liability for the provision of relief to these Catholic refugees, and it also wanted immediate steps taken to protect the Catholics of the north-east and arrange for a speedy return to their homes. The letter certainly underplays the plight of Southern Unionists, in part at least to minimise the financial liability the Provisional Government was undertaking. It takes no account of the number of murders committed, and the consequent panic among the Protestant population.

The hope that normal conditions would be restored in the course of the next two months did not prove justified, nor was the Provisional Government in any position, for some time to come, to keep its promise of protecting all citizens against violence or intimidation. A report in the *News-Letter* of 24 June said:

> The campaign either to exterminate or to expel from the twenty-six counties the Protestants of Southern Ireland proceeds unchecked, the IRA, where they do not actually take part in the outrages, making no attempt to safeguard the minority.

During the past week, the report said, five Protestant families had been evicted from Ballyhaise in Co. Cavan. In addition there had been trouble in Donegal: the IRA had imprisoned Loyalists in Inch Fort at Burnfoot, the Orange hall at Lifford had been attacked, and Protestant families had fled from Stranorlar to Northern Ireland.

On 26 June the *News-Letter* reported: 'Terror in County Donegal', and the *Whig*: 'Barbarous Outrages in the South'. The *Whig* story dealt with Tipperary and the increasing number of assaults on Protestant women. On Sunday morning, 25 June, an attack was launched on Inver parish church in Donegal while the Church of Ireland congregation was inside. The *News-Letter* report on 28 June said that fifty-six windows in the church were smashed, an attempt was made to batter down the door, and one elderly parishioner was beaten up. Then came news of an attack on a Protestant orphanage at Clifden in Galway. A destroyer had to be sent from the British base at Queenstown (now Cobh), near Cork, to evacuate the staff and inmates, thirty-two in all, Churchill told the House of Commons at Westminster.[21]

On 10 July the *News-Letter* was again reporting 'Rebel Terrorism': 'In all parts of Southern Ireland the Protestant inhabitants are suffering from the system of terrorism organised by the rebels.' Many had been robbed of property, many had had 'criminals' under the guise of refugees from Belfast billeted on them. In Donegal they had had the 'scum of the Nationalist population of Derry' billeted on them. Thousands had had to flee to England. 'There has been no such persecution in modern times of people on account of their religion, or their loyalty to the King', declared the *News-Letter*.

On 14 July in another comment on the Southern Loyalists' suffering the *News-Letter* compared it to the treatment of the Huguenots at the hands of the French. Southern Protestants were now the victims of ruthless persecution. Later in the year the *Whig* used the comparison of the Southern Loyalists with the Smyrna refugees – the Greeks forced to flee from the avenging army of Turkey's Kemal Ataturk in the summer of 1921.

In its first interim report in November 1922, the Hoare Committee said that in the period from 12 May to 14 October it had dealt with 3,349 applicants, many of them married men with large families. Not all of these were in need of immediate assistance, but of the 1,873 cases approved for emergency relief, about 600 were Protestant, and just over 1,000 Catholic. (Fewer than 100 of these cases were from Northern Ireland.)[22] These statistics reflect only those who actually applied for assistance; the Hoare Committee was not actively seeking business and presumably there were families who had the means to support themselves, or who had close relatives and friends in England to whom they could turn. Almost certainly most of these would be Protestant, so the total of Protestant refugees in the Hoare figures could be considerably understated. Many of the Catholic refugees from the south of Ireland were ex-RIC men, or former soldiers, both of which categories were frequent targets for IRA attacks.

Dealing with the situation at the time of writing, that is mid-October 1922, the report said the state of emergency still continued:

Refugees have not ceased to arrive in Great Britain, and the state of affairs in some parts of Ireland makes it likely that for some time to come men and women may be forced to fly for safety from their homes. The original idea, therefore, that the Committee's task would be completed within a few weeks has not proved to be correct.[23]

By October too the question of compensation, not just for this latest category of refugees post-May 1922, but for many other Unionists who had fled, or who had suffered damage to property or personal injury in Ireland since the Truce of 1921, was revealing itself as most complicated. It was a question that was to surface regularly for most of the 1920s, re-awakening bitter memories of the violence. Loyalists fleeing north into Northern Ireland were not covered by the Hoare Committee. Indeed no public funds were made available to assist them. A private committee was set up under the Chief Whip in Craig's Government, Captain Herbert Dixon. The Northern Government made strenuous efforts to have the Hoare Committee take responsibility for refugees going North, and, having failed in that, to get the Hoare Committee to reimburse Dixon's committee for money spent assisting such refugees.

There is no accurate record of the numbers who actually did flee North. In September 1922 Craig wrote to Churchill mentioning 'some three hundred and sixty [refugees] now being maintained by private generosity in Ulster'.[24] The money spent by the Dixon Committee was limited; in October 1923 Dixon sent a certificate of money expended to date, for £495.0s.6d., to the Home Office, seeking a reimbursement.[25]

There is an apparent discrepancy between this small amount of money spent by the Dixon Committee, and the frequent eye-witness accounts of hundreds, or even thousands, of Southern Loyalists arriving as refugees in the North. For example in December 1922, James Cooper MP told the House of Commons in Belfast that

> . . . in the County of Fermanagh you have at the present time a very large number of people indeed – hundreds upon hundreds of families who have crossed the Border from the Free State during the last twelve months. Every day I see four or five, sometimes six or seven, and sometimes more families coming from the County of Leitrim, the County of Longford, the County of Donegal and every county around the Border, and some of them have come to Fermanagh from Kerry.[26]

Cooper wanted a Government scheme to assist these people,

many of whom, he said, were fine citizens, citizens with money. But they could not find accommodation and the result was that 'very many good citizens are being lost to Northern Ireland'. Lost presumably, either because they were returning to the Free State or were moving on to Britain. (In August Spender had asked if the Government in Belfast should advise refugees to go on to Britain, where they would qualify for Hoare Committee aid.)

Some no doubt did so. What is clear is that there is no evidence of any large-scale transfer of population across the border at this period. The census returns, which are of limited use given the exceptional gap between the 1911 and the 1926 returns, contain no indication of any such movement. In the border counties of Fermanagh, Tyrone and Derry, where according to the eye-witness accounts of 1922 the refugees were ending up, there was a general decline in population.[27] The drop was similar for both Protestants and Catholics, so that the proportions remained almost exactly the same in all three counties in 1926 as they had been in 1911. The only exception was in Fermanagh where the very small Presbyterian population (1,264 in 1911) had grown by about 200 in 1926, when all other denominations had declined, possibly reflecting the movement of some Presbyterian families from Donegal and Monaghan. Derry city, the county borough, was also an exception, for there the Catholic population grew by 4,000, or almost 20 per cent between 1911 and 1926, almost certainly reflecting rural migration into the city during the First World War. Belfast's population was growing (7.3 per cent up in 1926 against 1911) but there too the religious denominations remained largely stable in percentage terms – Catholics and Presbyterians marginally up, Church of Ireland marginally down.

Nevertheless, Protestants were leaving the South in considerable numbers. The decline in the fifteen-year period between the 1911 and the 1926 censuses was by more than 100,000, or 32 per cent. Church statistics – both Presbyterians and Methodists published annual figures for congregational membership, either individually or on a family basis – give some indication of the pattern of decline. In almost all areas of the twenty-six counties it was particularly heavy during the war period, that is, up to 1919. Some stability followed until after 1921 when the figures dipped sharply again – the period including the withdrawal of British forces and administration, taking with them numbers of Protestant families. The number of Presbyterian families in Donegal declined by about 120 between 1920 and 1923, or less than 5 per cent, suggesting that there was no major permanent exodus from the county during its most troubled period.[28]

The most likely explanation for the accounts of hundreds, or thousands, of refugees crossing into the North, after allowing for some exaggeration, is that families, or in many instances some members of families, did leave their homes for a while, and travel North, but that they subsequently returned South of the border. As most of those involved would have been farmers or shopkeepers, there would have been considerable practical obstacles in the way of a quick and permanent exit. Much more likely is that wives and children would be sent North, possibly to relatives or friends, while one or two family members remained at home to look after the farm or business. Alternatively, where assassination was feared, menfolk would have travelled North, leaving the women to carry on until some degree of calm had returned. Certainly the congregational returns for Presbyterian churches in Donegal, listing the number of families annually, give no indication of a mass exodus, even in 1922, when Donegal Presbyterians were severely harassed. With the border as a new and not very substantial demarcation – no customs frontier existed, for example, in 1922 – such movement backwards and forwards short distances to familiar towns, and familiar people, would have been easy.

Nor is there any evidence of official British encouragement of Protestants to leave the Republic, as alleged by Collins. As has been seen, Churchill was anxious not to publicise the existence of the Hoare Committee and certainly did not wish to encourage refugees to come to England. Also, perhaps partly in response to pressure from Dublin, London refused to extend the Hoare Committee's mandate to looking after Southern refugees in Northern Ireland, and also refused to compensate Dixon for his private efforts on their behalf.

But even if the events of 1922 did not result in a large migration North of persecuted Southern Protestants, they must have had a great impact on Northern Protestant consciousness. The Belfast papers repeatedly talked of persecution, martyrdom, victimisation, assassination and expulsion. Potent parallels were drawn, both with Ulster's own experience in 1641, and with religious persecution elsewhere in history. In addition even the temporary flight into Ulster of numbers of Protestant families – into Newry, Enniskillen, Castlederg, Strabane, Derry – would have given many people their own first-hand evidence with which to support the newspaper stories. The experiences they related were often harrowing. One Limerick farmer told how sixty armed men had come to his house at 10.30 p.m., and put himself, his wife and four children on the roadside, while the house and farm were burned. He was forbidden to rebuild, or claim compensation, and had had to survive in the open air, with a shelter of corrugated iron against a wall.[29]

To most Ulster Protestants, reared on *Foxe's Book of Martyrs* and tales of horror of the Inquisition, the Free State in 1922 was behaving as they would have feared, but expected, a Catholic power to behave towards a Protestant minority. That the acts of violence or intimidation were not the work of the state, and were condemned by the authorities even if they failed to prevent them, were fine points lost in the horror of the time. Nor did the fact that many instances of intimidation arose from land jealousy, or were directly linked as reprisals to attacks on Catholics in Belfast, alter the perception of Northern Unionists that what was happening in the Free State was systematic persecution of Protestants. It was a perception that was long to remain, reinforced by the presence in towns and villages of the North of those families who did indeed move North and settle there, not in sufficient numbers to show up in census returns or to alter the religious balance in any area, but sufficient to personify the reality of Southern persecution.

PART TWO

8
THE WIDENING GULF

The outbreak of civil war in the South in the middle of 1922 undoubtedly took pressure and attention off Northern Ireland and its new administration. A weekly barometer of violence in the North 'attributable to Sinn Fein aggression' in the Cabinet papers in Belfast shows a dramatic plunge in the numbers killed and wounded from a record high in mid-May to very low figures indeed in early June. With only minor fluctuations, in late June, July and September, the graphs for both killings and woundings descend steadily almost to zero by November.[1] What had been a considerable military threat to the North had all but disappeared within a few weeks of the Civil War commencing.

Political pressure on the North too was eased by the outbreak of civil war. In May and June of 1922 Craig was being urged by Churchill to agree to a British Government plan for a judicial inquiry into the conduct of affairs in Northern Ireland – a suggestion vehemently resisted by members of Craig's Cabinet, particularly Dawson Bates.[2] The Provisional Government in Dublin had been pressing London for such an inquiry into the violence in the North – particularly the periodic attacks on Catholic areas in Belfast, the series of unsolved murders of Catholics in the city, and the serious and persistent allegations being made against the B Specials' behaviour in the city. Tallents, the civil servant sent to Belfast to report on the breakdown of the Craig–Collins Pact, and to assess the need for a full inquiry, wrote early in July to the Colonial Office saying that an independent judicial inquiry into events in Belfast should be ruled out.[3] The turmoil in the South, with the Provisional Government preoccupied and indeed in some jeopardy, made it much easier for the British Government to accept the Tallents recommendation, for hitherto much of the pressure for a judicial inquiry had been coming from Collins.

Not surprisingly, the Belfast papers contemplated the events in the South with something less than dismay. Under the heading

'Anarchy and Ruin', the *Belfast News-Letter* on 15 July commented: 'The rebels of Southern Ireland are hastening along the road to ruin. They are destroying property of all kinds, commandeering newspapers, closing post-offices, robbing banks. . .'

Nor did the *News-Letter* see the death of Michael Collins in August as a disaster. It commented on 24 August:

> He was a man of varying political moods, and no one could predict, even when he was fighting the Republicans, that he would not eventually lead them. He made speeches which could not be reconciled with his acceptance of the 'Treaty', nor with his position. As head of the Provisional Government he was required to be a loyal British subject, which he certainly was not, though he might have become one after the transition stage when the Constitution was ratified and the Free State fully established.

That comment reflected a hope that still persisted in the North – that 'settlement' was possible, that the South would, with the victory of the pro-Treaty forces in the Civil War, and the ratification of the Free State Constitution, accept the reality of partition and the new arrangements embodied in the Government of Ireland Act and in the Treaty. Such acceptance would leave the way open for the friendly rivalry that Craig and others had foreseen between two entities in Ireland, both loyal to the Empire, and each recognising the other's right to exist.

But even in 1922 it was not easy to hold on to such a fond dream. In October the Dáil, without its anti-Treaty members, debated the proposed constitution of the Free State. On 4 October the *Northern Whig* noted that all the Free State leaders did not 'even pretend to be reconciled to the inclusion of the Free State in the British Empire'. Two months later the Free State was officially in being, but in a comment on a speech by the new Governor General, Tim Healy, the *Whig* on 6 December was again acutely aware that being for or against the Treaty was not the essential point in the long term, but rather how one regarded it as a stepping stone to a Republic instead of a bargain imposing obligations on the two sides that had agreed it.

By mid-1923, when it was clear that the anti-Treaty forces had lost the Civil War, a more immediate threat to the Northern settlement had eclipsed Southern aspirations to a Republic. This was the Boundary Commission which, from this point until the end of 1925, hung over the Northern scene and dominated the public utterances of Unionist politicians and newspaper editorials and, indeed, news columns.

This revival of the prospect of the commission, which Craig and the Unionists had hoped they had killed by their refusal to participate in it, coincided with an event in London which greatly heightened Unionist nervousness – the resignation of Bonar Law, who had been Prime Minister since late the previous year. His resignation in May 1923, followed by his death in October, removed one of the few men in the Conservative Party whom the Northerners placed some reliance upon, though even he had caused surprise and dismay in 1921–2 by speaking in support of the Treaty. By then too the possibility of the Labour Party coming to power in Britain had forced itself upon the Unionists. In 1922 Labour had become the second largest party at Westminster, and in January 1924 the unthinkable happened, and Ramsay MacDonald became the first Labour Prime Minister.

History was beginning to repeat itself. In June 1921 Ulster Protestants were able to think that the struggle was over, and the Irish problem settled by partition. The Southern rejection of the Government of Ireland Act, and its negotiation of the Treaty, followed by the IRA assault on Ulster in early 1922 had threatened to unsettle everything. The Civil War had intervened, and in June 1923 the *Whig* could comment that 'peace and order reign throughout the Six Counties. Life and property are now as safe within the Borders of this Province as in any part of the United Kingdom.' Just at this point, the Boundary Commission resurfaced and the settlement was again in question. On 20 July Cosgrave nominated Dr Eoin MacNeill as the Southern representative on the commission. Craig repeated that Ulster would not nominate, and the commission could not therefore operate. But continued insistence upon the commission was a feature of the Free State general election of August 1923, and it was the main issue in Northern Ireland in the Westminster election in November of that year. By that time there had been official movement on the boundary with the British Government summoning both Northern and Southern representatives to a conference.

Only three constituencies were fought in the North in November 1923, two in Belfast, and the third in the key Fermanagh–Tyrone border two-seater. The return of two anti-Unionist candidates, in what was frankly called a border referendum in the two counties, heightened Unionist fears of boundary revision. On 10 December the *Whig* commented bitterly, blaming the result on the 'condition of the register', that the outcome would be

> . . . hailed as fresh proof that a large majority of the two counties are eager to break away from Ulster and to share in such blessings of 'Dominion Status' as higher taxation, reduced old-age pensions, two-penny postage, and general insecurity.

The boundary conference met in London early in 1924, and though the Unionists were still promising resistance to the death, Hugh Pollock indicated again, at the Ulster Unionist Council, that Belfast would be happy to make some accommodation if no 'arrogant claims' were made.[4] Most of that year was totally dominated by the boundary question. The conference summoned in London broke down in April, with the *Whig* commenting on 24 April that the situation was full of grave possibilities. A week later MacDonald's Government in London announced that the commission under the Treaty was to go ahead. Craig declared that he would 'not bend one inch' on the question.[5]

London got round the difficulty of Craig's refusal to appoint a representative to the commission by doing it for him. MacDonald's Dominions Secretary, J.H. Thomas, announced that effect would be given to the Treaty by means of legislation. 'A Bill to Coerce Ulster', was the *Whig*'s headline on 2 August, as it told its readers to prepare for the worst.

The passage of the legislation, and the creation and workings of the Boundary Commission, were by far the preponderant items of news in the Northern papers for the second half of 1924, and for almost all of 1925. Two elections during the period helped focus attention still more directly on the border. In October 1924 the Labour Government fell in London and a Westminster election was held. This meant that once again Fermanagh and Tyrone would be seen to be voting in a border plebiscite. This time the Unionists made no mistake, and helped by a nationalist split took both seats in those two counties, and indeed won all the Northern Ireland seats. To add to the Unionist euphoria, Labour was defeated overall, thus, marginally at least, reducing the threat to Ulster.

No doubt partly encouraged by the October result, Craig, in March 1925, dissolved the Northern Ireland Parliament and called the first general election in the North since the original 1921 poll that had preceded the creation of it. He specifically made it a border election, thus ensuring, or seeking to ensure, maximum Unionist solidarity at a time when his administration was coming under a deal of criticism over education and other administrative matters.[6] The critics were not entirely convinced, for the official Unionist monopoly of seats in the Northern parliament was broken, and three Labour men, four Independent Unionists, plus one Farmers' candidate were elected. None of these were anti-Unionist, but the result, certainly in Belfast, was something of a shock for the Unionist Party. On the nationalist side, Sinn Féin did poorly against more moderate Nationalists, who won ten seats against only two for Sinn Féin.

Overall, however, the election of April 1925 was no great setback for Unionism. The anti-Unionists ended up with twelve seats – the same as in 1921. The real victory, the *Whig* noted on 11 April, lay in the decision by the Nationalist members to take their seats in the Northern parliament for the first time, thus 'identifying themselves with the political life of this loyal self-governing province of the United Kingdom'.

Over the summer of 1925 speculation mounted on what the recommendations of the Boundary Commission might be, and Craig reaffirmed that the Northern Government would simply refuse to accept any findings not to its liking. When the *Morning Post* eventually leaked the commission's findings in November 1925, the reaction in Ulster was cautious, though there were signs that the changes proposed were rather pleasing to the Unionists. Caution turned to something like delight as Southern discomfort over the findings became evident. MacNeill resigned from the Free State Cabinet on 24 November 1925. A week later Craig and Cosgrave were at Chequers for discussions on the boundary, drawing a biblical quotation from the *Whig* on 30 November: 'Who so diggeth a pit shall fall therein', with the gloss that Cosgrave and company had dug their pit four years ago and were now crying for help from the bottom of it.

Before the end of 1925 a new boundary agreement confirming the status quo had been signed and ratified by Westminster and by the Dáil. Sunday 6 December was set by the Protestant churches as a day of thanksgiving in Northern Ireland. The following morning the *Whig* compared the deliverance to that at Derry more than 200 years earlier.

Despite some grumbling over the generosity to the Free State of the financial terms of the new agreement – Carson said these constituted a gift of £300 million to Dublin, and on 5 December the *Whig* noted sorrowfully that the British Government had surrendered once more to the Sinn Féiners – the year ended with something approaching general rejoicing in the North, on the Unionist side at least. Once again 'settlement' seemed possible. On 9 December, as the new agreement passed through Westminster, the *Whig* asked, 'was it peace?' Its own reply was that it was now up to the South to accept the hand of friendship held out both to the minority in the North, and to the Free State.

Christmas 1925, complete with snow in Belfast, was the happiest for five years. On 28 December the *Whig* reported:

> Christmas festivities throughout Ireland have been marked this year perhaps more than any other in recent times by the sentiment of peace and goodwill, for the spirit that made possible the Pact of Locarno and the Irish Boundary Pact, and the results therein achieved, have not failed to make their due appeal to the hearts and minds of men.

On 11 January 1926 the *Belfast Telegraph* greeted the New Year with a comment on 'The Real Unity' in which it said that a very successful beginning had been made to the career of the state of Northern Ireland as a political entity: 'There is no reason why the relations of Ulster with the Free State should not be of the best.' The boundary agreement, the *Telegraph* noted, had removed a serious cause of friction, though there was still wide divergence between the aims of the two states.

Early in 1926 not everything seemed designed to promote co-operation. The Cosgrave Government announced its decision to adopt its own coinage, which seemed to the *Telegraph*, on 20 January, a curious way of improving relations between North and South. Nevertheless, there seemed a real chance in 1926 that the two parts of the country would put their relations on a friendly footing. At the end of 1925 Cosgrave and Craig had exchanged messages, Cosgrave saying, 'I cordially reciprocate your earnest hope that we may get into closer touch in future for the common good', and reporting how well the final boundary agreement had been received in the South.[7]

In July 1926 the Governor General, Tim Healy, presumably at the suggestion of Cosgrave, wrote to Craig inviting him and Lady Craig to be guests at the Vice-Regal Lodge during Horse Show Week in August. Craig's reply, though declining the invitation, was most courteous, and implied that such a visit might be possible the following year.[8] It never took place, and it was another forty years before a Northern Prime Minister felt secure enough (wrongly as it turned out) to accept a formal invitation to Dublin. But at least one visit did occur in 1926. Éamonn Duggan TD, Cosgrave's Parliamentary Secretary, went to Belfast in April, and visited the Northern parliament. He was shown over the building by Craig's Private Secretary, and sat in the distinguished strangers' gallery.[9] According to the newspaper reports of the visit, during which he also met Craig, Duggan's purpose was to discuss matters in connection with the Free State Budget. At any rate it was a public visit by a Dáil member clearly representing the Free State head of Government, and seemingly it caused no great uproar in Belfast.

Great hopes for North–South co-operation were expressed at the June 1926 meeting of the Presbyterian General Assembly. The new Moderator, from a Dublin church, spoke of conditions being wonderfully improved in the Free State, of law and order, and of no religious disabilities. (Though he did have a complaint about the undue importance given to Irish in primary education.)[10]

The summer of 1926 was probably the high point of hopes for progressive and peaceful co-operation between North and South. But by November the IRA and extreme Republicanism had re-asserted themselves in the South, with armed raids on police barracks, setting alarm bells jangling in the Unionist mind. Cosgrave's firm tackling of the problem of this Republican violence – an immediate declaration of a state of emergency – won approval in the North. On 22 November the *Whig* noted that old poachers made the best gamekeepers, and on 8 January remarked that Cosgrave's Government was displaying a firmness in ruling the country that no British Government had shown since Arthur J. Balfour was Chief Secretary. But there was a return in the Belfast papers to frequent and lengthy dissertations on what was wrong with the South, on how unity was impossible, and on the folly and dangers of any sort of political dealing with Dublin.

As the Free State approached a general election in June 1927, Northern Unionist hopes and expectations were that Cosgrave would be confirmed in power. On 23 May the *Whig* commented that the North's only interest was 'a stable government beside us capable of maintaining law and order, and animated by a spirit of goodwill'. The present Government, according to the *Whig*, possessed both qualifications, and it added that de Valera would cause turmoil and strife, and should be given the *coup de grâce* by the electorate. But the electorate did not take the *Whig*'s advice, and instead there was 'an unlooked for rally to Mr de Valera's standard'. This 'retailer of empty shibboleths and stupid slogans' had been thought an extinct volcano, but instead Fianna Fáil had made major gains.[11]

With Fianna Fáil still not taking its seats in the Dáil, Cosgrave again formed a Government, but in August when de Valera did lead his party into the Dáil, Cosgrave was saved only by the vote of the Speaker. De Valera, already a bogeyman to Northern Unionists, was, from this point on, to dominate news from the South for the next twenty years, and to personify Northern perceptions of Irish nationalism and of the Irish state.

Between the June election and de Valera's entry into the Dáil, the assassination of Kevin O'Higgins, deputy to Cosgrave in the Free State Government, in Dublin on 10 July had had an enormous impact in the North. Not only was it a spectacular instance of political violence, but it also removed a man who had, it seemed to many Northerners, shown some glimmering of understanding of what they regarded as reality in Ireland. None in Cosgrave's Government, according to the *Whig* on 11 July, had a better claim to be a statesman:

> No one in an official position in the Free State had, we believe, realised more thoroughly the desirability of establishing friendly relations between Northern and Southern Ireland, or had more sensible ideas as to the means by which this object could be best accomplished.

His death, concluded the *Whig*, was a great misfortune for Ulster. The assassination was followed by the Government's assumption of Special Powers against the gunmen, termed 'Coercion in

Excelsis' by the *Whig* on 27 July and described, approvingly rather than otherwise, as the most severe coercion measures in 800 years.

Hopes of friendly co-operation between North and South faded. Instead, both politicians and editors in the North turned more and more attention to the speeches and statements of de Valera and his colleagues. Particular note was taken of a speech by Frank Aiken, one of the Fianna Fáil leaders, in the course of a by-election campaign in Dalkey, Co. Dublin, in August 1927.[12] In it Aiken said Fianna Fáil would use the machinery of Government in order to get a constitution 'that would recognise the independence and unity of the country'. They must sweep English authority out of the twenty-six counties, and then use the powers they had got in order to extend the sovereignty of the Irish people over the whole thirty-two counties. Aiken went on to say that Fianna Fáil did not support a standing army whose only object was crushing Irish Republicans. If the people stood by them, they believed they could secure the unification of the armed forces North and South.

Such apparent siding with the IRA was alarming to Northern Unionists, particularly as victory in the two by-elections could have brought Fianna Fáil to power. In an editorial the *Whig* on 22 August said Aiken had made it clear that Fianna Fáil did not accept the Free State Constitution as it stood, but were out to destroy it, and when that was done they were going to use their power to attack Northern Ireland. Once again the threat as perceived by the Unionists was the overthrow of the settlement, this time with the implication that armed force might be used in addition to negotiation and bargaining in London.

Cosgrave survived the by-elections and called another general election in September 1927. On 15 September the *Whig* again found it hard to believe that people would actually vote for de Valera: 'In any other country in the world, a foolish demagogue like Mr de Valera would have been discarded', yet in the Free State his party was almost as large as that of Cosgrave. Polling day brought no great consolation, for although he did not win, de Valera was not eclipsed.

It now seemed certain that de Valera would, one day, come to power. From 1927 on it was, for the Northerner looking South, a matter of waiting for him. Unionist horror at the idea of a Republic in Ireland was not just that this would mean the total rejection of the Empire, Commonwealth and all things British by the Irish state, but that by definition, a Republic could only be a thirty-two-county one. So determination to press ahead for a Republic meant determination to terminate the existence of Northern Ireland, by one means or another. The acute fear in 1927, illustrated by the reaction to Aiken's Dalkey speech, was that a major political force had emerged in the South that was professedly more interested in an accommodation with the Republican extremists and a common drive for the Republic than in the suppression of subversion and the consolidation of the institutions of the Free State.

On 31 January 1928 the *Whig* commented that the volcano of seditious violence in the South was no longer in eruption, but it was not yet extinct: 'It is clear that there is still a minority in the Free State that not only refuses to accept the Treaty settlement, but will not hesitate to resort to violence and bloodshed in the hope of upsetting it.'

In May 1928 the Northern Ireland Parliament renewed the Special Powers Act for a further five years. The Minister of Home Affairs, Dawson Bates, justified the move, while admitting that Northern Ireland was living in peace. The IRA, he said, was still in existence, and he referred to a recent trial in Dublin where evidence presented had spoken of monthly reports of the IRA in the North, giving details of ammunition dumps, and the disposition of firearms and stores under the control of the IRA.[13]

Early in 1929 de Valera caused excitement in the North by entering the state in defiance of an exclusion order, having himself arrested at Goraghwood Railway Station, and spending a month in jail in Belfast. In March of that year there were more IRA rumblings in the South. Forty young men were arrested in Dublin and taken to the Bridewell. Cosgrave said there was a deliberate and organised attack being launched against the foundations of ordered society in Dublin.[14]

That news might have helped Craigavon (Craig was created Lord Craigavon in the New Year's Honours List of 1927) decide it was time for another election in Northern Ireland. In mid-April he announced an election for 22 May and set about campaigning for Unionist unity and solidarity, in the face of attempts to revive an Ulster Liberal Party. His manifesto called for a 'strong united majority to carry on the work and so defeat all attempts to weaken the Constitution or force Ulster under an all-Ireland Parliament'.[15] The election saw the official Unionist Party recover almost all the ground it had lost to Labour and Independent Unionists in 1925. In this it was greatly helped by the fact that proportional representation had by then been abolished.

The late 1920s and early 1930s also saw a heightening of religious tension both within Northern Ireland and in the South, and a renewed attention by Northern Protestants to what they saw as the Catholic nature of Southern society and state. Major public events, such as the celebration in 1929 of the centenary of Catholic Emancipation, and the holding in Dublin, in mid-1932, of the Eucharistic Congress, highlighted in unmistakable fashion the strong identity between the Free State and Catholicism. This in turn was met by a marked increase in anti-Catholic rhetoric in the North, notably at Twelfth celebrations in July 1930, 1931 and 1932. In 1931 there were violent incidents surrounding Orange celebrations both inside Northern Ireland and in the Ulster counties of the South. It was in 1932 that Craigavon told a gathering of Orangemen at Poyntzpass, Co. Armagh, that 'ours is a Protestant Government and I am an Orangeman' – the first of two such declarations that were to hang around his neck.[16]

The last years of the Cosgrave Government had been notable from a Northern point of view for Dublin's continued efforts to modify the constitutional relationship with Britain, mainly through ending the right of appeal to the Privy Council, and for the continued activity of Republican extremists, now with the added menace of Communism, as in the recently formed Saor Éire. In October 1931 Cosgrave told the Dáil that a serious armed conspiracy against the state had grown for the past two years, and especially during the last nine months: 'One crime after another has been committed against the people and against the state. The conspiracy behind those crimes shows a growing readiness to usurp power by armed force.'[17] Emergency measures were taken, special military courts set up, and the IRA and Saor Éire proscribed.

The Free State's general election of February 1932 excited intense interest in the North. Cosgrave was seen as fighting to save

143

the Treaty, and maintain a reasonable economic relationship with Britain, as against de Valera's promises to revise the Constitution, abolish the oath of allegiance, and withhold the land annuities. There was the added dimension that Fianna Fáil had the support of the IRA, and in turn did not back the Government's stern measures against them.

The election saw defeat for Cosgrave, but less than guaranteed victory for de Valera. On 22 February the *Whig* was accepting that de Valera would head the Government, but only with Labour support, and that Labour would bring him down to earth. It was even anticipated that a year or two of executive responsibility would teach him to face reality.

But the reality of de Valera in power was quite different. On 10 March, his first day in office, he captured the largest headlines the Northern papers had available for his announcement that he would release the IRA prisoners, and for his symbolic act in sending two of his ministers, having just taken office, directly to Arbour Hill prison to visit the IRA men there, and to ensure that they were immediately given special status – in terms of segregation and conditions. From 12 March the Belfast papers were alive with headlines such as 'IRA Again Parade the Streets – Up the Rebels'. The *Whig* reported that platoons of the IRA were parading the streets of Dublin, opening recruiting bureaux and enrolling volunteers. In the editions of 14 March 30,000 people were reported welcoming the release of the prisoners from Arbour Hill. De Valera was termed the puppet of the IRA. In mid-March he released his next bombshell – his demand for the return of £30 million paid to Britain in land annuities. A few days later the ban on the IRA was lifted. That same week, in March 1932, he informed Britain that he intended to abolish the oath of allegiance.

That Easter the *Whig* on 28 March reported that the IRA had paraded in every important centre in the Free State. Some 2,500 had marched through Dublin 'in excellent military formation'. The following day full-page headlines in the *Whig* declared 'Wave of Republicanism Sweeps the Free State', 'Recruiting Campaign in Full Swing', 'Mr Cosgrave in Grave Danger of His Life'.

In a speech at the end of March in Dungannon, Co. Tyrone, Sir Hugh O'Neill voiced what was undoubtedly the view of most

144

Unionists on the latest disasters to overtake the South. The Free State, he said, was in danger of relapsing into Bolshevism and revolution. Secession from the Empire would mean that it would become

> . . . a petty, insignificant, so-called Republic, and its people aliens, without the status of British citizens. . . Lying to the western shores of Europe, divorced from all the great world movements and separated from the greatest and finest movement in the world today – which is the British Empire.[18]

What did this mean for Northern Ireland?

> The danger – and I think there is a great danger – is that there may be disorders; that there may be further attempts, as there were ten years ago, to create what they call a Republic for the whole of Ireland, and attempts to promote disorders in this, our very own province.[19]

But that was only part of the danger. A *Whig* headline on 25 April, on the publication of the exchange of notes between London and Dublin on de Valera's demands, read 'Free State Repudiates Settlement of 1921'. An editorial comment said that de Valera had raised again the old issues, and had attempted to bring the situation back to where it was before the 1921 settlement. That de Valera had never accepted the settlement was nothing new. But now he was the elected head of the Free State, and was clearly entering into a major dispute with Britain. As the *Whig* perceived, in a comment on 8 June, de Valera's real purpose was to bring Anglo-Irish relations into crisis, and to reopen the whole settlement as part of the negotiation to resolve the crisis. The knowledge that a British minister, and a Labour one at that, had travelled to Dublin to listen to de Valera's plans for Irish unity, if not actually to discuss them or negotiate on them, did nothing to calm Unionist fears or anger.

An editorial of 13 July summed up the *Whig*'s reaction to events in mid-1932:

> The change of Government has let loose not only the anti-British, but the anti-Ulster spirit in the South in a manner that, day by day for the last six months, has become more and more offensive to both Britain and Ulster.
>
> The destinies of the South today are in the hands of a coterie of Anglophobe agitators with no understanding or experience of

government who are driven forward in their extremist policy by a secret organisation and who seem quite prepared to go any length to bring Ulster under the control of the Free State.

That was not all; the editorial went on to note that Northern Catholics had changed their attitude towards de Valera. Some time ago he had been an enemy of the people, now he was a true, if somewhat impetuous, patriot:

The baneful influence of de Valera's policy is being exercised in the North in a direction which is decidedly prejudicial to peace and harmony here.

For the rest of the 1930s the 'baneful influence' of de Valera was a constant preoccupation of Northern Unionists. The economic war was seen as economic madness, plunging the country deeper into poverty, while on the constitutional side de Valera continued to dismantle the Treaty settlement, a process that culminated in the 1937 Constitution and the 1938 agreement with Britain on the Treaty ports and the economic war. The activities of the Republicans, and the fascist Blueshirt reaction to these, were prominently reported in the North and the picture conveyed of the South was of a country rushing headlong into anarchy, chaos and bankruptcy.

The immediate background to the 1933 election to the Northern Ireland Parliament was of IRA violence. On 8 October an RUC constable was shot dead in Belfast. On 13 October more than thirty IRA men were arrested in Belfast. What looked like a reprisal killing took place on 16 October. On 26 October a Unionist member of the Northern parliament, Major John Henry McCormick, who sat for St Anne's, was shot and wounded in the city.

In early November, Craigavon called a general election. His election manifesto declared that it was as necessary as ever for the Unionist Party to be returned to power

... with an overwhelming majority to enable us to defeat the designs of our enemies in their continued attempts to filch away the reward of our hard-won victories of the past, as well as to convince the outside world that we have in no degree weakened in our attachment to the Crown and Flag.[20]

More specifically he said that a 'certain extreme section' was continually menacing the peace and security of Northern Ireland,

and hoping to smash its parliament, and force it into the Free State under the domination of a Dublin government.

Since 1932 the Nationalists had again been boycotting the Northern parliament, partly because of de Valera's influence, and they stayed away until the end of 1933. Even then there was not a full return of Nationalist members, and for the rest of the decade they played a spasmodic and infrequent part in the Northern parliament.

From 1933 onwards there is evidence in the Northern papers of a more overtly hostile attitude towards Catholics in the North. This was particularly related to the border areas, and to a Unionist obsession with what was termed 'peaceful penetration'. Perhaps the most famous declaration on the subject was that of Sir Basil Brooke on 12 July 1933, when he appealed to Loyalists 'wherever possible to employ good Protestant lads and lassies' because there was a 'definite plot to overpower the vote of Unionists in the North', and Catholics were endeavouring 'to get in everywhere'.[21] At Keady, Co. Armagh, on the same day, Sir William Hamilton told the gathering that public offices were 'honeycombed with Republicans'.[22] Unionist and Orange speakers continued to stress this theme of 'peaceful penetration' and the need to protect Protestant employment throughout the 1930s. During the Second World War the issue became particularly sensitive, as skilled labour was needed in Belfast, and the Government had a hand in issuing work permits to those moving into the North.

There had been considerable Protestant alarm in the South in the last years of the Cosgrave Government over moves to end the right of appeal to the Privy Council – seen as a fundamental safeguard and a symbol of continued British citizenship. This alarm rose to something like panic with the victory of de Valera in 1932 and the re-emergence of IRA violence, some of it directed specifically at what were seen as Protestant targets – such as the November Armistice ceremonies.

De Valera's declared intention of dismantling the Free State Constitution added to the concern, involving as it did the removal of another Protestant guarantee, the Senate. But it was the hardship on sections of the farming community as a result of de Valera's economic war with Britain that prompted actions which had most impact in the North. Among those hardest hit by the effects of the economic war were the dairy farmers of east Donegal, most of them Presbyterian. In November 1934 about 8,000 of them signed a memorial sent to Belfast and London requesting reincorporation into the United Kingdom.

In 1935 there was sporadic violence against Masonic halls in the South, and much anti-Mason propaganda. In July this spilled over, in Galway, Limerick and other towns, into attacks on Protestants, demands for the expulsion of Protestant workers, and the burning of Kilmallock Church of Ireland church. These specific incidents were probably reprisals for what was seen as anti-Catholic violence in Belfast in July.

Throughout the mid-1930s the Northern papers reported constantly on the turmoil in the South, on de Valera's reluctance to deal with the IRA, on O'Duffy and his Blueshirts, and especially on the economy, with repeated comparisons of trade performances North and South. And all the while de Valera was moving towards his new Constitution, and the removal of most, if not all, vestiges of the British connection from the state. The background to this was the increasing certainty of a general war in Europe, and the frequently voiced fear in the North that the South would be no friend of Britain in such a conflict.

The year 1938 saw the culmination of Unionist fears and concerns when de Valera negotiated the end of the economic war, a financial settlement and the return of the Treaty ports. What he got out of the Chamberlain Government was bad enough in Unionist eyes – the *Whig* accused the British of 'reckless liberality' in the settlement, and deemed the handing back of the ports 'the final scuttle' – but much more serious was that de Valera had again raised the issue of partition directly with the British Government. (Characteristically Craigavon took advantage of the anger over the London–Dublin negotiations to call a Northern election in February 1938, using the Loyalist fervour to crush the breakaway Progressive Unionist Party.)

True, the British had not negotiated on partition, but on 5 May the *Whig* took serious note of de Valera's report to the Dáil on 27 April 1938, when he said that the agreement had removed all the major issues in dispute 'with the exception of partition'. He went on: 'I believe that with a united effort by the Irish people a settlement of that problem could also be achieved.' The *Whig* had no doubt that de Valera would make the new agreement 'the starting point of a renewed offensive against Ulster' and that he 'would look to his new found friends in British political life to smooth the path of his advance'. Even though the question of partition might be left aside for the present, the *Whig* predicted with remarkable accuracy that it would be revived 'when the Dublin Government believes Britain to be in a tight corner'.

That tight corner came early in the war, in June 1940, with the fall of France, and the secret offer from Churchill to de Valera of moves towards Irish unity in return for the South's participation in the war. To this offer Craigavon responded with apparently genuine shock and horror – it was 'treachery to loyal Ulster', he told Neville Chamberlain in a cable of 27 June 1940.[23] The Ulster Unionists' worst fears had been realised – the 1921 settlement was not only reopened in negotiations between London and Dublin, but London, under a Government led by, of all people, Churchill, was offering to deliver Ulster into a united Ireland.

It did not, of course, happen. The wartime experience drove North and South further apart and, at the same time, Northern Ireland and Britain closer together. Or so it seemed, and Churchill's ringing broadcast tribute to Northern Ireland at the war's end seemed to seal this new mutual indebtedness, while emphasising the gulf that de Valera's neutrality had opened between London and Dublin.

A MENACE TO PROTESTANTS

> Presbyterians are convinced that the power of the Church of Rome over her members would be used through an Irish Parliament and executive for the furtherance of the Roman Catholic faith and to the detriment of the Evangelical Churches. Under Home Rule the Church of Rome would undoubtedly be in a position to utilise agencies of popular government for her own aggrandisement. Against such misuse of the civil power it would be impossible for the minority to contend successfully. This evident danger renders Home Rule a menace to Protestants against which there are no possible safeguards.

Thus the Presbyterian Convention of 1912 declared its considered opposition to Home Rule.[1]

If self-government was a menace to more than one million Protestants in an undivided Ireland, what sort of threat did it pose to fewer than one third of that number in a Free State with an independence far beyond Home Rule? By mid-1922 Southern Protestants most certainly felt a persecuted minority, shown by the Church of Ireland deputation to Collins and Griffith in May 1922, asking whether they were to be allowed to remain in the country. In that atmosphere it was not surprising that they were dissatisfied with the safeguards included in the Free State Constitution for minorities such as themselves.

Half of the sixty members of the first Senate were nominated by the Government, which consulted with various bodies in deciding the names, to ensure representation for minorities not represented in the Dáil. Of these, it is estimated, sixteen were former Unionists.[2] In total, twenty-four Senators were not Catholics. Some former Unionist or Protestant representation in the Dáil was practically guaranteed by the three Dublin University seats. Proportional representation itself was seen as another guarantee to the minority. When the draft constitution was published in mid-June 1922, the *Belfast News-Letter,* on 16 June, endorsed the Southern Unionist view that the proposed Senate, with guaranteed Unionist, or former-Unionist representation, would not give adequate protection to the minority. Its news report of the draft did highlight the clause that said no law might be passed to endow any religion, to prohibit its free practice, or to give any preference on account of religion. But it added, tartly, that all depended on how this clause was interpreted in practice, and on what efforts the Free State Government might take to protect Protestants from persecution and spoliation, as they were receiving no protection at present.

Indeed the Free State Constitution contained none of the horrors that the Presbyterians in 1912 were regarding as inevitable, and in some of its provisions it was specifically guarding against such abuses. It was a much less 'Catholic' document than they, and most Northern Unionists, were expecting and was, in fact, far less Catholic than some leading Southern political figures would have wished.

The previous year Cosgrave had put some of his ideas in a letter to de Valera, apparently suggesting an upper house to the Dáil, 'consisting of a theological board which would decide whether any enactments of the Dáil were contrary to faith and morals or not'.[3] Moreover, Cosgrave said a guarantee should be given to the Pope that the Dáil would not make laws contrary to the teachings of the church, in return for which the Holy Father would be asked to recognise the Dáil as a body entitled to legislate for Ireland. The committee set up under Collins's chairmanship in January 1922 to draft a Free State Constitution had different ideas, though two of its members, Professor James Murnaghan and Professor Alfred O'Rahilly, produced their own minority draft which had a highly Catholic flavour.[4]

The Free State has enjoyed a good historical press for its treatment of the Protestant minority.[5] But the contemporary Northern view was entirely different. Throughout the inter-war years Unionist politicians and the Unionist newspapers frequently reported, and commented on, the 'persecution' of the Southern minority, and on the Catholic nature of the state and society in the South.

Who were the minority? In 1922 Churchill referred to 300,000 Unionists in the twenty-six-county area who might be forced to flee. If he was equating Unionist with Protestant, he was certainly over-estimating their strength. The 1926 census revealed a Protestant population in the Free State of only 208,000, a decline of

33.5 per cent, or 106,000 on the 1911 count. By mid-1922 much of that decline had already taken place, so the Protestant population was then almost certainly below 250,000. F.S.L. Lyons suggests that the term 'minority' applied properly to ex-Unionists, and that to equate these with Protestants would be a gross over-simplification.[6] But whatever their former politics, all Protestants after 1922 were, of course, a religious minority, and it was their welfare as a religious grouping that was watched with such interest from the North.

These people were also a minority in another, political, sense. They fully accepted the Free State, its Constitution and its institutions. They valued, and saw as permanent, their allegiance to the British Crown, their membership of the Empire and their British citizenship, all of which they saw enshrined in the Free State Constitution. When the Church of Ireland General Synod met annually in Dublin and sang 'God Save the King', as did Protestant schools at their annual prize days, they were not being 'former Unionists', or disloyal to the Free State, but were carrying out Archbishop Gregg's promise of allegiance to the new Constitution. In this they were very much a minority, for only they fully accepted the 1922 Constitution to the letter. Unionist pamphleteers made a favourite quotation out of Michael Collins's remark on the day the Treaty was signed, that once the Treaty Act was passed through the British House of Commons, and the evacuation of British troops completed, then 'the demand for full Republican rights must be conceded by Great Britain'.[7]

There was, therefore, a fundamental difference of attitude towards the new Free State, its Constitution and institutions, between the Protestant/former-Unionist minority, and the majority. This aspect of their minority status became increasingly acute as the Cosgrave Governments proceeded to remove the symbols of the Crown, and later as de Valera effectively overthrew the Free State settlement and replaced it with a *de facto* Republic.

There was a third dimension to the status of the minority – culture. The Irish language and Gaelic culture had become a fundamental plank in the Sinn Féin nationalist platform. The Constitution of the Free State afforded equal status to English and Irish, but the Government was committed to an ambitious programme for the restoration of Irish as the spoken language of the country. The majority either supported this cultural objective, or were prepared to give theoretical assent to it – though not without dissenting voices. The minority, as a whole, dissented from the objective of restoring a language most of them did not regard as historically theirs, and protested, frequently and strongly, against the considerable element of compulsion successive Governments embodied in their restoration programme.

These three minorities – religious, political and cultural – did not exactly overlap, but they did substantially, constituting a single minority that was most easily and most commonly identified as Protestant. Indeed, with the collapse of Unionist political organisation in the Free State, the only representative voices of the minority were those of the Protestant chuches, and particularly of the Church of Ireland. An assessment of the degree of toleration extended to Protestants in the Free State should, therefore, not be restricted to the question of religious freedom, narrowly defined, but must take account of the toleration extended to the political and cultural minorities too.

In December 1922 the Civil War meant the Free State was born in conditions of disorder, with the authorities still not fully able to keep Collins's promise of May to protect all citizens. The Irish Unionist Alliance papers document cases from the 1922–3 period of Southern victims of violence, along with complaints of the Free State authorities' handling of them, and particularly of the way the courts were dealing with the claims.[8] A letter from Co. Cork, dated 3 December 1928, filed with a Southern Irish Loyalist Relief Organisation minute book, reads:

> I beg to inform you persecution of Protestants in this area is still in full swing. A fat heifer, two years old, value £14, was taken off my lands on the night of November 26–27, just seven days ago, and I have received no assistance whatever from the Civic Guards in the search to trace her. A bullock was taken from a neighbour's farm a year ago – he is also a Protestant, but he did not report it to the Civic Guard, being afraid. I also hear four sheep were taken from a Protestant near Bandon.[9]

The theft of a fat heifer is not conclusive proof of religious persecution, but the letter indicates how some Protestants felt they were still the victims of such abuse.

Alongside this belief by at least some Protestants that they were still the victims of some degree of persecution, was the reality of the decline in the Protestant population. The drop from 1911 to 1926 was by one third, to 208,000. A loss of that magnitude, for whatever reason, had to have major impact, psychologically and organisationally, on the Protestant community.

Just how massive this impact was in some places can be gauged from the drop in Protestant population figures in many towns in the same period. Newbridge and Kildare, both garrison towns, saw declines of 88.9 per cent and 93.5 per cent in their Protestant communities; Midleton, Co. Cork, had a drop of 68 per cent; Tralee, Dundalk, Galway, Limerick and Bantry all lost more than 50 per cent of their Protestants; the decline in the second city, Cork, was 49.8 per cent, while Dublin lost 38.4 per cent.[10]

In some instances such blows were mortal – schools closed, churches were merged and families moved, either elsewhere in the Free State, or out of the country. The rate of decline was such that it contained the seeds for its own continuation, even after the upheavals of the First World War, the Anglo-Irish War and the Civil War were over. And continue it did, though not at the same disastrous rate. Between 1926 and 1936, another decline of 24,500 was recorded, or 11.8 per cent, and between 1936 and 1946 the loss was 14.2 per cent.[11] As Robert E. Kennedy has pointed out, the Catholic population of the twenty-six counties decreased only marginally between 1911 and 1926, by 2.2 per cent, and actually increased, if only barely, in the two latter periods.[12] Northern Unionists watched this outward flow of Protestants from the Free State, and had no doubt at all that it was the result of a deliberate policy of squeezing out.

After the trauma of 1919–23, Southern Protestants were, however, quick to express their appreciation of the relative stability of the first years of the Free State. Even before the Civil War was over, the Bishop of Cashel, Dr Miller, saying that Southern Protestants owed the same loyalty to the Free State Government as Northerners did to Belfast, added that so far that Government had shown no disposition to be unjust to them. The real danger arose from forces opposed to settled order.[13]

The Presbyterian General Assembly in June 1923 revealed a difference of perspective North and South that was to persist. The

State of the Country Report, presented by Pollock, who was also the North's Minister of Finance, highlighted the difficult year in the South. It contrasted the judicial fairness of the Northern Government in dealing with criminals with the summary executions in the South. It referred to crimes in the South perpetrated against fellow Protestants by fanatics. But, it continued, there were many well-documented cases where the greed of possessing their neighbours' property and goods was the inspiring motive, and where reprisals only provided an excuse for the expulsion of families, and the looting of neighbours' possessions.[14]

The report did dissociate the Southern Government from these atrocities, but it still provoked criticism from the Southern-based members of the assembly. The Revd Dr Osborne said it was not a true picture of the state of the country at the present time; there had been a vast improvement. The report was about the most dangerous, injudicious, misleading and inaccurate report that had been tabled in the assembly. It was slandering the Free State in which there was no general sectarian hostility and he proposed an amendment to it, which was carried, noting the encouraging progress that had been made in the South. Dr Corkey pointed out that the report had been prepared in May, based largely on statements made by Southern ministers. He added that Bishop Fogarty's statement, about persecution of Protestants, had also been made in May.[15] The difference was one on emphasis, not of facts. The Southern ministers were almost painfully anxious to stress the positive, while the Northerners were undoubtedly seeking out the negative.

A year later the incumbent Moderator of the General Assembly, the Revd R.W. Hamilton, speaking at a St Andrew's College dinner in Dublin, paid fulsome tribute to the Free State.[16] He was, he said, an Irishman to the backbone; the Free State Government had done magnificently in an unconceivably difficult situation. He could not imagine any set of men doing better, and he only wished that the Northern leaders would be more in the way of encouraging and admiring, rather than ridiculing, as they did far too much, these men in the South.

At the 1926 assembly the Moderator, a Dubliner, the Revd R.K. Hanna, reviewed the previous ten years, and combined regret at the dwindling of the Presbyterian strength in the South, with another tribute to the Government. In the south and west, he said, there had been what amounted almost to an exodus; a colleague had told him he knew of no congregation which was not weaker now by 50 per cent than it was ten years ago. But conditions had wonderfully improved:

> We are not aware of religious disabilities. . . As a minority we suffer from inconveniences; for instance the undue importance we consider is given to Irish in primary education. But in a new State and under trying conditions, our people say that the Government has done well.[17]

A very different line was taken two months later by Blackmen, the élite version of the Orange Order, in Co. Monaghan, many of them, presumably, Presbyterians. In resolutions at their August demonstration they protested against compulsory Irish, and against 'the continued exclusion of Protestants from any share in local appointments just because they are Protestants'.[18]

However, when the Presbyterians presented an address of welcome to the new Governor General, James MacNeill, in April 1928, there were no reservations:

> We can assure your excellency, as the representative of His Majesty the King, that the members of our Church are strong in their loyalty to their sovereign and in their fidelity to constitutionally established government. We are deeply interested in the welfare of our native land and are in hearty sympathy with the Government of the Irish Free State in their efforts to promote peace, prosperity and progress of all the people under their jurisdiction. We thoroughly appreciate what they have already done in this direction, and we can give the assurance that in all such efforts for the good of the people they shall have the hearty co-operation of all the members of the Presbyterian Church.[19]

But by June 1929 an important note of caution had entered into the Presbyterian position.[18] This time the tribute to the Free State Government from the new Moderator, the Revd J.L. Morrow, was qualified. After noting that relations with the Government were most friendly, he continued:

> While there is no interference with religious beliefs, no invasion of the rights of conscience, the Governments of both the Free State and Northern Ireland will have no more loyal citizens than the members of the Presbyterian Church.[20]

But he felt it necessary to offer some advice to both Governments – they should temper the wind to the shorn lamb in dealing with minorities. Catholics in the North and Protestants in the South were in equally helpless political situations:

> The one fear to be seriously entertained, especially in the Free State, is that the trend of legislation seen in compulsory Irish, in the attempts to build up a State economically self-contained, and to be heard in the cryptic and at times venomous utterances of the enemies of the Free State settlement with the British Government, and attempted but largely defeated in the censoring of literature, should be pursued till no Protestant with love of freedom and self-respect in his breed would consider the South a land to live in.[21]

The assembly was meeting in Dublin that year for the first time in twenty-five years, and the Revd Morrow had been selected Moderator, according to himself, because he had spent all his ministerial life in Dublin. It was natural therefore that he should have addressed himself particularly to the minority problem in the South. Behind the cautious phrases it was a remarkably strong statement. He was talking about 'a fear seriously to be entertained', and about a potential situation in the Free State which any Protestant might find intolerable. His concern was for the future, but he pointed to a trend in four areas of public affairs that he clearly saw as threatening the Protestant minority – compulsory Irish, censorship, attempts to destroy the Free State settlement, and the growing economic barrier between the Free State and the United Kingdom.[22]

Southern Protestants did indeed protest over the imposition of compulsory Irish. But though successive Free State Governments were generous in their treatment of Protestant schools – in allowing smaller schools to remain open, in providing some subsidy for travel to school, for instance – they were unrelenting on the question of compulsory Irish. Protestants and their churches based their objection mainly on the argument, which was not really disputed, that the time devoted to Irish in primary schools was having a harmful effect on the general standard of education. However, they did not object to the study of the language itself.

But the answer to that came from the Gaelic League's secretary in a letter to the *Church of Ireland Gazette* on 22 October 1926. Did they, the members of the Church of Ireland, want their church to stand in opposition to the national will, to deny Ireland's nationhood? Governments remained unrelenting, culminating in the attempt by de Valera's Government in 1942 to make it a criminal offence for parents to send their children to school outside the Free State in order to avoid compulsory Irish.[23]

It would, of course, have been illogical for a Government firmly believing in the necessity of reviving Irish, and totally committed to it, to have allowed one section of the community, however small, to opt out. It was the original belief, and the total commitment, that posed the threat to the minority – Irish identity as defined by the Free State was Gaelic, and had to be forced upon everyone, even those who manifestly were not Gaelic, and denied that they ever had been. Morever they were obliged to take their Gaelic medicine, even if it damaged their own non-Gaelic cultural standard. Free State toleration embraced the minority's religious beliefs and practices, not their cultural ones.

The Revd Morrow's reference to censorship was an indication that he was worried there might not be full toleration of the minority's moral principles either. The 1929 Censorship of Publications Act was a victory for censoring, not the defeat the Moderator had spoken of so hopefully. It was the most noticeable of the, admittedly few, acts of the Free State Government up to then that unquestionably enshrined Catholic values in legislation. Not only did it impose a literary censorship that was to become notorious, it also effectively banned any education on, or promotion of, contraception.

There had been evidence earlier of the strong Catholic influence on the Free State Government and legislature in matters of morality, though these had not provoked significant outcry from the Protestant churches. From early 1922 the Catholic Irish Vigilance Association had been pressing for censorship of films, including the exclusion of material used for 'propaganda purposes alien to Catholic and Irish ideals'.[24] The result was the Censorship of Films Act, 1923. The cinema and its possibly dangerous influence was feared by all churches at that time, and the Church of Ireland and the Presbyterian Church had actually joined with the Catholic lobby in seeking legislation.

Catholic influence was much more specifically present in the attitude towards divorce. Before independence, divorce was available in Ireland only through the passing of a private bill at Westminster. When the matter was raised by Éamonn Duggan TD in 1923, he was told by Cosgrave to consult the Catholic Archbishop of Dublin, Dr Byrne. Later in 1923, when the Attorney General, Hugh Kennedy, made a formal submission to the Executive Council on the question of divorce facilities, suggesting that these could be provided through private bills in the Dáil, Cosgrave promptly sought the advice of Archbishop Byrne and the Catholic hierarchy. The reply from Cardinal Logue was that it would be altogether unworthy of an Irish legislative body to sanction concession of such divorce no matter who the petitioner might be.

There the matter rested until 1924, when three private bills for divorce were lodged with the Dáil's new Private Bill Office.[25] The situation was considered by the Joint Committee on Standing Orders, which, in a report of June 1924, pointed out that the position was unsatisfactory from every point of view. Cosgrave sought to resolve it, in February 1925, by a motion in the Dáil telling the committee to amend Standing Orders to rule out divorce bills. The Senate was asked to join in the resolution. The Chairman of the Senate, Lord Glenavy, however, ruled the resolution out of order on technical grounds, in that a legal right was being removed by resolution when, in fact, this could only be done by enactment.

Senator James Douglas then proposed a compromise which, he claimed, was the only way to block divorce bills short of actually legislating against divorce. His suggestion was that Standing Orders be changed so that divorce bills would have to be voted on in a First Reading in each house. (Normally a private bill conforming to Standing Orders would be deemed to have had its First Reading in the Senate and could be defeated only at its second stage.) The rather odd logic of Senator Douglas's proposal was that as there was no chance of Dáil or Senate passing a First Reading of a divorce bill, no one would attempt to initiate one. It was an attempt to achieve the exclusion of divorce by resolution, without falling foul of Lord Glenavy's ruling.

The Douglas motion provoked a sharp debate in the Senate, which included W.B. Yeats's famous contribution denouncing the move as 'oppressive legislation':

> If you show that this country, Southern Ireland, is going to be governed by Catholic ideas and Catholic ideas alone, you will never

get the North. You will create an impassable barrier between South and North, and you will pass more and more Catholic laws, while the North will, gradually, assimilate its divorce and other laws to England. You will put a wedge into the midst of this nation. . . You will not get the North if you impose on the minority what the minority consider to be oppressive legislation.[26]

Yeats's plain speaking was not characteristic of the Protestant minority, and was generally regarded at the time as a lapse from good taste.

The Douglas motion was narrowly passed by the Senate, but rejected by the Dáil. Divorce remained theoretically available by means of private bill, but it was clear no such bill stood any chance of progress, and the three already presented were withdrawn. Nothing more was done on the subject by the Dáil until the enactment of the 1937 Constitution.

Not surprisingly, the reporting of this series of intricate events in the Belfast papers concentrated on the highlights – Lord Glenavy's ruling in March that the Government's resolution against Bills of Divorce was out of order, a 'direct violation of the Constitution' according to the *Northern Whig* on 6 March 1925. In a comment following Yeats's tirade, the *Belfast Telegraph,* on 15 June 1925, declared that the Free State was doing everything it could to make it impossible for Ulster to enter a Dublin parliament. The attitude of the Government towards divorce was another instance of how the Free State would trample on minority rights.

The Revd Morrow's other two points, the attempt to build up an economically self-contained state, and the intentions of the 'enemies of the Free State settlement', bear on the minority's political dimension. Protestants generally, as businessmen and as, mostly, inhabitants of border counties, were harmed by, and certainly felt threatened by, any economic barriers between the Free State and the United Kingdom. They had deplored the original Free State action, in April 1923, of erecting a customs barrier at the border by bringing in Free State tariffs. (Craig had called the decision a great error of judgement, and appealed to Dublin to postpone it for all time.)[27] They were certainly not prepared to pay an economic price for a political goal they did not desire – the lessening of ties between Britain and Ireland. This issue was to become much more critical in the years ahead, when de Valera was in power.

So too was the question of dismantling the Free State settlement. But this process had already begun, to the great indignation of Northern Unionists, and the considerable discomfort of the minority in the South. First to go were the obvious symbols of the British connection – the Union Jack, all reference to the King, either in parliament or in the courts. The King went, too, from the stamps at a very early stage, and later from the coinage. In practical terms such changes made little or no difference. But they did indicate that there was no room in the Free State for what the *Irish Times* had termed 'Imperial Irishmen'. It had used the phrase on 7 December 1921 in a key leading article indicating Southern Loyalist support for the Treaty. For them, it said, Ireland did not exist, and never would exist, apart from the Empire:

> If Ireland accepts the Empire with her heart, and not merely in the cautious wording of an oath; if she accepts them as Imperial Irishmen, they [Southern Loyalists] will joyfully come to her side.

Of immediate practical concern to the minority was the lengthy campaign by Free State Governments to terminate the right of appeal, from Irish courts, to the judicial committee of the Privy Council in London. In negotiations over the Constitution in mid-1922 Collins had tried to resist this judicial link, but it was included at British insistence, and was looked upon by Southern Loyalists as one of their major guarantees. It was questioned from the outset, and was a prominent item on the Free State's list of priorities, as it sought to expand Irish independence throughout the 1920s, mainly in the context of the Imperial Conferences of 1926 and 1930. But it became a major topic for public debate in 1928–9 when Cosgrave announced his intention to alter the Free State's Constitution. The minority was alarmed, and the Church of Ireland sent a delegation, led by Archbishop Gregg, to see Cosgrave in December 1929.

The delegation's submission began with a tribute to the fair and generous treatment afforded the minority, and continued:

> But we have viewed with very real concern the avowed determination of the Government to deprive the citizens of the State of the right to appeal to the Privy Council.
>
> This is a right which we believe to be secured to us by the Treaty

and the Constitution, and to which we have looked as a most valuable protection to the minority which we represent.

We have asked for this interview for the purpose of protesting most respectfully against the declared policy of the Government in this matter. We presume that it is their well-considered and settled determination, but the minority which we represent must not be taken as acquiescing therein. On the contrary, we desire to impress on the President of the Executive Council the fact that there is a feeling of grave disappointment – we might even say of alarm – on the part of those whom we represent.[28]

The Church of Ireland protest made no impression, and almost a year later, in November 1930, the Archbishop of Dublin was joined by the Primate, Dr D'Arcy, in a public appeal for the retention of the right. Their statement referred to the delegation that had gone to Cosgrave, adding that the reply they received did little to relieve their apprehension. Their statement continued:

We do not impute to the present Government of the Irish Free State any desire to invade our rights either of property or of religious liberty, but the present Government will not always be in office, and Ireland is a country in which religious distinction and prejudices exercise a dominating influence of a kind of which those not living in Ireland can have little or no experience. The position of the minority, a minority viewed with jealous hostility by elements of the population far from negligible, needs therefore the protection of such a safeguard for its fundamental Treaty rights.

The minority in the Irish Free State has loyally accepted the new order of things in Ireland; but it must be remembered that memories in Ireland are long, and that the removal from the Constitution of the safeguard referred to. . . while it may gratify the desire of Irishmen for independence, will inevitably weaken the security enjoyed by the members of a vulnerable minority, and as time passes lead most certainly to infringements of their liberty which they would be powerless to withstand.[29]

This statement, cautiously phrased, even obsequious, was probably the closest the minority ever came to calling 'foul' on the Free State. It made no difference; having fought hard at the 1930 Imperial Conference to have the right of appeal terminated by agreement, and failed, the Cosgrave Government pushed ahead with its own legislation to do it unilaterally. It was finally accomplished under the new Fianna Fáil Government in 1933.

Both the Revd Morrow's statement of 1929 and that of the Church of Ireland leaders of 1930 expressed their fears in terms of the future, of what might happen. As the *Whig* put it on 7 November 1930:

> The right of appeal is a valuable privilege to the minority in Southern Ireland, even under the conditions which prevail today; it might become still more valuable under conditions which may possibly arise in the future.

The 'conditions' in the writer's mind were no doubt the advent to power of de Valera. But they were already changing, for society in the Free State was, at the turn of the decade, becoming much more self-consciously Catholic and more assertively so. If in the 1920s the minority in the Free State were made painfully aware of their vulnerable position as Imperial Irishmen, and non-Gaelic Irishmen living in an anti-Imperial and pro-Gaelic Ireland, in the 1930s they had the added discomfort of ever more frequent reminders that they were living in a Catholic state.

By the late 1920s the Catholic temperature in the South was rising. Catholic action groups were campaigning openly for a more Catholic society in the new state, determined, according to one writer, 'that Irish life in the independent state should bear a frankly Catholic complexion and that Catholic power should assert itself unambiguously in social and economic terms'.[30] In 1927 the Catholic hierarchy had reaffirmed its prohibition on Catholics attending Trinity College Dublin, a ban that had been widely disregarded. But the National Synod of that year 'strictly and under grave penalty' forbade all priests and clerics to commend to parents or others that they should send adolescents to that university. The same synod, incidentally, issued no such ban on Queen's University Belfast, which also came within its area of pastoral care.[31]

The centenary celebration, in 1929, of Catholic Emancipation helped arouse Catholic awareness. Northern reporting of the great public events in Dublin noted that Cardinal MacRory and others had included much criticism of the Northern state in their addresses. In June 1929, the Free State accredited its first Minister to the Holy See, and six months later the first papal nuncio to Ireland for almost 300 years arrived in Dublin.

By 1930 the Censorship Board was beginning the work that

was to make it world famous. The same year saw the case of the Mayo librarian – when Mayo County Council's Library Committee refused to confirm the appointment, as it was obliged by law to do, of a new county librarian. The librarian had been selected for the job by the new Local Appointments Commission, but the woman in question was a Protestant, and a graduate of Trinity College. The library committee's stand was defended by the Catholic Dean of Tuam, Monsignor D'Alton, on the grounds that they were not appointing a washerwoman or a mechanic, but 'an educated girl who ought to know what books to put into the hands of the Catholic boys and girls of this county'. Protestant and Catholic views on such things as divorce and contraception differed, he argued, and if there were books 'attacking these fundamental truths of Catholicity' was it safe to entrust a girl who was not a Catholic with their handling?[32]

The Cosgrave Government insisted that the appointment stand, and when Mayo County Council refused to over-rule the library committee, it was dissolved, a commissioner sent in, and the librarian appointed. However, the libraries under her charge were then boycotted and she was transferred to another position. In a subsequent Dáil debate Fianna Fáil sided with the library committee, and de Valera himself said that an overwhelmingly Catholic county had the right to insist on a Catholic librarian. At the time of the row the *Church of Ireland Gazette,* on 5 December 1930, commented simply that it 'must inevitably increase the apprehensions which are felt by many as to the treatment which Protestants are likely to receive if certain elements in this Free State get their way'. In power, de Valera promptly reinstated Mayo County Council.

Anti-Catholicism was evident in Northern Ireland in the Twelfth celebrations in July 1931. One resolution put to all demonstrations was:

We desire to warn, in the most emphatic manner, all Protestants to beware of the insidious propaganda of the Roman Catholic Church, and of the danger of allowing the Vatican to interfere with Imperial and domestic affairs.[33]

Numerous speakers warned of the dangers of mixed marriages, and there were references to the role of the Catholic Church in Spain and Italy. There were also 'hostile incidents' at parades in Monaghan. More serious trouble occurred in August, when a large mob prevented an Orange gathering in Cavan. A bridge was blown up, and an Orange hall attacked. There were anti-Catholic riots in Portadown, Armagh and Lisburn.[34]

In November 1931 the League of Knights of Christ demanded that no foreign publication be allowed into the Free State until it had been examined by a competent authority and found to contain nothing offensive to the traditional standards of the people.[35] The English popular press was the target here, and two years later de Valera obliged, in part, by imposing a tax on imported newspapers.

The religious temperature was rising all around. The 1930 Education Act in the North was seen as grossly unfair by Catholics. This Act conceded demands made by the Protestant churches for much greater influence in the state school system. The temerity of the Church of Ireland in claiming St Patrick was denounced by Cardinal MacRory, who in 1931 outraged Protestant feelings by declaring, publicly, that the Protestant Church in Ireland was 'not even a part of the Church of Christ'. At the 1932 General Assembly of the Presbyterian Church, the Moderator denounced the Cardinal for 'an astonishing piece of medievalism'.[36]

In 1931 the Ulster Protestant League was founded in Belfast, an extremist Protestant group that harried Craigavon for his alleged moderation and, with unemployment at very serious levels and rising, had as its main objective the protection of Protestant employment.

Tension in 1932 was much higher again. De Valera was in power and he had released the IRA prisoners. In the North an Ancient Order of Hibernians parade in Co. Derry on St Patrick's Day was ambushed and two marchers wounded. In June the Eucharistic Congress in Dublin brought Catholic devotional fervour to a high point. Northern extremists responded, attacking parties of Catholics travelling South in several Northern towns.

The resolutions passed at the Twelfth demonstrations that year reflected the anti-Catholic mood:

> We emphatically protest against the arrogant, intolerant, and un-Christian pretensions fulminated by Cardinal MacRory and the clerical and lay spokesmen of the Church of Rome against the Protestant churches of Ireland, and we repudiate with all indignation his, and their, attacks on Protestantism, which we hold is the essence of civil and religious liberty. These attacks show the un-changing bigotry of Rome.[37]

The reference to Cardinal MacRory stemmed from his controversy with the Church of Ireland Archbishop of Dublin, Dr Gregg, arising from the latter church's own celebrations to mark the 1500th anniversary of St Patrick.

By July 1932 the Eucharistic Congress had been held in Dublin, marking a high point in Catholic enthusiasm, and also of Protestant distaste. Twelfth speeches in 1932 dwelt on the 'Romish influences and Papal power' in the South, on the 'idolatry of the Eucharistic Congress', 'a week's display of the emptiness of Romanism'. The Revd Louis Crooks thanked Cardinal MacRory for doing the Orange Order 'by far the best deed, and for giving it by far the most powerful support and impetus they had received for years'.[38]

These were the years of the extreme Protestant declarations of Craigavon and Sir Basil Brooke. On 12 July 1932 Craigavon told an Orange demonstration that 'ours is a Protestant Government, and I am an Orangeman', and on the following Twelfth Sir Basil Brooke appealed to Loyalists to employ Protesants wherever possible, and boasted that he himself did not have 'a Roman Catholic about my own place'. The following year, in a parliamentary debate over Brooke's speeches, Craigavon stated that he was an Orangeman first and a politician and an MP afterwards: they were a Protestant parliament and a Protestant state. This last remark, Craigavon said, was his reply to the boast in the South that it was a Catholic state.[39] (The first almost exactly mirrored a statement by de Valera in 1931 at the annual Fianna Fáil Ard Fheis that he was 'a Catholic first'.[40])

Certainly the leaders of Free State governments gave no indication of thinking for a moment that things were otherwise. In June 1929, when Charles Bewley became the first Free State diplomat to present credentials to the Pope, he spoke of the attachment of the Free State people to the Catholic faith and he begged the pontiff to impart an apostolic benediction to the Head of State, to the Government and to the people of the Free State.[41]

Analysing the votes cast in the very close election in February 1932, Seán MacEntee, shortly to become Finance Minister in de Valera's first Government, said it was significant that the Catholics of the twenty-six counties had spoken decisively. Of first-preference Catholic votes, he calculated, 640,000 had gone for a change of government, while only 480,000 had opted for a continuation of Cosgrave's regime.[42] Catholic votes, it seemed, were the only ones that really counted.

De Valera himself had no hesitation in declaring Ireland a Catholic nation. In a St Patrick's Day broadcast in 1935 he said that since St Patrick, Ireland had been a Christian and Catholic nation. All attempts through the centuries to force her from this allegiance had not shaken her faith – 'She remains a Catholic nation.'[43] Such remarks have never attracted the notoriety attached to those of Craigavon and Brooke, but they were noted in the North by Unionist politicians and press.

The plight of the Southern Loyalists became a common theme for most of the 1930s in the Belfast papers. In 1934 de Valera's moves to abolish the Senate and end university representation in the Dáil were seen as attacks on the safeguards and guarantees in the Treaty settlement, and as, in the words of Cosgrave, reported in the *News-Letter* on 9 May, 'an injustice to the Protestant minority'. The General Assembly of the Presbyterian Church in June was told of the economic plight of farmers in east Donegal, cut off from their markets, and hit particularly hard by de Valera's economic war with Britain. Added to that they were now faced with a yet more severe imposition of the Irish language. The Free State Government, Dr Corkey told the assembly, intended making Irish the sole language for infant schools from 10 a.m. to 2.30 p.m. each day. Their people, he said, were manifesting in their grievous plight the same patient faith and brave spirit that brought their fathers through similar difficulties in former times.[44]

The Twelfth demonstrations of July 1934 heard many references to the plight of the Free State Loyalists. Sir William Allen, Westminster MP and leading Orangeman, referred to Dr Corkey's statement showing how 'Protestants were being driven out of the South of Ireland'. William Grant MP said the South was a priest-ridden country under the heel of Rome, and Protestants were gradually leaving it. The Revd E.G. Dixon from Portstewart, Co. Derry, said that in the Free State there were many jobs 'where no Protestant need apply'.[45]

Later in July when Lord Hailsham, from London, tried to put another view, arguing that there was no justification for saying Loyalists were being penalised for their loyalty in the Free State, he was answered by the *News-Letter*. On 26 July it quoted the decline in the Protestant population of the twenty-six counties – down 32 per cent between 1911 and 1926, and probably down further since then:

> There is convincing evidence of a crusade against Loyalists in the Free State, but it is conducted under the guise of safeguarding 'the Catholic state' against the machinations of Freemasons. The property of these people is coveted, and the Free State Government aids and abets and even gives a lead to the work of spoliation.

It was all a terrible story of grievous wrongs, said the *News-Letter*.

Towards the end of 1934 there were reports of major discontent among the Protestants of Donegal, mainly on the grounds of economic hardship resulting from the new trade barriers on the border. The previous year an anonymous group of people calling themselves 'We, the Unionists of the Free State', had written to the Duke of Abercorn, the Governor of Northern Ireland, pleading for help. They were ready at any moment to go to Northern Ireland if they could sell their land. Were they to be left among the lions?[46]

In July 1934 a memorial had been sent to the Ministry of Home Affairs in Belfast signed by six people on behalf of 5,000 Protestants in Donegal. Craigavon advised that no action be taken on it. Then, in November, a second petition arrived from Donegal, addressed to the Cabinet. It said the situation had become more critical since their previous memorial. Recent legislation prohibiting the sale of potatoes to Northern Ireland, the new Northern Ireland milk scheme soon to come into operation and the Free State Beef Bill left them with no markets, and they were absolutely unable to meet the demands on them. If they could not pay, the bailiffs would seize their stock. Moreover the petitioners referred to reports that de Valera was about to declare a Republic, and make them foreigners and aliens in the British Commonwealth. Compulsory Irish was again listed as a grievance. They were on the verge of bankruptcy and ruin. They ended by asking if east Donegal and the Laggan district could not be transferred into Northern Ireland.

Less than a month later yet another petition signed by 7,368 'loyal subjects of the King' residing in east Donegal and the Laggan, was forwarded by the Irish Loyalist Imperial Federation to the Dominions Secretary, J.H. Thomas. This too declared that the petitioners felt their lives and property were not secure under the Free State Government, and called on the Imperial Government, as a party to the Treaty of 1921, to take steps to restore them their former rights and liberties. The petition, with London's draft reply, was sent to Craigavon, who asked the opinion of each member of his Cabinet on the draft. The consensus was that it should be more sympathetic. Pollock's comment was that he could not think of anything worse than the tragedy of these people: 'It is a dreadful thing that we can do nothing for these poor creatures in Donegal.'

The petitions had two immediate results. The Donegal Protestants were denounced in Letterkenny court by District Justice Walsh, who described them as anti-Irish bigots, engaging in treasonable activities.[47] And in Belfast Dawson Bates announced, in the Northern Ireland House of Commons, that the Government was willing to assist in every way in its power to arrange transfers, with exchanges of farm holdings, between discontented Nationalists in Northern Ireland and Free State Loyalists wanting to come North.[48]

The evidence of such bitterly felt discontent among Protestants in the Free State confirmed the worst Northern views of that entity. Reporting that the Ulster Unionist Council was taking steps to help Loyalists move North, making special financial arrangements for the purchase of land, the *News-Letter*, on 10 December, commented:

> During the past eighteen months there has been an almost constant drift of Loyalists from the Free State to Ulster, and not a few have been able to acquire land. . . The recent petitions from Donegal Loyalists have led to similar memorials by individuals in other parts of the Free State.

On 14 January 1935 the *News-Letter* devoted more than two columns to another major story on the 'Plight of Loyalists in Free State'. As the Cabinet files in Belfast show,[49] this article was prepared with the help of Hungerford, secretary to the Ulster Unionist Council, and was shown to Craigavon before publication. Its main purpose, perhaps, was to put pressure on the Government in London to help the Free State Loyalists. The article argued that because the Treaty contained specific safeguards for the loyal minority, the British Government had thereby implicitly admitted a duty to them.

But the article also held out little hope of help from Belfast. It did again emphasise the plight of the Loyalists, saying that 'the so-called safeguards have been cast to the four winds and their places filled with the most flagrant penalisation and persecution'. Shoals of letters, it was claimed, had come in from Southern Protestants seeking to move North. It also reported that prominent Church of Ireland men had recently considered a scheme to help young men wishing to purchase farms in Ulster, and there was a strong body of opinion in the Presbyterian Church that it should have a fund to assist the settlement of Free State Protestants in the North. Before quoting extracts from some of the letters received in Belfast, the author of the article said he had read much of the large volume of such correspondence arriving at the Ulster Unionist Council: 'Without exception they point to the fact that Loyalists are slowly but surely being squeezed out by the Government's avowed campaign to establish a Catholic state.'

While the main complaint of the Donegal Loyalists in 1934 was economic – the loss of markets for their farm produce and the burden of taxation – they frequently cited other disabilities, including the compulsion to learn Irish, and discrimination against them as Protestants or former Unionists, in the issuing of cattle export licences, and in the seeking of employment through labour exchanges. Termination of the right of appeal to the Privy Council, and the new citizenship legislation were also causes of alarm and complaint. In the event they got little help from either Belfast or London. The Ulster Unionist Council gave some *ad hoc* assistance by way of small sums of money to pay transport costs or, more often, to help with customs duties on the movement of possessions and stock.

The year 1935 saw a re-emergence of physical violence against Protestants in the South. In part it was directed against the Masonic Order, long a target for Catholic enthusiasts. In January 1935 the annual dinner of a Masonic Lodge in Cork was raided by armed men and the hall wrecked. Reporting the incident on 28 January, the *News-Letter* said it need cause no surprise, in view of the relentless campaign waged against the Masons by the Catholic Church – 'The wonder indeed is that Masonic Halls should be allowed to stand in that land of tolerance and freedom on the other side of the Border.'

In the summer of 1935 anti-Protestant feeling spilled over into violent acts in several parts of the Free State, fuelled by reports of disturbances in Belfast in July, which were seen as another anti-Catholic pogrom. The attacks began on Saturday 20 July when a mob rampaged through Limerick, attacking homes and shops owned by Protestants. That weekend three Protestant halls were burned in Clones, among them the Masonic hall and a Plymouth Brethren place of worship. Early on Monday morning a group of men attacked the Church of Ireland church at Kilmallock, Co. Limerick. The door was battered down and the church set on fire and destroyed. The attackers then broke windows in the rectory and attempted to enter it. Another Protestant home was attacked, and the windows of a Protestant-owned shop broken.[50]

An attack had been made on another Church of Ireland building, at Trim, Co. Meath, where raiders had smashed a large stained-glass window on the Saturday night. An attempt was made to set fire to the Masonic hall in Kells, Co. Meath. At Listowel, in Kerry, shots were fired early on Sunday morning into the Bank of Ireland premises – also the home of the manager and his wife who were Protestants. At Athboy, Co. Meath, homes of Protestants had the words 'Remember Belfast' painted on them. In Letterkenny, Co. Donegal, Protestant-owned shops had their windows smashed. In Dunmanway, in west Cork, where Protestants had been murdered in 1922, slogans were painted in tar on the streets saying 'Watch Belfast'. 'Orangemen Beware' was written on the pavements outside the shops of Protestants in Enniscorthy, Co. Wexford.

On Tuesday 23 July the trouble spread to Galway, where dock workers paraded through the town calling on Catholic workers at mills and other places to come out on strike until all Protestant workers had been dismissed. According to the *Irish Times* report of 24 July, large numbers of workers complied and joined the parade. *Gardaí* had to draw their batons and charge the crowd when Electricity Supply Board workers refused to join the protest. Earlier in the day at Galway docks the SS *Dun Aengus*, which served the Aran Islands and Connemara, was not allowed to sail until its chief engineer, a Protestant, had left the ship. In Limerick dockers refused to discharge cargo from a coal ship owned by

171

Kellys of Belfast. The Galway incident was reported in the *News-Letter,* on 25 and 26 July, as 'The campaign to drive Protestants out of employment in the Free State continues.' It added Sligo as another centre of similar trouble, and later in the week reported four cottages owned by Protestants in Co. Cavan burned, and Waterford dockers also refusing to handle a Belfast ship.

The Church of Ireland Archbishop of Dublin, Dr Gregg, protested publicly over the attacks in Kilmallock, and received an assurance from the Government that the damage would be repaired and the perpetrators brought to justice.[51] However, on 25 and 26 July the *News-Letter* reported speeches by Seán MacEntee and de Valera, which indicated clearly that both regarded these attacks as reprisals for events in Belfast. De Valera said that they knew the fundamental cause of these unfortunate happenings. There was a power outside the country which had created this situation.

Catholic protests at their treatment in Northern Ireland were met by citing the fate of Protestants in the South. On 21 August the *News-Letter* said safeguards for Protestants had been wiped out by the deliberate act of the Southern Government: 'And what of the Catholic state which we are unblushingly told it is the aim of Mr de Valera and his colleagues to establish?'

A year later, on 7 November 1936, the *News-Letter* was still reporting distressed Loyalists leaving the South. Another article by a special correspondent said that judging from the increased numbers making their way into Northern Ireland, Loyalists were finding it more and more difficult to live in the Free State. During the past two or three years scores of Cavan and Monaghan families had crossed the border. He said the numbers involved were reflected in the increased membership of Orange lodges such as the Cavan Defenders No.1327 now meeting in east Belfast, with a membership of one hundred, having had only eleven when founded a few years earlier.

By 1937 the Northern Unionist view of the Free State was unshakably fixed – it was a self-proclaimed Catholic state, in which the Protestant minority, while allowed to practise its religion, was the victim of deprivation of its constitutional rights, of cultural discrimination, and of economic policies which were, by design or accident, reducing it to poverty. The conclusive proof that Protestants were being 'squeezed out' was that they were undeniably leaving the Free State. Between 1926 and 1936 another drop of roughly 12 per cent, or 25,000, had been recorded in the Protestant population.[52]

There was, therefore, no great outcry at de Valera's overtly 'Catholic' Constitution of 1937. Indeed the Presbyterian Moderator, at the 1937 General Assembly, thanked God for it. It was remarkable in modern times to find a Constitution based on a definitely Christian attitude to life. Ebenezer Bain, from Dublin, noted with pleasure that under the Constitution the rights of the Presbyterian religion had been amply secured, and he went on to acknowledge the respect and consideration shown to Presbyterians, not only by those in authority in the Free State, but by their Catholic fellow countrymen.[53]

On 7 May the *Church of Ireland Gazette* did not think much of the Constitution, deeming it to belong to the realm of fantasy and humbug. But it did accuse it of serving badly the real cause of Irish unity, and cited a catalogue of its provisions which 'cannot reasonably fail to alienate the North'. Among these were the prohibition on divorce legislation, and the recognition of the special position of the Catholic Church as guarding the faith 'professed by the great majority of the citizens'.

But Craigavon himself had no objection to that particular clause, Article 44, 2, or so he said in an exchange at Stormont in June 1937. Challenged once more by a Nationalist member over his 'Protestant state' remark of three years earlier, he replied:

I made that statement at this box very shortly after one of the leaders of the Free State had made a statement that the Free State was a Catholic state, or a Roman Catholic state. It was made to clear the air, but does not necessarily mean all that Hon. Member reads into it. Let me go a step further. The Free State Bill just passed by the Dail says in Article 44, number 2, that the State 'recognised the special position of the Holy Catholic Apostolic and Roman Church as the guardian of the faith professed by the great majority of the citizens'. I have no objection to that. . . I would far rather see a religious community than a non-religious community. At the same time, while the Government of the South is carried on along lines which I presume are very suitable to the majority of Roman Catholics in that part. . . surely the Hon. Member will admit that the Government of the North, with a majority of Protestants, should carry on the administration according to Protestant ideas and Protestant desires.[54]

Early in 1938, after the new Constitution had come into operation, the *Northern Whig,* on 7 February, followed a similar line. Taking up the special recognition of the Catholic Church in Éire, it added:

> In other words the South possesses a Catholic Parliament for a Catholic people. Those Protestants in the area governed by Dublin are living under a system of Government dominated by the philosophy of the Roman Catholic Church. . . Southern Loyalists, moreover, complain that through the actions of the Roman Catholic organisations, appointments in the public services are given almost exclusively to applicants belonging to that faith. Disabilities of much the same character are suffered by Protestants in town and country. The result is that the Protestant population is little more than half as numerous as when the Free State was established.

The appointment of a Protestant, Douglas Hyde, as President under the new Constitution cut little ice: there was little or no comment on his appointment at the time.[55] At his installation in June 1938, a Dublin Presbyterian minister, the Revd R.K. Hanna, said it was a gesture of goodwill towards the minority. Two weeks later, at a Twelfth of July celebration in Belfast, the County Grand Secretary, Mr Barlow, said it was so much eyewash. Protestants had no place in the public life of Éire or the Government of Éire, or positions under it; the corporation and other public bodies were closed to them. The two or three hangers-on who found place and profit in the Government of Éire were not worthy of the name.[56]

The Unionist view of the South was put succinctly by the *Whig,* on 23 June 1938, in a leading article commenting on the installation of President Hyde:

> It has long been apparent that the narrow and fanatical type of Nationalism which Southern Republicans have fostered, and in support of which they have forced on the people a language that most of them do not want, is hardly distinguishable from the tribalism of the most primitive peoples. The tribal spirit is at the very core of Mr de Valera's political philosophy, but never before has it been so clearly revealed in his public utterances. To him, Ireland is the home of a people having no racial, political or cultural affinity with the British nation.

174

10
AN ABSURD FANTASY, A DEAD HORSE

When the first Dáil addressed the free nations of the world in January 1919, it listed among the justifications for Irish independence the fact that the language of Ireland, as well as the race, the customs and traditions, was radically different from the English.[1]

The use of Irish in the first Dáil was the element in its proceedings that drew most comment from the Northern papers. This elevation of Irish to a key position in Sinn Féin nationalism was to become something of an obsession for Northern politicians and journalists looking South. On 22 January 1919 the *Belfast News-Letter* reckoned nine-tenths of the population did not speak it. The *Northern Whig*, the same day, charitably granted that one-eighth did, adding, 'Whether Nationalist patriots relish it or not, Ireland is not only English speaking, but her whole intellectual life, even in the South, is entirely bound up with England.'

When de Valera addressed the Sinn Féin convention in Dublin in April and talked about minority difficulties in the country and Sinn Féin's ability to settle them, it was his reference to the Irish language that again drew most comment from the *News-Letter* on 10 April 1919:

> It is to be taught as a living language in every school in the country, although it is absolutely dead in the greatest part of it. The millions of people who cannot speak or read it are compelled to learn it if they want either to do business or retain employment. English may be taught as an extra subject – like Latin, Greek or any of the modern languages, but generally it is to be suppressed, for is it not a language of heretics?

As an indication of its seriousness about the language, Dáil Éireann appointed a Minister for Irish in October 1919, almost two years before it was decided a Minister for Education was necessary. J.J. O'Kelly was the appointee in both cases, but siding with de Valera in the division over the Treaty, he was replaced in Collins's Provisional Government by Fionan Lynch. Lynch soon attracted the attention of the *News-Letter*. On 30 January 1922 it carried a report under the double heading 'A Provisional Despot', 'His Gaelic Zeal'. This said that Lynch had ordered the education board to make Irish a compulsory subject in schools that year. National school infants were to be faced with a compulsory bilingual programme. This was to be a cause of much practical concern to Southern Protestants over the next two decades, and something about which they protested regularly to the Dublin Government. It was a grievance which was much reported in the Northern papers.

When the Free State's Constitution was published in June 1922, the *News-Letter*'s report on 16 June highlighted the guarantee of religious equality in it, but the editorial comment was on the language – on the position of Irish as the national language:

> This provision is inserted as a concession to the sentiment of nationality, but its absurdity is apparent when the fact is remembered that in the last census there were fewer than seventeen thousand people in the whole of Ireland who spoke Irish only, while those who were able to speak Irish, but generally used English, formed only 13.3 per cent of the population.

The significance of the language, as it had been seen by Sinn Féin for decades, was not lost on Northern observers. Commenting on 30 November 1922 on the passage of the Irish Bills through Westminster, the *Whig* declared that the men to whom the twenty-six counties were being handed over had proclaimed their intention to revive the Gaelic civilisation. This did not mean reproducing the Ireland of Brian Boru, but setting up 'something as much unlike the British civilisation as possible'.

But the *Whig* could never resist the temptation to extract as much fun and ridicule out of the use of Irish as possible. In September 1923, when Professor Michael Hayes was appointed Speaker in the Dáil, Cosgrave complimented him on his ability to conduct the business of the House in the Irish language. This, said the *Whig* on 20 September 1923 was an interesting accomplishment

> . . . but so far as the bulk of the members of the Dáil are concerned, Professor Hayes might make half a dozen blunders in every sentence or even discourse to the House in Armenian. . . without any risk of being called to account.

The continued concern of Southern Protestants over compulsory Irish in schools was faithfully reported in the Belfast press. In August 1924, a Relief of Derry celebration in Castleblayney, Co. Monaghan, saw the assembled Orangemen and Apprentice Boys passing a resolution giving hearty support to the Free State Government in its establishment of law and order. The resolution added that

... while we are quite in sympathy with the promotion of the study of the Irish language so long as it is voluntary, we must protest in the strongest manner against it being made compulsory in our schools, except where the parents of the children so desire.[2]

Formal protests came also from the Protestant churches. In May 1926 the Bishop of Limerick told the Church of Ireland General Synod meeting in Dublin:

There is no question of deprecating the study of the old language. We regret that this particular policy was forced on the country without consulting the parents or teachers; the majority of the people are against it. We regret compulsion. We have no wish to discourage the teaching of Irish, but we have every wish to discourage the compulsion placed upon our people. Those of us in the country see how the whole progress of children has been put back by compulsion.[3]

He regretted that teachers had been taken away from their schools

... in vain search of trying to get a knowledge of this difficult language... As a patriotic Irishman it is a matter of deep grief to me that the children now growing up promise to be among the most uneducated people in Europe.[4]

A month later the Presbyterian General Assembly, while listening to tributes from its new Moderator, the Revd R.K. Hanna, to the 'wonderfully improved conditions' in the Free State, also heard him complain of 'the undue importance we consider is given to Irish in primary education'.[5]

Almost a decade later the General Synod was still worried about the impact of the primacy given to Irish on general standards.[6] The synod was told, by Canon Hedges for the education board, that teaching through Irish was an experiment fraught with danger. The board regarded with very considerable apprehension the tendency to make Irish such a key subject, not only in schools, not only in public offices, but also in various aspects of social life. To make Irish such a key subject was almost to imbalance the whole system of education.

A comprehensive statement of the Church of Ireland's complaints about the language policy was contained in the report of a survey of Protestant elementary schools in 1938–9 carried out by the church's board of education.[7] It found that the school curriculum had been restricted in an undesirable fashion by the exclusion of several practical subjects such as drawing and domestic economy, apparently because pupil development had been retarded by the demands of learning Irish or, worse still, learning through Irish. Teachers too were being put under constant strain by the language programme, both in their teaching, and because without Irish-language qualifications they were excluded from salary benefits. The report also said no progress was being made anyway in making Irish a spoken language. It noted that there was a definite tendency for Protestant parents to remove their children from national schools and send them to private institutions, or to Northern Ireland, in order to avoid compulsory Irish.

Not surprisingly, the Belfast papers were less than restrained in their reporting and commenting on the subject. The *Whig* headed its report on the Gaelic League conference in Dublin in January 1925, 'The Gaelic Folly'. On 2 January it noted that the league was in a bad way, and proceeded to pour scorn on the efforts to restore the language:

> The Free State Government, it is true, is backing the League. It has decreed the wasting of a certain amount of time, money and teachers' nerve tissue by the infliction of instruction in Gaelic on the unfortunate pupils in Southern schools, and has made knowledge of the language a test for the appointment of certain officials.
>
> Few of its acts have been more unpopular with the majority of Free State citizens – which is saying a great deal. To sentimentalise with a total lack of sincerity over the supplanting of Gaelic by English is one thing; to be compelled to learn an obsolescent and quite useless language is another.

In the middle of 1925 the Mulcahy Commission's suggestions for the Gaeltacht areas provided more scope for the *Whig*. On 18 June it noted the proposal that some islands should become 'Gaelic reservations' where nothing but Gaelic would be spoken, 'and the inferior tongue of Shakespeare, Bunyan, Milton, Synge, Yeats and AE "verboten"'. At the same time the *Whig* also related how Frank Fahy, Secretary of the Gaelic League, had told the commission that he knew only one person able to take dictation in Irish, and transcribe it on a typewriter. He himself had to write out his letters and give them to a typist.

On 29 September 1925 the *Whig* was in less jocular mood, denouncing the 'high-handed policy' of the Department of Education on Irish and declaring that the Minister, then Eoin MacNeill, was one of the most unpopular men in Ireland. Under the heading 'A Dead Horse', an editorial commented:

> The Gaelo-maniacs of the Free State are still busily endeavouring to force an obsolescent and unwanted language on a reluctant people. Proofs that they are flogging a dead horse are daily multiplying, but they persist in efforts that are making them increasingly ridiculous in the eyes of the world.

Not surprisingly, compulsory Irish was added to the list of reasons why the North would not consider unity with Dublin. In one of its periodic rehearsals of the arguments against unity, the *Whig* on 28 February 1927 said this:

> We know full well the difficulties with which its [the Free State's] leaders are confronted, but we also know that liberty there is much more restricted than it was with us. Imagine your children being compelled to spend one fourth of their school life learning the Irish language. That is what is actually happening in the Free State. . . Whatever interest the Irish language might have for philologists, it can be of no help to anyone fighting the battle of life. . . These are people who do not mind wallowing in poverty if they can only indulge in dreams.

Northern politicians as well as editors found the language a useful piece of ammunition. In October 1927 the Minister of Finance, H.M. Pollock, delivered a speech on what was by now a familiar theme – how events in the Free State justified the existence of Ulster. What, he asked, would parents say if their children were compelled by statute to waste part of their time studying Gaelic, a language of no practical application outside its area of use, and of very little use even there?

> English is the mother tongue of the Ulster people, and to compel the children of the province to acquire a language which is dying

a natural death would be as insanely tyrannical as to force the teaching of Kaffir or Abyssinian on them. We have been delivered from less desirable things than the Gaelic incubus by remaining in the United Kingdom, but protection from this nuisance is not a negligible boon.[8]

Compulsory Irish in the schools, as well as being a long-standing grievance with the Protestant churches, was also a matter of general controversy. Disputes in 1932 over the impact of the time devoted to Irish on the general level of education were well reported in the Belfast papers.[9]

Full play was given in 1937 to Gaelic League calls for stronger measures to enforce the use of Irish. On 26 March the *News-Letter* said the League was out of funds, but Gaels were not easily daunted: 'They say, in effect, that if the people do not take kindly to the study and use of language, they must be compelled to do so, and the Government is urged to take steps accordingly.' It listed some of these recommended measures – no civil sevant under fifty to get promotion or a salary increase unless he could work through Irish, and a legal requirement on all newspapers to carry one page daily in Irish.

It may be somewhat surprising then that the Northern Ireland Government not only permitted the teaching of Irish in schools in the North, but actually subsidised it. Admittedly the subsidy was extremely modest – £1,500 a year – and was withdrawn in 1933, but public elementary schools, beyond doubt exclusively those under Catholic management, continued to teach it. In 1936 the Nationalist MP, T.J. Campbell, told Stormont that 10,000 children in elementary schools in Northern Ireland were then learning Irish and another 1,200 in secondary schools. According to.the Parliamentary Secretary to the Minister of Education, John Robb, Irish could be taught as an optional subject in elementary schools, as could French or any other language, but that no extra fees were paid for the teaching of any language. In secondary schools Irish could be taught as part of the ordinary curriculum, and its position in certificate examinations was similar to that of any language other than English.[10]

The occasion of that debate was a recent regulation designating Irish as a foreign language in the school curriculum. This, claimed Campbell, revealed a provincialism and obscurantism that were almost unthinkable. He reminded the House that 90 per cent of place names in Northern Ireland were Irish, and could only be properly appreciated by a person with a knowledge of Irish. He noted that an Irish name, Lisnagarvey, had been given to the new BBC radio transmitter near Lisburn and added, 'Only Philistines and withered pedagogues would try to degrade Irish.' His question, addressed to the Prime Minister, brought a reply from Craigavon in moderate, if patronising, terms:

> What use is it to us here in this progressive, busy part of the Empire to teach our children the Irish language? What use would it be to them? Is it not leading them along a road that has no practical value? We have not stopped such teaching; we have stopped the grants. . . simply because we do not see that these boys being taught Irish could be any better citizens.[11]

Campbell's point about the naming of the new transmitter, which was opened just a few days earlier, is interesting. It had been expected that it would be called Blaris, the name of the townland where it stood outside Lisburn, and which already was, and was to remain, its popular designation. But, as the *News-Letter* reported on 20 March, an eleventh-hour decision altered this to Lisnagarvey and the Governor, the Duke of Abercorn, so named it on 20 March 1936. The *News-Letter* approved: it was a 'happy thought, for the district name suggests much that is old and historic in Ulster, while the transmitter is the last word in modern scientific and engineering invention'. In her diary Lady Craigavon says the name Lisnagarvey was suggested by her husband.[12] It would be wrong to read too much into this, for Lisnagarvey, the old name for Lisburn, was in common use in the town by various sporting and cultural organisations, many of them exclusively Protestant. The town's highly successful men's hockey club was – and is – Lisnagarvey.

In the 1930s Irish phrases still cropped up in odd places in Northern Ireland – the Duchess of Abercorn photographed under a banner reading *Céad Míle Fáilte* at the opening of a sale, for example. Nor is there evidence in Northern sources for the fear expressed by Southern Protestants that the Irish language, with its invocations of the Virgin Mary and the saints, was a means whereby 'unwary Protestants are familiarised with Roman ways of thought'.[13] But there was growing hostility to the language as part of the political weaponry of Irish nationalism. This hostility was expressed by the *Whig* on 27 April 1933, when it commented on the announcement that the Government was ending its grant to the teaching of Gaelic in Northern Ireland schools. This was a luxury Northern Ireland could not afford, the paper said. It would be sounder, continued the *Whig*, to subsidise Esperanto than to pay grants for the teaching of the 'moribund Gaelic'. The demand for instruction in it was not the outcome of a spontaneous movement on the part of any section of the Ulster people:

> Rather it is one of the by-products of an agitation which is not cultural but political, having for its ultimate object the severance of the Province from the United Kingdom, and its absorption into the Free State.

'Pro-Gaelic' and 'Anti-British', concluded the *Whig*, were practically synonymous terms.

The position accorded Irish in de Valera's new Constitution of 1937 was listed by the *Church of Ireland Gazette* on 7 May 1937 as one of many features of that document certain to alienate the North. But it also cited the language as a main reason for dismissing the Constitution as window-dressing, humbug or fantasy. Noting that the Irish version of the document was to be the legally authentic text and that Irish was to be the official language of the country, it said this was an absurd paradox when Irish was a language understood by perhaps 10 per cent of the people. (This figure, it added, might be an over-estimate if applied to the Free State, and was certainly a gross exaggeration if applied to Ireland as a whole.)

The great emphasis placed on the language first by Sinn Féin nationalists, and then within the independent Irish state, proved a real bonus to Unionist politicians and propagandists. In terms of newspaper coverage of the South it occupied much more space than, for instance, the original Unionist concern over Catholic domination of an Irish parliament. The insistence by Sinn Féin that language was an essential badge of nationhood could be turned around and used to disprove the existence of a distinct Irish nation. Only a small minority of people in Ireland spoke Irish, therefore no distinct Irish nation existed, or at least no longer existed in the twentieth century.

If the ground was shifted to argue that historically the Irish nation did exist, that it had been forced, in part, to adopt English but that it was now embracing the language again, that too suited the Unionist case, for if it proved anything, it proved that there were two distinct peoples on the island of Ireland. As Pollock said in 1927, English was the 'mother tongue of the Ulster people', a phrase by which he and fellow Unionist politicians invariably meant the Protestants or Unionists of Ulster.

It also fitted in neatly to the way Unionists liked to distinguish the two peoples in Ireland: the one – themselves – hard-headed, realistic, practical; the other, dreamers, idealists, impractical to the point of foolishness. As Craigavon and others repeatedly asked, what use was the Irish language? What stronger proof of wrong-headedness and foolish idealism could be found than the attempt by an English-speaking state in the twentieth century to replace English with the patently dying and antiquated language of a small minority? And at great financial cost and even greater cost to the educational health of the state.

The language question also gave Unionists the chance to present Irish nationalists not just as misguided idealists, but as fools and hypocrites. This was most evident in the ridicule poured on the first Dáil, and was also the theme of the many reports dealing with the activities of the Gaelic League. Finally, the language issue frequently strengthened the case of those who saw authoritarian, if not dictatorial, tendencies in Free State Governments, particularly under de Valera. The language was being 'forced' on an unwilling population. Children were being 'compelled' to learn it.

Evidence of widespread opposition to the compulsory language policy was not hard to find – Unionist politicians and newspapers did not have to quote solely from Southern Protestant sources. A great many others in the South publicly denounced it as foolish, authoritarian and harmful. But the treatment of the Southern minority in regard to the language was of special interest in the North, and of considerable value in bolstering the Unionist case. While English was officially recognised as a national language under both the Free State and 1937 Constitution, compulsory Irish in schools and the imposition of Irish-language requirements in certain professions and in the public service, constituted an official policy of forcing upon a well-defined minority a culture that it regarded as alien.

The lengths to which Dublin was prepared to go to do this, rather than the policy itself, constituted the real offence. In 1932 de Valera's zealous Education Minister, Thomas Derrig, had a private preparatory school in Wexford – patronised by Protestant families – prosecuted because Irish was not taught in it. The case was lost on appeal. But in 1942 Derrig introduced, and the Dáil passed, a Bill which would have effectively compelled all parents to have their children taught Irish, even if they were sent to schools outside the state. (Protestant parents in border counties and elsewhere often sent their children to school in Northern Ireland.) As a result of the Bill, parents could have been prosecuted under the compulsory school attendance law if their children were at a school anywhere – Northern Ireland, England – that did not teach Irish. President Douglas Hyde referred the Bill to the Supreme Court and it was ruled repugnant to the Constitution.[14] But it had been passed by the Dáil and the Senate, and de Valera himself had spoken in its support.

In its approach to the language, the nationalism of Sinn Féin and the Free State was at its most exclusive and most irrational. It was a gift to Unionist polemicists. Both the depth and the nature of the Unionist objections to the language do not seem to have been appreciated in Dublin. There was a fond assumption that individual, and usually antiquarian, interest in the Irish language among a minority of Ulster Protestants indicated an underlying readiness to embrace Gaelic culture and language restoration. Irish as an antiquarian interest, as one aspect of Ireland's mixed cultural heritage was one thing – but Irish as an essential element in an Irish identity, as a compulsory language in schools and in other areas of life and at the cost both of money and, as de Valera himself admitted, of the strength and quality of English-language culture was something entirely different. Dublin's language policy was, to the Northerners, economic and cultural madness – obscurantist nationalism at its most extreme.

NO MATERIAL ADVANTAGE

It is reported from London, said the *Northern Whig* on 25 January 1923, that the Free State is bankrupt. Kevin O'Higgins had warned the Dáil of the danger of economic collapse.

It was a theme that was to vary little over the next thirty years. The Southern economy was a favourite topic for Northern editors and for Unionist politicians, though in this area as in others there is little evidence of serious study of the problems of the South, or of the positive efforts made by various administrations to estab-lish a measure of control over that economy. The evidence to hand in the state of the economy to prove the Unionist case, and the folly and the wrong-headedness of Irish nationalism, was irre-sistible. It must also have been of great comfort to look regularly at an economy and a society that seemed heavier hit even than Northern Ireland by the hard times. Commenting on the 1923 Budget of the Cosgrave Government, the *Whig* on 14 April termed it 'The Fruits of Anarchy' and noted that the Free State had ended the year, its first full year, with a debit balance of £2.5 million – 'a very large amount for a small and poor country'.

But national deficits meant less than the cost of a stamp, and on 22 June 1923 the *Whig* noted in a leading article that the postal service in the Free State was now dearer than in Ulster, and less efficient. Lady Spender, in her diary for June 1923, recording a tour of the border with her husband and Tallents, reports that people were crossing from the Free State to post their letters in Northern Ireland, saving half a penny.[1]

The income tax was higher too, as the *Whig* recorded on 6 August 1923. On 28 April 1924 the same paper published a table of comparative taxation levels, North and South. Income tax, at 5s., was 6d. higher in the Free State; corporation tax, at 1s., was double the rate in the North, beer was taxed at £5 a barrel, £1 higher, postage was 2d. against 1½d. and parcel post was 9d. as against 6d.

Over the next two years Northern readers were told that the

Free State was 'the most heavily taxed country in the world'; that its taxes were 'the highest in Europe'; that it was 'the sick man of the British archipelago'; that the burden of taxation in the Free State was 'higher than in any other country in Europe in proportion to the population', and that the Free State was the poorest state in Europe with a cost of living twelve points higher than in the North. For good measure those reports also carried the news that 'the cost of living has gone up enormously, and the whole economic fabric is quickly going to pieces'; that there was 'semi-starvation and poverty' in the Free State, and, possibly, famine.[2] In 1924 when a Luke Duffy told a Labour Party conference in Dublin that he was concerned about the indolence and inefficiency of the people running Southern industry, and running it on antiquated lines, without expert and intelligent direction, he was sure of good coverage in the 15 March columns of the *Whig*.

In January 1927 Pollock, the Northern Minister of Finance, made a speech on the economic problems facing the Free State. It was quite impossible for the South to keep up the same standard of living as Great Britain, of old-age pensions, or of unemployment benefit. 'Apart from the religious, the educational, the political and the sentimental sides of the question, the Free State has not a single material advantage to offer us', he said.[3]

On 16 April the *Whig* used the state of the South to answer Nationalist criticism of the economy in the North. Taxation in the North was too high, it agreed, but it was much higher in the Free State. There too the administration was inferior, education was much below the Northern standard, old-age pensioners received worse treatment, and there was no widow's pension at all. Earlier that month Andrews, the Minister for Labour, had rejected a proposal for reciprocity between North and South in the payment of unemployment benefit. It was impossible because the North paid 18s. for a man, and 2s. for each child, while the Free State paid 15s. and 1s. Moreover the North had extended benefit while the South did not.[4]

The Northern papers noted in 1927 that the Free State was again unable to balance its Budget, and in fact never had. The *Irish Independent* was quoted as saying that as year succeeded year the hope of attaining a balanced Budget seemed to recede, and would never be achieved unless expenditure was checked and reduced. Northern Unionists regularly attributed part of the South's economic ills to foolish expenditure – on a large standing army, on a Foreign Minister who was deemed unnecessary in a member state of the British Empire, on foreign diplomatic missions, which were even less necessary, and on the compulsory promotion of the Irish language.[5]

The picture was not so gloomy at the beginning of the 1930s. On 1 May 1930 the *Whig* gave prominence to its report of Ernest Blythe's Budget. He had produced, it said, the most satisfactory financial statement that had appeared since the establishment of the Free State. The following year was even better: for the first time the publication of the estimates showed that the Free State was able to announce that revenue would meet expenditure. But the Northern reader's attention was drawn to the figure of £70,000 expenditure on 'establishments abroad', to the cost of the army, and to the lower social benefits in the South, as reported by the *Whig* on 12 March 1931. But world recession was by then hitting everywhere, and the Belfast papers carried stories on the slums of Dublin, and on distress among the farmers. In November 1931 a supplementary Budget in the South put 6d. on income tax.[6]

After de Valera's accession to power in 1932, the economic picture of the South became yet more dire. On 25 April 1932 the *Whig* commented on the rising unemployment in the Free State, noting that the trade situation was bad, but could be immeasurably worse as a result of de Valera's 'act of folly' in challenging Britain over the land annuities.

By mid-1932 the Free State farmers were already feeling the adverse effects of de Valera's policies. On 5 August the *Whig* commented that as Ulster looked across the border 'she sees a country helpless in the grip of a double tyranny calling itself patriotism, a tyranny which is deliberately setting about bleeding the country to death. . . As the result of a combination of bad faith and foolish obstinacy, it is bringing its only industry to the verge of ruin.' In September 1932 the decline in the Free State's economy was shown up in the trade figures for the year ending that July. These revealed the worst adverse balance since 1927, and the July figures showed a remarkable slump in livestock exports.[7] If under the Cosgrave governments the South's economic woes had been due in part to foolish government spending, under de Valera they were perceived to be the (much more serious) result of a deliberate and suicidal policy. By 22 October 1932 the *Whig* saw the Free State drifting to complete ruin, with the suppression of de Valera the only hope of saving it. The hunger marches in Dublin of late 1932 confirmed this view.

A graphic description of hardship in Dublin was given to a meeting of the Loyalist Relief Association in London in April 1933 by a Mr Somerville, a member of the Irish committee of the association. They were, he said, going through a time in Ireland when no one knew what was going to happen. People were starving; it was pitiful to go through the streets of Dublin and see men, women and children dragging themselves about. The whole trade of the country was going, and the few people in jobs were gradually being dismissed.[8]

On 12 August 1933, with the Blueshirts active, the *Whig* noted that Southern politicians seemed to be concentrated on mutual maledictions, party feuds and the marching of men, and meanwhile the country was committing economic suicide. Exports were down by 47 per cent from 1930–31, and the adverse trade balance up from £11.5 million to £14.5 million. On 20 January 1934 the *Belfast News-Letter* had even more dramatic figures; the Free State's total trade was down from £103 million in 1930 to £55 million by November 1933. Up to 125,000 people were on public assistance. The South's trade had been brought to the verge of ruin and the country seemed to be heading for bankruptcy and anarchy. In such circumstances the *News-Letter,* on 25 January, dismissed the plans for industrialisation put forward by Seán Lemass, de Valera's Industry Minister, as 'flights of fancy'. Lemass talked of the current industrial revival, but it was a pity, said.the *News-Letter,* he could not say where the new factories were. That same month de Valera's claim that he was pleased with the progress of his self-sufficiency programme, that everything was working out as anticipated, was deemed 'absurd' and 'moonshine' by the *News-Letter* on 30 January.

In mid-1934 the economic state of the South was brought to the attention of Northern Unionists in a more direct way. At the General Assembly of the Presbyterian Church in June, Dr Corkey, the Moderator that year, spoke of the plight of the numerous Presbyterian small farmers in Donegal. They had, he said, a great body of loyal people in Donegal:

> Most of them belong to the farming community and are passing through most difficult times. Their market towns where they sell their produce and buy their goods are Londonderry and Strabane. They are now completely cut off from these towns by the boundary and high tariffs and these people, among the most loyal in the British Empire, have no market in which to sell their cattle or produce, and in common with the farmers of all classes in Donegal, can see nothing in the future but black ruin.[9]

The economic hardships suffered by Presbyterians in Donegal, and by Protestants elsewhere in the South, attracted much Northern attention in 1934 as Southern Loyalists sought to move North.[10] The *News-Letter* may have been overstating it on 13 August, when it put the headline 'Economic Ruin of Free State' over a report that Guinness was to open a brewery in London to avoid the tariff wall, but Ireland's few large exporting industries were suffering, and there were reports that Jacobs, the biscuit manufacturers, were pulling out, and also Gallahers, the tobacco firm. In November 1934 the North's Attorney General, A.B. Babington, had more impressive statistics: Free State exports in 1924 had been worth £50 million – in 1934 they were worth only £16 million.[11]

The first returns from the 1936 census suggested to the *News-Letter* that things were even worse than they seemed. There had been a small (6,000) decrease in the Free State population since 1926, not the increase expected, and not the 40,000 increase which, according to the *News-Letter* on 29 August, Lemass had been citing to explain the high level of unemployment. Total emigration for the decade was given as 170,000.

The North too had severe economic problems in the 1930s, but it was not, like de Valera, trying to abolish free trade, and it did have substantial manufacturing industries. These two factors enabled Pollock to quote, in the Northern Commons in March 1937, some conclusive-sounding figures. The total trade estimates for 1935, he said, were £92 million for Northern Ireland, and £57 million for the Free State: 'In other words, the trade and wealth of Ulster was almost twice as great as that of the Free State.'[12] Some years earlier Lemass had, as the *News-Letter* put it on 3 November 1934, taken the Blythe line that the Free State should make economic, social and political conditions within its area so attractive that the North would want to come in. At that time the *News-Letter* commented that Ulster nationalists must despair when they looked at the South.

Ulster Unionists looking South, on the other hand, found considerable consolation. As the *Whig* reported on 5 August 1932, Ulster had plenty of burdens of its own – heavy taxes, a quite too-expensive Government, a huge workless army and a serious setback to her two chief industries, 'but undoubtedly never since 1921 has she looked across the Border with more gratitude for the opportunity then given her of "contracting out" of the Free State than she does at the present moment'.

Frequent accounts in the Northern papers of the economic and social plight of the South in the inter-war years, particularly in the 1930s, were useful boosts to Unionist morale, for conditions in Northern Ireland were undoubtedly also extremely difficult. Unemployment in the entire period was rarely below 20 per cent. In 1932 a total of 76,000 was registered as out of work in the North, or more than 27 per cent. For most of that decade the level of unemployment was above 25 per cent. Health and welfare services and benefits were very bad, as was the standard of housing, all well below the general level in the United Kingdom. It was the inadequacy of the welfare services that led to the unusual combination of the Protestant and Catholic workers of Belfast in street protests in 1932.

In such circumstances it was very convenient for the Unionist leadership to be able to draw attention to the still worse state of affairs in the South. In addition to providing some modest encouragement to the general morale of the hard-pressed Northerner, such comparisons helped keep the internal political debate in Northern Ireland focused on the Unionist–Nationalist confrontation. If partition and the creation of Northern Ireland had not resulted in general prosperity inside the North then the plight of the South could be cited as proof positive that life in a united nationalist Ireland would be even worse. The condition of the South could be pointed to as an indication of the correctness of a basic tenet of Unionism, which was that the economic prosperity of the island of Ireland was dependent on the closest possible ties with Britain. Moreover, particularly after 1932 and the opening of de Valera's 'economic war' with Britain, the damage to the South's economy resulting from the actions of its own Government could be adduced as evidence of the peculiar obscurantism of Irish nationalism.

As in the case of the restoration of the Irish language, this willingness to damage the immediate and real interests of the country in pursuit of a distant nationalist goal, or perhaps, as Unionists believed, in furtherance of a spiteful vendetta against Britain, heightened the Northern perception of Irish nationalism as something verging on the ludicrous. Northerners also pointed to what they deemed internal contradictions in Dublin's economic policies, in so far as they were 'partitionist'. In 1923 Craig had made much of the fact that it was the Cosgrave administration that created the physical border in Ireland by instituting its own tariffs and setting up the customs machinery along the border. It was, said Craig, a great error of judgement, for without it there was no such thing as partition.[13]

A decade later Andrews returned to this theme of the South as partitionist when he told a meeting in Derry in 1934 that it surprised him sometimes that those in the Free State most opposed to the geographical boundary should be the very people 'who by means of normal and abnormal tariffs are giving effect not only to a constitutional but also an industrial and commercial boundary of very great importance'.[14]

Both Andrews and Craig were scoring debating points, but there was a more serious underlying Unionist concern that Dublin was using economic and, particularly, trade policy in a deliberate attempt to hurt Northern Ireland. This was one accusation made in 1923, but between 1924 and 1931 North–South trade was little affected by the border.[15] Its total value remained remarkably constant over the period, despite dwindling prices for most goods. But loss of market for specific products would have tended to confirm the argument that Dublin's policy was anti-North.

After 1932 the picture was rapidly altered. By 1936 exports from North to South had dropped to one-third of the 1931 level.[16] De Valera's whole confrontation policy with Britain from 1932 on, centred on the withholding of the land annuities and the tariff war, was perceived in the North as a strategy to destroy the Treaty settlement and reopen the question of Irish unity. Within that general strategy, the imposition of new tariffs and restrictions on Northern goods entering the South was seen as an attempt to bring pressure directly on the North through damaging its economy.

In 1932 Spender noted in his 'Financial Diary' that Northern Ireland was the 'butt of the tariff war with the Free State'.[17] A memorandum said there were strong arguments to justify an annual grant from the Imperial Government to Northern Ireland, among them the fact that conditions in the Free State, for which the Imperial Government must assume a large measure of responsibility, had hit Northern Ireland very materially.[18] In discussions with the Treasury in London in mid-1935, Pollock said the British Government's row with de Valera had seriously affected business and the receipt of income tax in Northern Ireland. Britain's trade with the Free State had been cut by 32 per cent but Ulster's by 61 per cent.

With negotiations approaching to end the tariff war, Northern Ireland was asked by London, in late 1937, to indicate its attitude. A memorandum from Belfast claimed that Northern Ireland found itself virtually excluded from the Free State market. The value of exports and re-exports across the border from North to South had dropped from £5.4 million in 1929 to £1.6 million in 1936, 'largely due to the prohibitive import duties and more recently to import restrictions imposed by the Government of the Irish Free State'.[19] Belfast's complaints went back to the original duties imposed by the Cosgrave Government in 1923. The memorandum claimed that the Custom Entry Duty, of 6d. on every consignment entering the Free State, had had 'the most damaging effects upon the trade of Northern Ireland wholesale houses, whose business was spread over a large number of retail firms'.[20] An appendix to the document gives statistics for goods imported into the Free State from Northern Ireland from 1924–36. The share of total imports which came from the North dropped from 11.4 per cent to 1.4 per cent or from £7.8 million to £0.5 million.

London did not accept the Belfast case in full. The Home Office took the view that although the border had been harmful to Belfast, there was no evidence that could be sustained 'that Irish Free State policy has been deliberately discriminatory against

Northern Ireland'.[21] But there was sympathy and support in London for Belfast's insistence that Britain should not relax her tariff duties against the Free State without reciprocation from Dublin. In the face of de Valera's determination to continue to protect his economy, and his infant industries, London pushed the idea of special concessions that would allow Northern Ireland goods free entry into the South. But this was firmly rejected by de Valera, at least partly on the grounds that he would not agree to anything that might stabilise partition, and give Northern Ireland all-Ireland free trade.[22]

In the event, the last-minute intervention by Craigavon in the dealings with London, up to then in the hands of Andrews and Brooke, meant a dropping of Belfast's demands and acceptance of an agreement that gave Northern Ireland little additional advantage in its trade across the border. Six months later, in November 1938, Spender was writing that the benefits promised to British trade under the agreement were quite illusory:

> The facts are that British imports into the Free State have gone down by ten per cent whilst the exports into Great Britain from the Free State have gone up by twelve per cent, and in the case of Northern Ireland, by no less than twenty-four per cent since the Agreement was made.[23]

At the time of the agreement, Unionist opinion was more concerned with relief that partition did not, after all, get a mention, and at what the *Whig* on 26 April 1938 termed the 'reckless liberality' of Britain in returning the Treaty ports than it was in the financial details. But the *Whig* did add that it regarded London as having been scarcely less generous on the financial agreement than it had been over the ports. This conformed to a pattern the Unionists had noted since the Treaty in 1921, of a willingness on the part of London to concede extremely generous financial terms to Dublin. It did nothing to dispel Unionist fears that a similar generosity, also at their expense, might be forthcoming at some future date on political and constitutional questions.

> A revolutionary and well-armed force which holds that its objective
> can be achieved only by resort to arms.

That was how the *Belfast News-Letter*, on 14 March 1934,
described the Irish Republican Army, in more restrained mood
than usual in Northern references to the IRA. Its image as a
sinister and ruthless terrorist organisation was cemented in
Unionist perceptions in the first years of Northern Ireland's
existence, particularly during the Belfast and border areas
violence of the first half of 1922. Its continued existence in
ensuing decades, evidenced by spasmodic periods of violent
activity, kept vividly alive the Unionist view of Irish nationalism
as having, at best, an ambivalence towards the use of murder and
terror in pursuit of its political goals.

Collins's undertaking in the 30 March 1922 Pact with Craig
that IRA activity in the North would cease was based on an
assumption, by both sides, that Collins had authority over such
activity. The rapidity with which IRA activity in the North
decreased as civil war spread in the South confirmed the Unionist
view that the IRA was essentially an external threat. It was to the
South that Unionists thereafter looked for evidence of its survival
or revival.

The Civil War, and the Free State Government's handling of it,
established a distinction in the Unionist mind between the administration of the new state and the IRA – a distinction which, if
anything, heightened the image of the IRA as an organisation of
extremists, of desperate and ruthless terrorists. But the distinction
was not complete, for even though the official policy of the Free
State was that force could not solve the Northern problem – a
policy enunciated by Collins before the Civil War, though not
necessarily espoused by him, and by Cosgrave and others after it –
moves by the Cosgrave Government to assert the full independence of Ireland raised again the spectre of a Republic, which
could, by definition, only be a thirty-two-county unit.

The events of 1924 in the Free State, which included mutiny in the Free State Army and an armed attack on British soldiers and their families at Cobh, near Cork, were indications that the IRA had not died with the Civil War, and were well publicised in the Northern press: as were the by-election results in that same year which showed an increase in support for Sinn Féin – the Republican side in the Civil War and the political arm of the IRA.

The possibility of renewed conflict involving the North was discussed by the Belfast Government in the same year. At a Cabinet meeting in August Dawson Bates raised several contingencies they might have to face as the result of the findings of the Boundary Commission. One was the Free State Government, or its successor, 'having recourse to arms to enforce their views'; another was renewed attacks by Irregulars; a third was the possibility of the North resisting, by force, findings unacceptable to it.[1]

Such eventualities did not arise, and the agreement between North and South confirming the existing boundary, signed in December 1925, removed them as possibilities. But by that time the IRA had begun to reorganise itself, ending its allegiance to the Sinn Féin 'Government' of de Valera. It had indicated its new energy by engineering the escape of nineteen IRA men from Mountjoy Prison in Dublin on 25 November 1925.

The optimism that was seen in Northern Ireland in 1926 was shattered by the re-emergence of the IRA in November of that year. First came disruption of the Armistice Day ceremonies in Dublin and then, on 14 November, a series of attacks on twelve *garda* barracks around the country, resulting in the deaths of two *gardaí*. These raids were reported in the North as armed rebellion, as a 'Republican Uprising'.[2] The Cosgrave Government's prompt proclamation of a state of emergency heightened the drama. Readers of the Northern newspapers were left in no doubt that the IRA was back in business.

Eight months later, in July 1927, the news of the assassination of Kevin O'Higgins in Dublin reawakened all the Unionist horror of the Sinn Féin gunman. Once again the stern Government response in the taking of special powers served as much to emphasise the seriousness of the threat as to reassure Unionists that subversion would not be tolerated. That same month a raid on Tallaght military camp near Dublin captured the headlines in the Northern papers.[3] In political terms a still potent IRA was useful to the Craigavon Government, ever anxious to emphasise the need for unity, but the alarm in 1927 was not entirely unfounded. Bowyer Bell says of the situation in 1927:

> In the four years since the dump-arms order, the IRA had done much: reorganised, maintained the structure and kept up the line to Clan na Gael in America. . . The scattered remains of the defeated army had been integrated into a large, covert, revolutionary underground force still dedicated to a second round.[4]

There was little action from it for the next four years, but Northern awareness of the IRA as a potential threat did not diminish. It was, if anything, increased by Fianna Fáil's Republican rhetoric, and the conviction that the next election would bring de Valera to power.

On 29 October 1928 the *Northern Whig* noted that de Valera was devoting a lot of attention to Northern Ireland, and threatening to do terrible things to it if it refused to go into 'his little tin-pot Republic'. It warned the Government that Ulster had been caught by surprise when murder and arson extended North in 1921, and a second blunder of that kind should not be made. It was known that 'desperate efforts are being made to revive the Republican movement in the North'.

When the next violent action in the South did come in August 1931, it was not immediately presented by the Northern papers as the work of the IRA. On 13 August the *Whig* referred first of all to 'southern rowdyism', and 'organised ruffianism', which it said, 'was seething in Southern Ireland as the result, chiefly of Republican activities'. The object of the immediate trouble, according to the *Whig*, was to prevent Relief of Derry Orange celebrations being held in Monaghan and Cavan in mid-August:

> The episode shows very significantly the temper and spirit of the Southern Republicans, and their eagerness to provoke a clash with the North. . . Further South brutal political murders have been committed and a state of organised terrorism prevails.

The reporting was scarcely muted: 'Amazing Scenes in Cavan', 'Sensation Follows Sensation', followed by an account of several young Republicans attacking an Orange hall.

An incident in Armagh, when the IRA seized six local men as

punishment for using the name IRA, prompted the *Whig* on 11 September, to comment that this was symptomatic of a real menace to public order and established authority, and showed that, in spite of all precautions, the IRA was still at work in Ulster. It was certainly still at work in the Free State, as the measures taken against it that October showed. Once again there was extensive Northern reporting, both of the IRA activity itself, and of the firm hand of the Cosgrave Government in dealing with it.

But the open support given by the IRA to de Valera and Fianna Fáil in the 1932 election, de Valera's immediate abolition of the military courts and freeing of the IRA prisoners, and the major role played by the IRA in the 1933 election, all reawakened the Northern Unionist belief that there was a real threat of violent attack on the Northern settlement from the Free State. In March 1932 graphic reports of IRA platoons openly parading in the streets of Dublin, enlisting volunteers, of 30,000 people welcoming the released IRA prisoners, must have spread alarm in the North. They prompted the *Whig* to comment on 15 March: 'It is not Mr de Valera who is in control of the Free State; it is the Irish Republican Army.' By his actions, said the *Whig*, de Valera had given the IRA a new prestige and impetus, and the South was now confronted with a perpetual menace to its peace. These were sinister influences de Valera had set loose – 'the evil spirits of rebellion sent forth on a nefarious errand, certain to create intense bitterness on both sides of the Border'. As the *Whig* put it two days later, the IRA was not brought into being to settle a constitutional question like the oath, which de Valera had promised to abolish, thereby enabling the militant Republicans to enter Dáil politics, but was 'the instrument by which the Republican extremists hoped to set up an all-Ireland state, separated from Great Britain and dominated from Dublin'.

On 17 January 1933 the *Whig* gave a full-page headline to a report that the IRA had provided a guard for de Valera at the opening of the Fianna Fáil election campaign in Roscrea, Co. Tipperary. Several thousand IRA men, the paper said, had acted as his escort.

In fact, as far as Northern Irish territory was concerned, there had been little or no significant IRA violence for almost a decade. Then, in October 1933, an RUC constable was shot dead in Belfast, and in the same month, a Unionist MP, Major J.H. McCormick, was shot and wounded in the city. More than thirty leading IRA men were arrested in a round-up by the RUC. By that time Northern Ireland had been in existence for more than twelve years, the settlement with the South in the form of the Treaty and the Free State for almost as long. Yet the political turmoil in the South, the revival of the IRA and its reappearance in the North kept alive the Unionist fear that the settlement was under threat.

On 14 March 1934, the *Belfast News-Letter* summarised the continued threats to Ulster's security: the settlement of twelve years ago was repudiated by all nationalists, de Valera was arguing that a lasting settlement had to be on the lines of a united Ireland, and the other Southern parties put unity in the forefront of their aims. Ulster's nationalists were wrangling over whether unity should be achieved by physical force or other means. Some suggested unity by 'peaceful penetration' or through the Labour movement. A section of the English press talked of federation.

> There can be little doubt that a considerable body of Nationalist opinion would not object to the use of force in order to compel the Ulster people's submission to the rule of a Dublin Parliament.
>
> A revolutionary and well-armed force, which is pledged to the establishment of an all-Ireland Republic, holds that its objective can be achieved only by resort to arms... The danger of such attacks is a real one, for there is abundant evidence of the ramifications of this organisation in the Six County area, of its aims and objectives, and of its plan of campaign. It is restrained only by the realisation that the Ulster authorities would deal ruthlessly with any revolutionary outbreak within this area. If, however, Unionists were to permit divisions within their ranks, if by any action of theirs, the authority of the executive should be weakened, then Ulster would be struck as venomously as when the Administration was new and still untried.

It was clearly in the interests of the Unionist establishment to stress the danger from the IRA, but in 1934 that organisation was much more than a figment of Unionist imagination. Equally useful to Craigavon's Government was the Fianna Fáil rhetoric on the North. In March 1934 Seán T. O'Kelly, Vice-President of the Free State executive, declared in a speech:

> We will use every effort to establish a Republic for the Thirty Two counties of Ireland. That is our aim and if the gun is necessary, the

people have the Government to direct the army, and they have the volunteer force behind them.[5]

In Southern terms such speeches may well have been designed to bring Republican militants to accept Fianna Fáil leadership and, therefore, the institutions of the state. But in the North they were taken as straightforward support for armed action against Northern Ireland. Commenting on the O'Kelly speech, the *News-Letter* on 30 March noted that it had not been repudiated by the Government, and might therefore be assumed to represent secret official policy, revealed in a moment of indiscretion.

Less than two weeks later what was presumed to be an IRA raid on the Braidwater Mill in Ballymena, Co. Antrim, resulted in the theft of sixteen B-Special rifles.[6]

By 1934 the sectarian temper in the North had risen considerably, inflamed partly at least by the Ulster Protestant League, which had been formed in 1931 mainly to protect Protestant employment. There were disturbances in Belfast in 1934, involving attacks on Catholic houses, and again in 1935, culminating in serious rioting at the Twelfth of July. Over that summer more than a dozen people died in disturbances in Belfast – the worst period of violence since the summer of 1922. The IRA had been in action, and of the dead, eight were Protestants, assumed to be the victims of IRA gunmen. In July when the violence was at its height, *gardaí* raided an IRA training camp in Co. Louth, near the border, and arrested twelve men, all from Northern Ireland. Up to 100 were in the camp when it was raided.

As in 1922, the events of that summer in Belfast were presented in the South, and often in Britain, as Orange assaults on Catholics, or even as a pogrom.[7] In the Unionist press the reporting of daily, or nightly, violence was of a series of disturbances or outrages. Often the reader would have required a knowledge of the confessional geography of Belfast to identify which side was aggressor and which side victim. But again as in 1922 there was intense Unionist resentment over the blaming of 'Ulster', or the Northern Government, for the deaths and violence. The basic cause of sectarian rioting, regretted and deplored by Unionist spokesmen and press was, in their eyes, nationalist or IRA provocation.[8] The year 1935 ended with the IRA in rather spectacular action again – raiding Campbell College in Belfast in search of arms, but being surprised by the RUC.

The following year began with another much noted speech by Seán T. O'Kelly, in which he said, according to the *News-Letter* on 8 January, that ministers in the Fianna Fáil Government did not deny Ireland the right to use force, if necessary, in attaining complete independence. The murder by the IRA in March 1936 of Vice-Admiral Henry Boyle Somerville, aged seventy-two, at Castletownshend, Co. Cork, awakened obvious echoes of 1921. A month later the RUC captured thirteen leading IRA men in a raid in Belfast.

By 1936 the shadow of war among the major powers was already over Europe. A statement by the IRA leadership, read at Easter marches in April 1936, was noted by the *News-Letter* on 13 April. The statement referred to the possibility of war and said Irish patriots should be ready 'to take advantage of [Britain's] difficulties and weaknesses to assert the independence and unity of their country'. By mid-1936 the IRA had become a sufficient challenge to de Valera's regime in the South for him to move against it, proscribing it in June, and on 21 June mounting a massive show of *garda* and army strength to prevent it marching to Bodenstown, Co. Kildare. But he had tolerated its open existence for four years. As the *News-Letter* commented on 11 July 1936, it had taken him 'a long time to discover that the existence of armed bands of revolutionaries menaced not merely the public peace, but the very foundations of the state'.

The clamp-down by Dublin on the IRA, plus the distraction of their involvement in the Spanish Civil War, meant a sharp decline in the IRA as a force, or threat, in Ireland, North or South, from 1936 on. But it did not disappear. There was trouble at a 1937 Easter parade at Milltown Cemetry in Belfast. In July there was bombing and shooting in Belfast following the Loyalist demolition of a Fenian monument. Later that month, during a visit to Belfast by the new King George VI and Queen Elizabeth, there was a series of IRA attacks on customs huts around the border, an attempt to mine a train carrying B Specials from Derry to Belfast, and some explosions in Belfast.[9]

In August, the Portrush home of the Minister of Home Affairs, Dawson Bates, was raided by the IRA, apparently in search of documents. The *Whig* commented on 5 August:

Even if the IRA was inactive, there was usually a minister or Unionist politician to remind the Northern public of its existence. In February 1938 Sir Wilson Hungerford, secretary of the Ulster Unionist Council and a Junior Whip at the time, declared: 'We know there is a criminal conspiracy to overthrow the Government of Northern Ireland', and he claimed correspondence seized by the RUC showed there was still an IRA plot afoot.[10] A month later, almost on cue, a bomb exploded at an army recruiting office in Belfast, followed by another thrown at a police barracks, and on 28 March a landmine exploded near the technical college, sufficiently large to merit a full-page headline in the *Whig* on 29 March. At the end of May an explosion at a house in Leeson Street in the lower Falls area revealed a big IRA arms dump, 'enough to blow up half the city', according to the *Whig* on 30 May, and enough certainly to justify another full-page headline.

In December the Government banned planned anti-partition meetings, Bates asserting that during 1938 thirty-five 'outrages' had been committed in Northern Ireland, 'for the purpose of intimidating Loyalists'.[11] Just before Christmas thirty-four IRA men were arrested in Belfast. The IRA, according to the *Whig* on 23 December, was intensifying its campaign of violence and terror in Ulster.

The bombing campaign in Britain, launched in January 1939, ensured headlines for the IRA. Explosions occurred at various centres throughout Britain for the first eight months of 1939, culminating in the Coventry bicycle bomb of 25 August which killed five people and injured sixty. With the concentration on Britain, there was little IRA violence in Belfast in 1939. But on 3 September the IRA shot and seriously wounded a soldier in the city. That same day Britain and Germany went to war. Twenty-three years earlier, when armed Irish Republicans had fired on British troops at the height of the First World War, the event had shocked the Empire. The firing on 3 September 1939 was of little note. IRA action against Britain was expected, particularly in time of war. But it still confirmed to Ulster Unionists, and to a new generation of them, that the IRA and the Irish nationalism it claimed to represent, was so virulently anti-British that it would side with Nazi Germany against Britain.

It is arguable that after 1924 the IRA was a negligible force in Irish life, apart from its revival from 1931 to 1936. But it never went away, and it proved an ever-useful bogeyman for Craigavon and the Unionist leadership seeking to preserve the solidarity of the Northern Protestant population. But it was more than just a bogeyman, for it repeatedly proved that it existed – by allegedly assassinating Kevin O'Higgins in 1927, by asserting itself in considerable strength from 1931 onwards, by making its contribution to the killing in Belfast in the summer of 1935, and by its sustained bombing campaign in Britain in 1939.

The IRA may not have killed O'Higgins. And at various times in the period it was not a monolithic organisation controlled from one centre, but disparate scattered fragments. But to most Northern Unionists, and to their newspapers, the three initials meant any form of violence and terror in the name of Irish nationalism. The IRA itself manically clung to its claim of continuity as the embodiment of Irish Republicanism. The one group of people on the island least likely to dispute that claim were the Ulster Unionists.

A SOURCE OF WEAKNESS

In 1912 Bonar Law had predicted that Home Rule would mean a second government at the heart of the Empire that could be a source of fatal weakness to Britain in time of war.[1] In 1921 Britain's security was a key element in the Treaty negotiations. Lloyd George laid down three main principles on the British side – allegiance, the Empire and defence.[2] In the Treaty itself, Article 7 gave Britain not just the Treaty ports as military bases in times of peace but any harbour or other facilities it might require in time of war or strained relations with a foreign power.

These specific arrangements, plus the fact that the whole Treaty was based on continued Irish allegiance to the Crown, and on a relationship with Britain similar to that of Canada, were assumed to ensure that a self-governing Ireland, within the Empire, would pose no problems of defence or foreign policy for Britain. In the post-Treaty negotiations on the Free State Constitution, the draft presented by Collins and Griffith to London included an article on external relations, giving the Free State the right to make its own treaties with foreign powers. This was rejected by Britain as incompatible with the Treaty, and was dropped by the Irish.[3] What did remain in, however, was Article 49, which said that except in the case of invasion, the Free State was not committed to active participation in war without the consent of its parliament. When the draft constitution was published in June 1922, this Article was seized upon by Northern commentators. On 16 June the *Northern Whig* remarked:

> If there were no other points of difference between Ulster and the Free State, this deliberate preparation for neutrality in the next great war would constitute one sufficiently grave to rule out permanently all idea of union with the South.

In the inter-war years statements and actions of Free State politicians in the area of external relations were among those most reported and commented on in the North, frequently in the context of the South's likely behaviour in a major European conflict. The whole question of the Free State's constitutional evolution, above all its relationship with the British Crown and with the Empire or Commonwealth, was an abiding preoccupation of Northern Unionists in the period. That relationship was part of the settlement embodied in the Treaty of 1921, the Free State Constitution, and the agreement amending the Treaty of 1925. A change in the relationship would mean altering the settlement.

Any attempt to alter that settlement was a matter of the utmost concern to Ulster Unionists, even if a particular alteration did not bear directly upon Northern Ireland; the settlement was sacrosanct, yet the Unionists were only too aware that no party in the Free State so regarded it. The de Valera faction and the more extreme Republicans repudiated it; Collins had described it as a first step. So Northern attention on the South was indeed focused on this area of constitutional change, to a considerably greater extent than on any other aspect of Southern life or politics.

The topic may be divided into three overlapping aspects: first there was Cosgrave's tampering with the settlement, beginning with the removal of the Imperial symbols, and culminating in his major assault on the right of appeal to the Privy Council; this was followed chronologically by de Valera's deliberate dismantling of the settlement and his attempt to renegotiate it in its entirety, including the North; and running through the whole inter-war period was the gradual assertion by Dublin of an independent foreign policy, leading to neutrality in the Second World War.

In November 1922 an article in *The Free State* – regarded in London at least as an official organ of the Government in Dublin – spelled out Cosgrave's attitude to the new Constitution:

> If we use this Constitution properly, if we regard it not as a perfected edifice but as a foundation on which to build, if we never fail in moments of conflict to take the strongest line of action to enforce our interpretation of the dispute, we cannot fail to develop our present status into one of complete independence. . . We shall be able to ignore England so completely that her Monarch and his trappings will drop out of our Constitution unheeded.[4]

The trappings began to disappear almost immediately. The new state did not use either the British national anthem or the British flag. It did not formally replace either of them, but the tricolour was in general use, and it was neither politic nor safe to fly the Union Jack. In 1926 Cosgrave told the Dáil that it was not considered necessary to introduce legislation to legalise the national flag, 'which has already been established. . . by usage'.[5] 'The Soldier's Song' was the popular anthem of the Sinn Féin revolution, but it was not formally adopted either, though by 1926 usage too had made it the national anthem.

Both flag and anthem were carry-overs from the Sinn Féin rebellion. The Volunteers in 1916 had sung the one, and hoisted the other over the GPO. In Northern eyes, as in the eyes of those who used them, they were the symbols both of rebellion and of an Irish Republic. On 17 December 1924 the *Whig* complained in an editorial:

> The Free State is supposed to occupy the same position in the Empire as Canada or Australia, but a colonial coming to the South of Ireland would have great difficulty in discovering the nexus between the Free State and the rest of the Empire. The flag which is flown and loved by the Colonies is anathema to the Free State. The King, who is the living symbol of the Empire, finds no place in the Free State Parliament, in the Free State courts, or in the Free State administration.

From the outset, the Free State administration showed a determination to dispense with every element it could of British ceremonial. The new Constitution came into force by Royal Proclamation on 6 December 1922, and the Governor General, T.M. Healy, formally addressed a joint meeting of Dáil and Senate on 12 December – following the British practice of the address from the throne. But ceremony was kept to a minimum; the Governor General had a guard of honour, and a bugle was sounded, but he arrived by motorcar, not carriage; and the Labour Party boycotted the session.

Following the general election, the Governor General again formally addressed both Houses in October 1923, outlining, as he had done in 1922, some legislative proposals of the Government. But this was the last time he did so. The practice was stopped, partly, according to Donal O'Sullivan, who was Clerk of the Senate, because of the Government's desire to keep the Crown's representative in the background, and partly to offset de Valera's attacks on the Treaty. But it was also, he added, to a large extent the result of the repugnance felt at that time in Government circles to what were regarded as British symbols.[6] The Governor General, on the King's behalf, still had to sign Bills indicating that they had received the Royal Assent, but there was no formal ceremony in Dáil or Senate declaring that the Royal Assent had been given.

Neither Senate Chairman nor Dáil Speaker wore wig and gown in the Westminster fashion, nor did clerks in the chamber. When the courts were reorganised under the Courts of Justice Act, 1924, there was an attempt there to abolish the traditional wigs and gowns, and enquiries were made as to what the Brehon law judges might have worn in ancient Celtic Ireland. Ridicule killed such ideas and the traditional court dress remained. But the Act had replaced the jurisdiction of the Lord Chancellor with that of the Chief Justice (not the Lord Chief Justice) of Ireland.[7]

From the Free State point of view all this was a conscious attempt to confirm the continuity of the state from the first Dáil, and the Sinn Féin courts of 1919 onwards, an extremely important exercise in the light of the situation in 1922–3. This continuity was underlined in the numbering of the parliaments of the Free State, which are dated not from the legal creation of the Free State in December 1922 but from the first Dáil's Declaration of Independence in January 1919. The first parliament of the Free State is officially the third Dáil. But to the Northern Unionists these moves were evidence of the bitterly anti-British nature of the new state in the South, and also of the determination of the leaders of that state to regard the Treaty and the Free State Constitution as anything but a final settlement.

The central element in the legal, or technical, as distinct from the symbolic, tampering with the settlement was the question of the right of appeal to the Privy Council. Collins and his team had resisted inclusion of this right in the Free State Constitution, but had had to concede. However the right was not absolute; Article 66 of the Free State Constitution declared decisions of the Supreme Court final and conclusive, not capable of being reviewed by any other court or tribunal whatever. It went on to say, however, that nothing in the Constitution should impair the right of any person to petition the King for leave to appeal, or the right of the King to grant such leave. But that could imply, as the Irish side in the Treaty negotiations had apparently been assured, that the right of appeal would be exercised only with the permission of the Irish Government or Supreme Court.[8] The Free State Government tried to have this position confirmed at the 1926 Imperial Conference, and indeed went further to argue that the Free State had the authority to terminate the right. This was not successful, though the report of the 1926 conference seemed to confirm that appeals would go forward only with the approval of the Supreme Court in Dublin. And there was an assurance from Lord Birkenhead, former Secretary for India and an influential figure in the 1926 conference, that the matter would be dealt with at the next Imperial Conference in 1930.[9]

It came up again before that, in the context of the League of Nations in 1929, when the Free State signed, without reservation, the Optional Clause, accepting the jurisdiction of the International Court of Justice. Britain and the other dominions signed too, but with a reservation excluding internal Commonwealth cases. From August 1929 the Northern papers were writing of a campaign in Dublin against the Privy Council. When the Optional Clause was signed in Geneva, the *Whig* was, on 20 September 1929, 'frankly disappointed' that the Free State had put itself in the wrong in Geneva, by putting the Hague Court in the place of the Privy Council.

Throughout 1930 the topic provoked a stream of editorials in the Belfast papers, culminating in October with the Imperial Conference in London, and Dublin's attempts to have the right of appeal finally buried. The fact that the conference did not specifically concede the Free State's case gave scope for a note of triumphalism in the Belfast reaction, though the Cosgrave Government subsequently promised unilateral legislation. This was eventually passed under the de Valera Government as the Constitution Amendment (no. 22) Act of 1933, to change Article 66 and remove the right of appeal. This legislation was subsequently deemed valid by the Privy Council itself.

The main concern of the Cosgrave governments was to build on the foundation of the Treaty and achieve full Irish independence, not to reshape the British Empire. But there was at least some sign on the Irish side of a concept of the Commonwealth that was not incompatible with such independence. Collins, in a 'Personal and Unofficial' memorandum sent to Chamberlain in late 1921, had discussed the crisis in relations between Britain and the Dominions, and argued that Ireland could accept, not the present legal status of the Dominions, but the real position they claimed and had, in fact, secured:

> It is essential that the present *de facto* position should be recognised *de jure*, and that all its implications as regards sovereignty, allegiance, constitutional independence of the governments, should be acknowledged. An association on the foregoing conditions would be a novelty in the world. But the world is looking for such a development, and it is necessary if the old world of internecine conflicts is to emerge into a new world of co-operative harmony.[10]

Collins's idea was remarkably close to what happened – if not by 1931 then certainly in the post-colonial era after the Second World War.

Despite some examples of strong British resistance, as over the right of appeal to the Privy Council, the Free State's constitutional evolution, up to 1931, was achieved by reasonably amicable negotiation, helped by a generally sympathetic and understanding approach from London. But Northern Unionist perception of the change in these years was entirely different. The removal of the symbols of royalty was seen as petty and vindictive, and in some instances deliberately insulting to the Governor General, the personal representative of the King. Both the removal of the symbols and the moves to end the right of appeal were particularly resented by the Southern minority, and that was a resentment that communicated itself quickly to the Northern Unionists. It was also a resentment, and a fear, that the Unionists were ready to use in efforts to alert British opinion to the dangers of the Irish situation. One Irish Unionist Alliance writer, summarising events up to 1930, had this to say:

> It will thus be seen that the aim of the Free State Government is to translate into actual terms the constitutional theory of the absolute co-equality of a Dominion with Great Britain, not for the purposes of consolidating the Empire, but to assert their own independence regardless of the interests of the Empire.[11]

A major factor that prevented the Unionists seeing the constitutional evolution in a positive light, indeed in any light other than a sinister and treacherous one, was the shadow of de Valera. When Church of Ireland leaders appealed for retention of the right of appeal in 1930, their fears were specifically expressed with reference to the possibility of a change of Government.[12] These fears had been present at least since Fianna Fáil re-entered the Dáil in 1927, placing the Cosgrave Government in a precarious position.

De Valera's campaign in the January 1932 election was on the particular issues of the oath of allegiance and the land annuities, rather than an outright rejection of the Treaty and the Free State Constitution. Immediately after his narrow victory he said he would consult the electorate again before denouncing the Treaty. But even before he had taken office, he had again raised the question of partition. If relations between Ireland and Britain were to be placed on a foundation of really lasting peace, he said in March 1932, this wrong would have to be righted.[13]

In office, later in March, he gave Britain formal notice that he intended abolishing the oath, and that land annuities would be withheld. This was reported by the *Whig* on 23 March, under the heading 'Mr de Valera Forces a Constitutional Crisis'. The gauntlet was being thrown down; it was a direct challenge. The document delivered to London could only be the work of a Government 'affecting to regard the Free State as already a Republican country, dissociated from the British Commonwealth of Nations'.

On 12 April, when it published the texts of notes exchanged between Dublin and London, the *Whig* used its largest headline to declare: 'Free State Repudiates Settlement of 1921'. An editorial that day encapsulated what was to be the Unionists' convinced attitude to the whole of de Valera's dealings with Britain right through the economic war, the 1938 negotiations, up to the Second World War itself and the crisis of July 1940 – that he was deliberately provoking a crisis in Anglo-Irish relations in order to bring the whole settlement of 1921–2 into question, and into negotiation, and to make the ending of partition the price he would exact for a new settlement and peace between Britain and Ireland.

A meeting between de Valera and the Dominions Secretary, J.H. Thomas, in early June 1932, raised the fears again. Once more the *Whig*'s biggest headlines on 8 June were used to report 'Mr de Valera's New Move to Annex Ulster' and his statement to Thomas that the removal of the oath and the unification of Ireland would do much to secure lasting peace between the two countries. The Free State, according to de Valera, was ready to make sacrifices for unity. Here was a new menace to Ulster, said the *Whig*.

Ten days later Unionist opinion was outraged when Thomas disclosed just what de Valera had proposed in their Dublin talks – a plan for recognition of a united Ireland as a Republic, with some sort of association with the British Commonwealth in some circumstances and for some reasons, and the recognition of the King as head of the Commonwealth. The gulf between North and South was wide before, commented the *Whig* on 18 June, now it had become a chasm that could never be bridged.

There is evidence that de Valera did not, in fact, actually believe in 1932 that he had any real hope of negotiating a deal on partition.[14] But not surprisingly, for most Unionists the rhetoric was the reality, and the newspaper reports, and the politicians' speeches for the rest of the 1930s continued to present de Valera as a constant threat to Northern Ireland's existence.

It was not just his rhetoric. In office he continued and intensified some policies of the Cosgrave governments. The Governor General continued to be downgraded, and was publicly and deliberately slighted by the new Fianna Fáil administration in mid-1932. Major headlines were given in the Belfast papers, for example the *Whig* on 26 April 1932, to the incident when two senior ministers, Seán T. O'Kelly and Frank Aiken, walked out of a dance in Dublin given by the French Minister on the arrival of the Governor General James MacNeill and his wife. There were similar headlines on 20 June when the Government failed to invite the Governor General to a state reception for the papal legate in Dublin for the Eucharistic Congress. It was headline news again in July when the major row between the Governor General and de Valera was made public. MacNeill defied the Government and published the correspondence between himself and de Valera, which included his allegation of 'calculated discourtesy' by members of the Government towards himself, and his demand for an apology.

The drama was heightened by de Valera's despatch of *gardaí* to the Dublin newspapers on the night of 10 July, with orders to them not to print the correspondence. They did not, but Northern and British papers did, and efforts were made to prevent their entry into the Free State. By Monday afternoon de Valera had to retreat, and he withdrew his ban on publication by the Dublin press. In a comment on 12 July the *Whig* said:

> At the very moment when the Loyalists of Northern Ireland are renewing their declaration of fealty to the Crown and their devotion to Protestant principles, the Free State Government is giving the world an almost incredible exhibition of peevish narrowness and discourtesy to the King's representative. The contrast between the two attitudes illustrates anew the impossibility of any sort of fusion between North and South. The accumulated acts of the de Valera Government within the space of a few months have done more to accentuate the division between Ulster and the Free State than any other circumstance or influence.

To de Valera's sins of breaking treaties, repudiating debts and encouraging revolution and disorder, the *Whig* could now add the charge of muzzling the press.

The unfortunate MacNeill was to make the Belfast headlines once more – on 4 October 1932 – when he was, in effect, dismissed by de Valera. The *Whig* said there had been no more discreditable episode in Free State politics since the advent of the de Valera Government than the series of insults heaped upon the Governor General, culminating in his dismissal. It was the motive behind the act that gave it its significance. If the Dublin Government made no move to replace the Governor General, would London acquiesce?

> If so, it will be the first step to scuttling out of Southern Ireland altogether. The constitutional issue involved is of the first importance. . . It may be that we are all now at the beginning of a great constitutional struggle, on the outcome of which the future status of the Free State, inside or outside the British Empire, will depend.

It did not happen in quite that way, but between 1932 and 1936 de Valera had indeed accomplished something of a revolution in the Free State's constitutional position – so much so that his new Constitution in 1937 changed little in this regard, and excited no great consternation, even in Belfast. A new Governor General, Donal Buckley, was appointed in late 1932, but he never lived in the Viceregal Lodge in Phoenix Park, and performed no public or ceremonial functions beyond the basic minimum, such as the signing of Bills.

The Abdication Crisis of 1936 gave de Valera the opportunity to rush through legislation effectively abolishing the office of Governor General and removing the British monarch from the Free State Constitution. From then on the Chairman of the Dáil summoned and dissolved parliaments, and signed Bills. The legislature consisted, not of 'the King and two Houses' as the 1922 Constitution had stated originally, but of 'one House', the Senate having pre-deceased the King in this regard.

De Valera had already terminated the right of appeal to the Privy Council, abolished the oath, withheld the land annuities, removed both the Senate and the university representation in the Dáil, and, as far as Irish law was concerned, terminated the British citizenship of all Irish men and women (through the Irish Nationality and Citizenship Act of 1935). This progressive demolition of the Treaty and the settlement based on it was chronicled in detail in the Unionist newspapers in Belfast. On the abolition of the oath, the *Whig* commented on 3 April 1935, that it was a definite and deliberate breach of the Treaty. What the Free State had done, was to repudiate the Treaty by a series of violations of its provisions. Much more was to follow, and every step was towards a Republic.

The link between the dismantling of the Treaty settlement and the drive towards an all-Ireland Republic was constantly stressed by the Unionists, but it was also a regular feature of de Valera's rhetoric. As the *Belfast News-Letter* reported on 4 April 1935, on the passing of the Citizenship Bill by the Dáil, de Valera declared: 'The fight will be completed only when every inch of the soil of this country is under the control of a government elected by the majority of the Irish people.' A few days later he told the Dáil there would never be fundamental peace amongst the Irish people until the Republic was reached. In June 1935, when the Privy Council itself eventually ruled that the Free State had the right, under the Statute of Westminster, to abolish the right of appeal and to abrogate the Treaty, the *News-Letter* on 7 June declared the decision of momentous importance: it was the burial of the Treaty.

So the new Constitution of 1937 was no surprise. Indeed if there was anything unexpected about it, it was that it stopped short of actually proclaiming a Republic, though its Republican character was in no doubt. On 1 May 1937 the *News-Letter* said it was a Republican constitution designed, as de Valera was frank enough to proclaim, to regularise a position already attained, in which every sign and symbol of British authority disappeared.

The link with the Commonwealth – de Valera called it association with, not membership of – survived only in the continued use of the King, at the discretion of the Dublin Government, to sign letters of credence of Irish representatives abroad. This preservation of a link, de Valera was later to explain, was considered desirable 'because there was another problem that remained to be solved and because it represented a distance to which I thought our people might go towards meeting the sentiment of the people of the Six Counties'.[15] But technical association with the Commonwealth combined with total rejection of the symbols and authority of the monarch, and even of British citizenship itself, cut no ice at all with 'the sentiment' of the Unionists. Moreover, the progressive assertion of an independent Irish foreign policy, now clearly presaging Irish neutrality in the next major European war, made the South's continued technical association with the Commonwealth meaningless to the Unionists, or still worse, hypocritical.

That the Free State always intended having its own foreign policy was made clear right at the beginning in December 1922, when the new Free State Government followed the lead given by the Dáil and the Provisional Government, and appointed a Foreign Minister. Even before that when the Provisional Government decided in August 1922 to name a new Foreign Minister to replace the dead Arthur Griffith, the Northern papers took strong exception to the move. On 30 August the *News-Letter* said that as the Free State would not be an independent nation, it would not have a foreign policy of its own, and therefore no need of a Foreign Minister. On 11 September the *Whig* noted that no Dominion in the British Empire indulged in the luxury of a Foreign Minister. In 1924 when Desmond FitzGerald announced that the Free State was to appoint a representative in Washington, DC, which no other Dominion had, the *Whig*, on 12 April, declared that this would mean the Empire speaking with two voices, not one. No doubt a representative would be sent, too, to Berlin.

In September 1926 the Free State again asserted its independence by seeking – unsuccessfully – an elected seat on the Council of the League of Nations. The *Belfast Telegraph*, on 25 September, could not contain its indignation – the thing was ridiculous, the Free State would have one vote, the same as the United Kingdom, if it was elected. It was all part of the policy of pin-prick where Imperial interests were concerned.

By 2 June 1928 the shadow of de Valera was prompting the *Whig* to ask if, under a Republican Government a few years hence, the Free State could be relied upon to accept a lead from Britain 'on any momentous international question'. There was only one possible answer, and a single jarring dissentient voice, in a crisis where Imperial unanimity and harmony were all-important, might well be the herald of disaster.

In September 1930 the Free State sought again, this time with success, a seat on the council of the league, producing from the *Whig*, on 24 September, a reminder of the fable of the bullfrog and the fox. It reported that the Irish representative, Seán Lester, had protested at the Free State being classed as part of the British group, and had declared that Ireland was an independent state with complete control over its foreign affairs. Could the Free State, the *Whig* asked, be a sovereign state with full control over foreign affairs and a loyal member of the British Empire? Ulster should ask itself if it had over the border, not a loyal colony, but a power which had the right to declare itself an enemy. However, by the mid-1930s it was apparently accepted, even in Belfast, that the Free State would attempt to follow a policy of neutrality in any European war.

Neutrality would be clearly difficult to maintain if Britain was using the Treaty ports, and exercising its rights under the Treaty to other facilities. By 1936 de Valera was asking for the ports back, and for the end of the undertaking. With war increasingly likely, the matter was far from academic. In July of that year Seán T. O'Kelly warned England that she could not count on Irish friendship in 'political and international difficulties', while she countenanced partition.[16]

The heightened nationalist rhetoric that surrounded the adoption of the new Constitution in 1937 indicated to the Northern Unionists that another major drive against partition was on the way. In October 1937, de Valera told the Fianna Fáil

214

Ard Fheis that they should move forward on the basis of the Constitution to secure the unity of the country. The time was ripe for launching a campaign to bring in Ulster. In an editorial on 14 October the *Whig* asked how Ulster was to be brought in – by propaganda, by force, or was it to be 'subjected to political coercion from Westminster at Dublin's instigation'? The writer assumed that one element in the campaign against Ulster would be for Dublin to seek to use Britain as an instrument of coercion; negotiations on the trade war were inevitable, and de Valera had already said he would make the unity of Ireland an indispensable condition of any agreement.

John Bowman, in his very detailed account of the 1938 negotiations, makes the point that de Valera was aware, from his contacts in 1937 with the Dominions Secretary, Malcolm MacDonald, that real progress on partition was not possible, and that the discussion of the matter in the talks with Neville Chamberlain in early 1938 consisted of the re-statement of known positions, rather than in any sense a political negotiation. He also suggests that when announcing that the talks with Chamberlain were on, de Valera said only, to some extent reluctantly, that partition would be on the agenda.[17] The presentation of the news in the Belfast papers was somewhat different: on 13 January 1938 the *Whig* carried the announcement of the coming talks between de Valera and Chamberlain under its largest full-page headline, 'De Valera's New Bid for All-Ireland Republic'. Partition, it quoted de Valera as saying, was definitely on the agenda.

When the talks opened in London on 17 January Ulster Unionists watched with apprehension. Not only was partition being discussed between London and Dublin, it was happening against the background of a grave European situation, the probability of war, and the knowledge that de Valera had in his hands the powerful, if not trump card, of the South's attitude to Britain in such a war. It was not, said the *Whig* on the same day, an occasion for panic, but the talks were fraught with momentous possibilities. De Valera, it said, intended pressing to the uttermost his demand for the yielding up of Ulster as an essential condition for a new pact with Britain.

Craigavon, having called a general election in the North immediately upon hearing the news of the London talks, found it very much in his interest to emphasise the danger to Ulster in the talks. *The Times,* in a leading article, had dismissed the danger that Northern Ireland would be forced into Éire as 'entirely imaginary', to which the *Whig,* on 17 January, replied that no one believed that the British Government was about to hand over Ulster:

> But there is a danger that is far from imaginary. It is that Mr de Valera may present the question of defence in such a light that British Ministers may be tempted to re-open the whole question of Irish unity in return for pledges of co-operation between Dublin and Westminster in the event of actual or apprehended war.

The *Whig*'s analysis of the dangers facing Ulster turned out to be well founded. The 1938 negotiations ended without any deal or pledge on partition but during them MacDonald several times advocated a British declaration on partition that would have been no less than a *nihil obstat* to a united Ireland, and possibly support in principle, subject to Ulster's agreement.[18] Two years later such a declaration was part of the package offered to de Valera by Churchill after the fall of France, a package that fits almost exactly the *Whig*'s description – a reopening of the whole question of Irish unity in return for pledges of co-operation between Dublin and Westminster on the war.

In October 1938 de Valera again drew attention to the danger posed to Britain by partition in the event of war. In his *Evening Standard* interview, quoted in the *Whig* on 18 October, he said the present situation was highly dangerous:

> We have definitely committed ourselves to the proposition that this island shall not be used as a base for enemy attacks on Great Britain. It is possible to visualise a critical situation arising in the future in which a united free Ireland would be willing to co-operate with Britain to resist a common attack. Let me say that the chances of such co-operation in the event of a European war are very, very slight while partition lasts. If such a war occurred while the British forces were in occupation of any part of Ireland, Irish sentiment would definitely be hostile to any co-operation.

Then in a passage that was almost a script for the dialogue of the summer of 1940 de Valera continued:

> Let England say to the Government of Northern Ireland: 'You say you are loyal to us. You wish to see England strong. Very well, here is an opportunity to settle that last remaining cause of quarrel between the two countries – a quarrel which will weaken England as long as it lasts!'

This was described by the *Whig*'s editorial writer on 18 October as an attempt by de Valera to frighten the British public into the belief that unless the Government at Westminster yielded to his demands, the South would accentuate Britain's difficulties in the event of a war. It was tantamount to a threat, or an ultimatum. In short, said the *Whig*, it was Hitler's technique.

At the outbreak of the war in September 1939, Éire's neutrality was accepted as inevitable. It was not until the following spring, when the war became more menacing, with the fall of Belgium and Holland, that Northern comment became really bitter. De Valera's strong statements at the League of Nations denouncing others for paying lip-service to the fundamental principles of the league were recalled, and contrasted with his own attitude in 1940, as one small nation after another was invaded. As the plague of war spread steadily across Europe, 'threatening all that is meant by civilisation, Éire's contribution to the cause is the lip-service which Mr de Valera properly denounced a few years ago, coupled with a determination to remain aloof', said the *Telegraph* on 14 May.

By June 1940 Éire's neutrality was of immediate and vital strategic importance, for after the fall of France an invasion of Ireland, possibly of Northern Ireland, by German forces was a distinct possibility. Measures to ensure the adequate defence of the island were a British imperative, and partition was clearly an obstacle to achieving such measures. As Bowman says, for the first time since its enactment twenty years before, partition was seriously questioned by London.[19]

In the British offer conveyed to de Valera on 29 June it was more than questioned. In return, not for Éire's entry into the war but for agreement to co-operate with British forces in its own defence, Éire was promised a British pledge of support, in principle, for Irish unity, which would take the form of a solemn undertaking that 'the Union was to become at an early date an accomplished fact from which there will be no turning back'.[20] A joint North–South body was to be set up to draw up the Constitution of the Union.

As the war situation deteriorated, Craigavon's Government had anticipated pressure from London on the question of some gesture towards Dublin. Spender had noted in his diary in May that things were so serious that there was no knowing what sacrifices it would be right for Northern Ireland to make.[21] On 5 June Craigavon had met Chamberlain in London and had, it seems, been told that an accommodation had to be found with de Valera, and Ireland would have to defend itself as a unit.[22]

The proposals that London was putting to Dublin during the second half of June were, of course, secret. From Craigavon's peremptory rejection of them at the end of the month it seems he, too, was unaware of their detailed contents. But it was obvious that something far-reaching was afoot. On 24 June the *News-Letter* published a letter from Dr James Little, Unionist MP at Westminster for Down, outlining a proposition he said had been put to him in the House of Commons, 'if it were not possible for the two Irelands to come together for the duration of the war and unite their forces against the common enemy'. His own reply was, he said, that while not abating his religious faith and political ideals, he was prepared to stand by the side of any man in defending the land of his birth and love against Nazi domination. In an editorial comment on the Little letter, the *News-Letter* said the kernel of the problem of the defence of Ireland as a whole was the Éire Government's policy of neutrality, and there seemed little likelihood that it would be abandoned.

Craigavon received a copy of the penultimate British proposal on 26 June, the same day on which it went to de Valera. This envisaged the South immediately joining the Allies, and the setting up of a North–South defence council in return for British acceptance of the principle of a united Ireland and the immediate creation of a North–South body to work out the practical details of such a union.[23] Craigavon's reply was an outraged telegram to Chamberlain: 'Am profoundly shocked and disgusted by your letter making suggestions so far-reaching behind my back and without any preconsultation. To such treachery to loyal Ulster I will never be a party.'[24] On 29 June he delivered a speech in Kirkistown, Co. Down, which was in fact a public reply. Unable, of course, to disclose details of what Chamberlain had been proposing, he referred to a recent speech in the Dáil which, he said, contained sinister evidence that something serious was afoot:

> I wish therefore to declare that I will be no party, directly or indirectly, to any change in the Constitution conferred upon Northern Ireland. Nevertheless in the interests of both North and South I am prepared to enter into the closest co-operation with Mr de Valera in matters of defence, provided he. . . takes his stand as we are doing, on the side of Britain and the Empire, clears out the German and Italian representatives from Eire and undertakes not to raise any issue of a constitutional nature.[25]

Craigavon went on to stress that his main concern was not to put his hand to any plan that would imperil the United Kingdom and the Empire. There had been vague suggestions that Ulster should agree to a united Ireland. The supreme consideration for all within 'our beleaguered islands' was the safety of the whole United Kingdom, and he was glad to think that Ulster's firm attitude in the past had literally saved the situation. An all-Ireland parliament would have meant all-Ireland neutrality.

The speech was something of a pre-emptive strike by Craigavon. He no doubt feared that London could put him under tremendous pressure by appealing publicly to Ulster to come to terms with de Valera in order to save the Empire. By portraying whatever was afoot as blackmail of London by de Valera, he was strengthening his ground, though he must have known that the initiative was coming from London, not Dublin. Just what would have happened had de Valera responded to Churchill's offer cannot be known. By speaking out publicly, Craigavon may have helped ensure de Valera's rejection of the offer, and that may have been part of his intention, though the evidence seems to be that de Valera would have turned it down anyway, not least because he and almost everyone else felt sure Britain was losing the war.

Within a week the episode was largely closed by de Valera's flat rejection of the British initiative. Craigavon presumably heard of this from Churchill when the two met in London on 7 July. On 11 July Lady Craigavon recorded in her diary her husband's epigrammatic comment: 'It is finished, it will not be raised by me again. . . We are closing the gates again as our ancestors did at Derry.'[26] But, as Craigavon must have realised, the gates had been closed not by himself, or by the Imperial Government, but by de Valera. The long-predicted neutrality of the South had indeed turned out to be a menace to the security of the United Kingdom and the Commonwealth, but de Valera's dedication to it had, in turn, proved to be of enormous value to Unionist Ulster. After de Valera's rejection of the overtures of 1940, Ulster's loyalty became of crucial importance to the British war effort.

In early June 1940 the Unionist position was more vulnerable than at any time since 1921. Had de Valera taken up the British offer and agreed to some measures of joint defence of the two islands, then the Northerners would have come under irresistible pressure. But the danger to Unionist Ulster was only as real as the chances of de Valera abandoning neutrality and those, according to the Unionist perception of both de Valera and of Irish nationalism as it had evolved, could only have been slight.

In effect the war years, and Irish neutrality, were confirmation of the complete gap that had opened in Ireland between North and South. They were also, in Unionist eyes at least, proof of that aspect of Irish nationalism that Unionists had perceived first during the First World War, that it was somehow inherently anti-British, that the new Irish identity consisted in a large part in rejection of a British identity and therefore in rejection of Northern Unionists. On 28 May 1941 the *Whig* noted, what it called,

... Eire's childishly wishful blindness to her own interests... imperilling her neighbours, and the whole cause of Christian democracy, freedom and civilisation itself. Even de Valera's King Charles' head – so-called Partition – is more firmly riveted on by his obduracy.

14
AN AGGREGATION OF PEOPLE

> Before we can talk of Ireland a nation we must make her one. A nation, politically speaking, is an aggregation of people whose interests are identical; and the interests of Ulster with the rest of Ireland rather than being identical are antagonistic.[1]

Thus commented the writer James Stephens in 1916 before Sinn Féin had completed its annexation of Irish nationalism. But he was perceptive enough to know that John Redmond had been rejected by the people and that a new phase, if not a new era, had been reached in Anglo-Irish relations. In that same book, *The Insurrection*, Stephens upbraided the Irish Parliamentary Party for its neglect of the Ulster question and its failure to do anything whatsoever to allay Northern fears and distrust. Hence his axiom that the Irish nation still had to be created. His own view was that Ulster's fears were economic:

> The safeguards which Ulster will demand, should events absolutely force her to it, may sound political or religious, they will be found essentially economic, and the root of them all will be a watertight friendship with England, and anything that smells, however distantly, of hatred for England, will be a true menace to Ulster. We must swallow England if Ulster is to swallow us, and until that fact becomes apparent to Ireland, the Ulster problem cannot be even confronted, let alone solved.[2]

Barely two years after Stephens wrote that, more than one million Unionists living in Ireland found themselves confronted with a new Ireland, or at least a new assertion of Irishness, that far from swallowing England, rejected it, and identified the connection with it as the never failing source of all ills. In addition, the nation whose independence the Sinn Féin movement set out to achieve from 1919 onwards was based on an idea of Irishness, on an assertion of national distinctiveness, rather than on the reality of the Ireland of the day. This new Irish nationalism was a much more potent mixture than that of the late nineteenth and early twentieth centuries, reaction against which had given birth to Irish Unionism. One vital difference was that, in Stephens's phrase, it

221

smelled of hatred for England, and far from distantly.

In 1914 the concept of the United Kingdom of Great Britain and Ireland was still generally accepted even in Ireland, a concept that included several nations and nationalisms, but one over-riding British identity. That identity, itself a sort of nationalism, was strengthened by the war, for it was the conflict with Germany that ended Ulster's rebellion and bound both Northern and Southern volunteers into the common cause. It was against this background of a heightened sense of common identity that the Easter Rising exploded in 1916. It constituted the most strident statement that no such common identity existed. Ulster Unionism, meanwhile, had dramatically reasserted its loyalty or, as the Unionists would have argued, had confirmed the true nature of that loyalty. By 1915 Carson was Britain's Attorney General and by 1917 he was in the War Cabinet. By 1916, James Craig, his lieutenant in rebellion in 1912, was a junior minister at Westminster.

The Rising was also a reassertion of the armed-force tradition in Irish nationalism, a strand that had been a minor thread since the United Irishmen rebellion of 1798. The Sinn Féin movement, as it developed from 1917 onwards, took over much more than the armed-force tradition, but it looked back to the Easter Rising for its inspiration, and violence was initially its most spectacular manifestation. The violence from 1919 onwards was of a new order. It was one of the earliest examples of the use of terrorism and guerrilla tactics in armed pursuit of a political end. Till then, terror to achieve a political goal had been almost entirely a Russian phenomenon. The Boers had used guerrilla methods against the British and possibly the Irish had learned lessons in South Africa but the combination of terror and guerrilla warfare, used by Sinn Féin in Ireland from January 1919 on, was unknown in western Europe.[3]

The horrors and squalor of the Great War had been cloaked by patriotism, honour and the military ethic. The very term 'great' lent a suggestion of nobility to what was happening, at least to corporate perception of it. By contrast, hit and run murder in a civilian setting – in a Dublin street or a country road – had no such cloak. The violence was directed towards the withdrawal of British power but it was exercised in Ireland; the immediate victims of it were those who supported British power, initially the Southern

Unionists, then the Northern Unionists and after June 1921, the Northern state. In the short space of about two years Irish nationalism had become identified, in Unionist eyes, with this new form of political terrorism.

It was the extent and the unprecedented nature of this violence that dominated the reporting in the North of the events in Ireland from 1919 to 1922. Two aspects of the violence had particular impact. The first was the extent to which the Southern Protestant minority were seen to be the victims of attack. The menace posed to Protestantism by Catholic power was part of the credo of British Protestantism but even closer to hand was the historical fear Irish, and particularly Ulster, Protestants had of violence at the hands of the Catholic Irish. The many references in 1920–22 back to the stories of massacres of Protestants in Ulster in 1641 are evidence of this.

Even if some, perhaps much, of the violence against Protestants in the South between 1919 and 1923 was incidental – that is, Protestants being attacked not because of their religion, but because of their identification with British rule – it is a factor that has been generally underestimated. It was almost certainly far more widespread than has been acknowledged in most accounts, and the reports of it reaching the Unionist community in the North added mightily to a fear that lay right at the heart of the Northern Protestant mentality.

The second aspect of the violence of 1919–22 of particular importance was its impact on the Protestant working class in urban areas of the North, especially in Belfast. The level of violence, notably in the first half of 1922, was unprecedented. Sniping, bomb-throwing and assassination added new dimensions to the sectarian strife with which Belfast was familiar enough. While much of that violence, probably more than half, was directed against Catholics, the Unionist perception was that Sinn Féin–IRA activity was the root cause of the state of the city; reprisals were to be deplored but would not have happened had not the IRA been active. Certainly not all IRA actions could be termed as in defence of the Catholic community – bombings of crowded tram-cars, incendiarism, the assassination of Twaddell, all confirmed the Unionist view that an evil conspiracy was at work.

It was in these working-class Protestant areas of Belfast that

Orangeism, strongly flavoured with anti-Catholic bigotry, was already rife. The addition in this period of urban terror carried out by the IRA, an organisation controlled and armed by the self-proclaimed Irish nationalist state, greatly inflamed this bigotry. Belfast's Catholics – though not all of them – professed allegiance to that state and in many cases enrolled in the IRA. The Orange mob had long identified its Catholic neighbour as a political opponent, a despised rival – after 1922 he was a mortal enemy.

Brief periods of intense personal experience can so cement attitudes and perceptions that these remain long after the particular events constituting the experience have passed. The events of 1919–22 in Ulster were extraordinarily dramatic – a new boundary, new political institutions, an emerging independent Irish state as a neighbour, and communal violence and terrorism of a type that no other city in Europe, outside the Soviet Union, had yet witnessed. The cause of this enormous upheaval was clearly identified as Irish nationalism, and that in turn profoundly influenced future Unionist attitudes towards both the new nationalist state and towards the Nationalist neighbour – the Northern Catholic.

But the whirlwind of 1919–22 abated even more rapidly than it had begun. The outbreak of Civil War in the South led to a swift end to violence in the North and a reduction in political pressure from London on the Craig Government. Even the much-feared Boundary Commission came to nothing. Internal Nationalist opposition to the new institutions dwindled as the campaign of non-cooperation collapsed and Nationalist politicians entered the new parliament. The Protestant community in the North was left a measure of peace in which to contemplate the evolution of the Irish nationalist state across the border.

But by then Sinn Féin nationalism had established itself in the Unionist perception as something alien, anti-British, and which certainly excluded the Ulster Protestant on grounds of identity, culture, religion and economic interest. Over the next two decades the generality of Northern Protestants looking South, usually through the window of the Belfast press, found little reason to change their perception, and quite a lot to confirm it. Admittedly, this scrutiny was less than comprehensive and far from scientific. Unionist editors and journalists were actively seeking the sort of coverage of Free State affairs that would appeal to their readers and confirm existing perceptions. But in this the Belfast papers were reflecting the widening gulf that had opened between North and South. Northern editors saw the Free State not as a prime area for news coverage but rather as one which produced stories only where events there touched on the perceived interests of the Northern Protestant reader.

What they reported was not untrue. The Irish state was increasingly asserting its independence and seeking to go beyond the Treaty of 1921, both as regards its own sovereignty, and as regards the partition settlement. The Irish state did place great emphasis on the Irish language, did make it compulsory in schools, did spend a great deal of money on its restoration, did go to extraordinary lengths to try to force the language on all and did ignore repeated appeals from the Protestant minority for a moderate approach on the language.

The Irish state progressively enshrined Catholic principles in its laws and Constitution; its leaders did not hesitate to proclaim their, and its, Catholicity; the state ignored the protestations of the Protestant minority over the Catholic attitude of the state to divorce and censorship, and over what the Protestants saw as the removal of their guarantees from the Free State Constitution. That minority did decline disastrously and while its members protested their loyalty to the Free State, it was clear that they were expected by the state to volunteer as subscribers to an 'Irishness' that took scant account of their cultural and political identity.

Nor were the Belfast papers wrong when they reported that the Southern state had severe economic difficulties, that there was poverty, unemployment and emigration, that taxes were generally higher there and benefits lower, and that it cost more to post a letter in the South than it did in the North. Donegal Presbyterians did petition *en masse* in 1934 for transfer back to the North because they believed they could not survive economically.

And politicians of all parties in the South did maintain their pursuit of Irish unity with the ultimate goal of an independent Republic and the severance of any link between Ulster and Britain. Much of this may have been rhetoric, but the rhetoric often indicated an ambivalence towards the use of force against the

North and the agents of violence, the IRA, never quite disappeared from the scene. Nor was the distinction between them and the legal authorities in the new state always clear, most noticeably was it confused when de Valera first came to power.

Unionism had its origins in the perceived threat posed by Irish nationalism to certain sectors of the people living in Ireland, particularly the Protestants of the north-east. This view of nationalism as a threat was spectacularly enhanced by 1916, 1919–22 and by events thereafter. Northern Unionist papers were, therefore, reflecting the real interests of the community they served when their coverage of the South, and of nationalism generally, concentrated almost entirely on those aspects which demonstrated the threat. Their coverage of violence inside the North was governed by the belief that the root cause of all violence, including reprisals and police excesses, was the Sinn Féin–IRA assault on the Unionist community. In their daily output the Unionist newspapers were both reflecting a perception that existed, and helping confirm and extend it.

On the other hand it was obviously difficult for a nationalist to understand that perception. By 1921 the Sinn Féin rebellion had become the Anglo-Irish War and was sanctified as such by Britain's negotiations with its leaders and the Treaty settlement. If the nationalist cause was thus a just one, how could it suddenly become totally unjustifiable, indeed criminal, in one corner of the island? From 1919 onwards, the Unionist could feel that his perception was a legally correct one, given that the United Kingdom of Great Britain and Ireland was the lawfully constituted unit, and that Northern Ireland, after June 1921, was the lawful creation of legitimate authority. The tragedy was, and perhaps remains, that the nationalist perception is not precise and legalistic, but historic and emotional, drawing its own legitimacy from what it asserts once was, or should be, rather than from present reality.

It is these conflicting perceptions, rather than biased reporting or corrupt journalism, that give the reader almost totally contrasting accounts of events in Ireland, according to the newspapers he reads. The balance of concentration in Unionist reporting of the period indicates that the threat of violence was less immediate than that posed by Dublin's constitutional machinations and by negotiations between London and Dublin. The constant fear of Unionists throughout the period was that of the reopening of the settlement.

The Irish problem has been neatly expressed in terms of a double minority, that is of the Catholic or nationalist minority in the North, and of the Unionist or Protestant minority in the whole island.[4] From a Unionist perspective the real problem was the triple minority, with the third minority being the Unionists within the United Kingdom of Great Britain and Northern Ireland. When the Northern Unionists accepted the Government of Ireland Bill early in 1920 they became the constitutionalists in Ireland – espousing and implementing the policy of the Imperial Government for the country, while Sinn Féin rejected it, and opposed it with arms. Yet the reward for their support was an almost immediate invitation from London to join in negotiations with those who had been fighting against Imperial policy, with the object of revising the settlement. The provision for a revision of the North's boundary in the Treaty was a real, and possibly disastrous, weakening of that settlement.

London's dealings with the Provisional Government in its post-Treaty difficulties brought more forceful reminders to the Unionists of their minority status within the United Kingdom. If Imperial interest decreed that every effort be made to preserve the Provisional Government and the Treaty, then Northern Ireland's interests came second to that Imperial one. In Unionist eyes London was frequently wrong in its assessment of where the Imperial interest lay, with the result that Unionists simply saw a readiness in London to accommodate Dublin at the expense of Belfast.

In the turmoil of 1921 the Unionists clung to the Government of Ireland Act and set about working the institutions created by it, only to find that the Act itself was shifting in the storm. This chronic sense of insecurity, particularly as regards London's intentions, was to be a key characteristic of Unionist behaviour for the next half-century. If de Valera realised in 1921 that any concession over the North could come only through negotiations with London, the Northern Unionists were not far behind him coming to the same conclusion. The Treaty, the pressing ahead with the Boundary Commission, British connivance in Cosgrave's

227

progressive removal of British symbols, similar British flexibility in the face of de Valera's much more radical assaults on the settlement – all fuelled Unionist fears of a sell-out by London of Ulster's interests. The most dramatic confirmation of Unionism's parlous position as a friendless minority within the United Kingdom came in the summer of 1940, when even Churchill was ready to offer the North to de Valera as the price of his limited co-operation in the war.

This awareness that Unionists were not, after all, masters of their own fate was a key factor in the evolution of internal politics within Northern Ireland. It ensured a continuing premium on maximum Unionist unity. Every election Craigavon fought, he fought on the border, on the preservation of the union with Britain and the fight against Irish unity. Of the five elections to Northern parliament held before the Second World War, four were directly related to events in Dublin, or involving Dublin. The first in 1921 was, inevitably, entirely on partition and the creation of Northern Ireland. That of 1925 was called early by Craig to coincide with the work of the Boundary Commission and the threat it posed to Northern Ireland. The poll of November 1933 was called against the background of widespread disorder in the South, with the IRA active, the Blueshirts organising, and de Valera's economic war in progress. IRA violence had reappeared again in Belfast, with Major McCormick MP being shot and wounded in the city a month before polling.

The election of February 1938 was Craigavon's response to de Valera's new Constitution with its assertion of sovereignty over Northern Ireland, and was held when Unionist indignation and alarm over the negotiations that had just opened in London between Britain and de Valera were at their height. A decade later Sir Basil Brooke called an election, in February 1949, in response to Éire's move to a Republic, and to the energetic anti-partition propaganda campaign of 1948.

Craigavon was criticised for exaggerating the threat to Ulster's constitutional position in order to silence opposition from within Unionism, which he undoubtedly did. As a tactic, the use of the green bogey was very successful. Over the years it saw off various strands of independent Unionism, most notably W.J. Stewart's Progressive Unionist Party in 1938. But Unionism tended to fragment towards the right, towards more extreme Orange positions rather than towards moderation and Craigavon's recourse to the nationalist threat meant he was stealing the extremist's Orange clothes as a means of containing him. As a result, the centre of gravity of Unionism moved steadily towards the right.

This was particularly noticeable in the 1930s, as anti-Catholicism became a much more explicit ingredient in the language of the Unionist leadership, and as Basil Brooke built his ladder to the top on the threat posed by the Catholic, or disloyal, minority. But the move to more sectarian positions in the 1930s was also certainly a response to what was happening in the South – the intensification of the overt Catholicism of society and state, and the aggressive nationalism of both de Valera's rhetoric and his dealings with Britain. The nature of the Southern state and the actions of its leaders provided ammunition for Craigavon and others that kept Unionism together, but it also provided a reality, and an actual threat, that dominated the thinking, not just of the Unionist leadership, but of the whole Protestant community in the North.

This perception of Irish nationalism as a constant threat to the Northern state helped promote the rigidifying of the political divide inside Northern Ireland along religious lines, perpetuating the concept of the Catholic minority as 'disloyal'. Far from making Ireland a nation, as Stephens had urged in 1916, the new Irish nationalist state had helped ensure that the interests of Ulster with the rest of Ireland not only remained antagonistic, but had become much more so.

The *Northern Whig* was never one to understate its opinions. Its comment, on 21 December 1938, on the GAA's decision to remove President Hyde from its list of patrons because he had attended a soccer match between Ireland and Poland gives a flavour of the extent of Unionist rejection of the new Irishness. The *Whig* found the ruling

> ... symptomatic of the spirit of primitive tribalism that passes current for enlightened Nationalism in Southern Ireland. It is a travesty of patriotism and of culture; it engenders sectional hatreds, restricts and distorts the outlook of thousands and makes its advocates the laughing stock of more advanced and progressive nations.

Had things gone that far? Was the gulf totally unbridgeable? It had not necessarily seemed so at an earlier stage. In a comment, on 18 August 1925, the *Whig* took strong exception to the decision by the 'Free State Nationalist fuglemen' to set up a separate medical register for the Free State just as they had tried, without success, to set up barriers in literature, art and sport. On a still higher plane had stood, hitherto, said the *Whig,* the unity of the Irish medical profession. This unity was something the *Whig* was not prepared to relinquish:

> When Ulster declined to join the South in separating from Great Britain it did not surrender its title as part of Ireland, nor renounce its share in those Irish traditions in art, in learning, in arms, in song, in sport and in science that were worth preserving in a united form.

The question of identity was not one Northern Unionists anguished over much in public, either in political speeches or in newspaper articles. The term 'Ulsterman' was generally deemed sufficient and conveniently could embrace either a British or Irish emphasis as occasion demanded. But the creation of an independent Irish state on part of the island, and a state embodying and proclaiming an Irishness that patently excluded 'Ulstermen' put an increasing strain in the inter-war years on this unity on a higher plane.

Partition had left a great many institutions and bodies unpartitioned. Most notably the churches had remained all-Ireland organisations – the Catholic Church because it tended not to recognise the partition of the country, the Protestant ones by deliberate decision,[5] based on the view at the time that partition was a political arrangement within the British Commonwealth and not the creation in the South of a sovereign, independent state. Both Protestant and Catholic, in their different ways, were subscribing to an Irishness they believed was to continue, despite political separation.

The same was true for most sporting organisations, and initially, for the legal and medical professions. The Royal Irish Academy, dating from 1785 and the senior learned society for both humanities and science in Ireland, survived partition and in 1924 was generally welcomed when it held a meeting in Belfast and presented an address to the Governor. On 4 January the *Whig* noted that it was to remain the Royal Irish Academy of all Ireland and was thus a 'symbol of national unity in literature, science and art'.

The academy, like the churches, was part of the unity referred to by the Moderator of the Presbyterian Church at the General Assembly in 1922.[6] Dr Strahan had told the Assembly that Presbyterians must maintain their unbroken ecclesiastical unity. This higher unity in Ireland, he said, was quite compatible with political separation.

There persisted a reluctance on the part of Unionists to forego the name 'Irishman' or to relinquish it to the South. St John Ervine, the North's most noted writer during the period and the biographer of Craigavon, invented the term 'Eireans' to describe the citizens of Éire, rather than concede the term Irish.[7] In 1933 Sir Joseph Davison, one of the more bigoted Orangemen, told a Black demonstration at Tandragee that he was 'proud to be an Ulster-Irishman'.[8]

At a political level there had long been a sensitivity to the term 'Ireland'. In 1923 Craig had complained to London about the use of it to refer to the Free State in the estimates for 1923–4, insisting that the distinction between the Free State and Northern Ireland should always be made clear.[9] After the 1937 Constitution came into effect it was de Valera's weakness for the Irish language and his incorporation of the name 'Éire' into the English language version of that Constitution, that avoided subsequent embarrassment, and Éire rapidly became the English name, not of the whole country but of the twenty-six counties only.

But outside politics, Northern Unionists raised no objections to the continued use of 'Ireland' and 'Irish' to designate their churches, their sporting organisations and international teams, and even the congress to which their trade unions belonged.[10] Nor did they see political danger in the appellation 'Northern Ireland', though popular usage much preferred the term 'Ulster'. Both names firmly attached the Northern state to Ireland – the one by incorporating the word, the other by using a territorial designation traditionally Irish. It took an Englishman, Spender, to point out the degree of illogicality and even danger in this and to suggest changing 'Northern Ireland' into 'North West Britain'. This, he argued in 1935, would make it clear that the area was part of Great Britain and would avoid giving some substance to those who argued it was part of an Irish nation.[11] But in putting forward his suggestion, Spender agreed that it might appear 'quite absurd', 'almost mad', and so, presumably, it did to the Northern Cabinet, for no more was heard of it.

Perhaps a decade later Spender's suggestion might not have appeared quite so absurd, for the distinction between 'Irish' and 'British' had been confirmed and deepened by Éire's neutrality in the Second World War. In 1949, during the talks over the Ireland Act, Brooke sought to have the name 'Northern Ireland' changed to 'Ulster'.[12] The reality of Irish neutrality, particularly after the fall of France in mid-1940, was further confirmation of the 'foreignness' of the Southern Irish state and of the concept of Irishness it embodied. It became increasingly difficult for Northern Unionists to retain another, higher concept of Irishness. The unity of the churches remained, as did that of most sporting bodies. But it was a unity that derived from the internal traditions and organisation of the institutions themselves, rather than from a lingering 'higher unity'.

The posture and actions of Dublin were also factors in weakening the arguments of the small minority of Ulster Protestants prepared to criticise the actions of the Unionist Government, and while not necessarily dissenting from the basic Unionist position on the constitution, to advocate much more liberal and flexible attitudes towards both the Northern minority and the Southern state. Some such people did emerge in the 1930s, including a small group at Queen's University in Belfast, who used the pages of the *New Northman* to attack the Special Powers Act and what one writer called 'the junta of self-seeking politicians who call themselves Ulster'.[13] One article in 1938 went as far as to urge a positive response to de Valera's proposals for Irish unity put forward in his *Evening Standard* interview of October of that year.[14] It was to this small group at Queen's that Major General Hugh Montgomery turned in 1938 to seek support for his idea of an Irish association, later to become the Irish Association for Cultural, Economic and Social Relations.[15]

But even the *New Northman* was far from happy with some aspects of the Southern state. In an editorial, in the summer of 1937, on the draft of de Valera's new Constitution, it criticised the Free State over its ban on divorce, its prohibition on the sale and importation of contraceptives and its censorship of literature. The attitude of the Free State Government on these matters, it said, was regrettable. Where the 'not unchallenged doctrines' of one church were embodied in law by the state, complete religious liberty could not be said to exist. The legislation against birth control, it said, was a more grievous danger to individual liberty than a Special Powers Act, and had caused more death. The editorial ended with the hope that before de Valera's envisaged united Ireland had come about,

> . . . we shall have seen a great change in the attitude of the Southern Irish politicians towards the freedom and sanctity of married life, the freedom of the Press, religious toleration and the liberty of the individual citizen, especially in the more personal side of his or her life.

Even when arguing that de Valera's offer of federal status in 1938 was an excellent basis for negotiation, one regular contributor to the *New Northman* felt obliged to point out serious defects in the Free State:

> If Irish Nationalists want to enlist the support of Protestants, it will be to the more liberal Protestants that they must look. The absence of divorce laws and the existence of a system of censorship are calculated to alienate the sympathy of those Protestants who would otherwise be inclined to lean towards the unification of the country.[16]

Effectively, neutrality in the Second World War was the final
chapter in the evolution of the Irish state to independence and
assertion of sovereignty. It was also, in Northern Unionist eyes, the
final rejection by Irish nationalism of all things British. Subsequent
analysis of Éire's position during the war has emphasised the
friendly or benevolent nature of that neutrality towards the Allied
cause, but there was no such perception among Northern Unionists
at the time, or since. 'Is it not abundantly clear,' asked the *Northern
Whig* on 17 May 1945, 'that the motive for neutrality lies in the still
deeply ingrained anti-British feeling that exists in Southern Ireland, a feeling so strong that even the great moral issues of the war
could not move them out of their narrow bitterness?'

If neutrality was the final chapter, de Valera's visit to the
German Minister in Dublin on 2 May 1945 to offer condolences
on the death of Hitler was an ill-tempered slamming of the book.
On 5 May the *Belfast News-Letter* commented that 'resisting all
inducements to take sides in a war in which civilisation is at stake,
she [Éire] shed an official tear over the grave, if it were known, of
the instigator of the conflict'. The condolences on the death of
Hitler, and the broadcasts of Churchill and de Valera later in May
focused attention at the war's end on the neutrality of the South.
Reporting Churchill's speech the *News-Letter*'s headline on 14
May declared: 'Mr Churchill exposes Eire's Shame'. On de
Valera's reply it noted on 17 May that the kernel of the broadcast
was the justification of neutrality on the grounds of partition:

> We seem to recall an occasion when Mr de Valera was at some
> pains in dissociating his Government's policy of neutrality in a war
> from the question of Partition. Yet today he treats the two things as
> cause and effect, conjuring up the unedifying picture of a disgruntled
> people – certainly a disgruntled government – sulking in its tent at a
> time when civilisation itself was at stake.

The *Whig* on 17 May in an editorial comment on the condolence
call, added a reference to de Valera's 'ill-natured and totally

uncalled for protest against the landing of [American] troops in Northern Ireland' in January 1942.

The South had, despite its neutrality, felt considerable impact from the war, and many of its citizens fought and died in the British Army. But the contrast between the neutral South and the war-stricken North was still stark, both in physical and material terms, and in the psychology of the war effort. The contrast was tragically heightened by the German air raids on Belfast in April and May 1941 when, in the space of a month and four nights of raids, almost 1,000 Belfast citizens died and great devastation was caused.

On 10 November 1942 a writer in the *Belfast Telegraph* reported that people in Dublin did not seem to take the slightest interest in the war: 'Owing to this mental detachment there is in Dublin an easy-going atmosphere and life is utterly devoid of any sense of urgency. In the streets and shops, people seem to have plenty of time.'

In a new and real sense North and South were worlds apart. If the war and neutrality proved, to Unionists, the inherent hostility of Irish nationalism towards Britain and the British, they also both underlined the worth of Ulster Loyalism, and its importance to Britain. The wartime experience, in short, proved one of the oldest Unionist arguments – that Britain simply could not, in strategic terms, afford to have all Ireland outside its control.

Most recent writing on Irish neutrality in the Second World War has stressed the positive contribution of that neutrality to the Allied cause, often with the conclusion that the South contributed more to the Allied victory by staying out of the conflict than it would have by joining in. But this should be qualified by two points: first the concept of 'friendly' or benevolent neutrality was formulated only after the United States entered the war. In a speech in December 1941 de Valera spoke of the ties of blood and friendship between Ireland and America, but said the policy of the state would remain unchanged: 'We can only be a friendly neutral.'[1] Robert Fisk describes de Valera's friendly neutrality as his concession to America's entry into the war.[2]

Moreover the entry of America helped change the war situation fundamentally from what it had been in July 1940 when de Valera had rejected Churchill's overtures. Then British defeat had seemed a certainty. After American entry, an Allied defeat was, to say the least, unlikely. So it is hardly surprising that the later benefits to Britain from Éire's neutrality meant little to Northern Unionists who remembered July 1940 and who, at any rate, found even friendly neutrality in such a conflict abhorrent.

Churchill's victory broadcast of May 1945, with its dismissal of de Valera and its tribute to the friendship and loyalty of Northern Ireland encapsulated and confirmed the Unionist view of the war experience as a vindication of Unionism and the final unmasking of Irish nationalism. Unionists basked in the praise, which came also from America, Dwight D. Eisenhower paying tribute in Belfast in 1945 to the part played by Northern Ireland as a staging post for American troops: 'If Ulster had not been a definite, co-operative part of the British Empire and had not been available for our use, I do not see how the build-up could have been carried out in England.'[3]

In the course of the war Ulster's contribution by way of ship and aircraft manufacture and food production had already been recognised. In 1943 Churchill had said that the bonds of affection between Great Britain and the people of Northern Ireland had been tempered by fire and were now unbreakable.[4] By war's end the stimulation of the war effort had lifted the Northern Ireland economy out of depression. By 1944 unemployment was down to below 5 per cent. Jobs in shipbuilding in 1945 stood at 20,000, almost three times the 1938 level; the new aircraft industry was employing 23,500 and employment in engineering had doubled during the war.[5] The economic gap between North and South was thus widening, and the creation of the British welfare state, extending to Northern Ireland in the postwar years, established a social and economic gap of substantial proportions between the two parts of Ireland. These new realities, added to the enormous political gap caused by Éire's neutrality, strengthened and deepened partition, and gave it a quality of permanence that should have put Unionist fears to rest at last.

But it did not seem like that to Unionists. Their first postwar shock was the landslide victory for Labour in the British general election of July 1945. Labour was not officially committed to a united Ireland, and indeed one of its leading figures, Herbert Morrison, had joined enthusiastically in the wartime tributes to Ulster's loyalty, but Labour's back-benchers contained those who were, and the Irish vote was important in some British constituencies. Pro-Irish Labour members banded together to form the Friends of Ireland, and they, along with others, continued the campaign begun by the National Council for Civil Liberties in 1936 against the discriminatory nature of Unionist rule in Northern Ireland.

This 'anti-Ulster' activity in Britain, as Unionists termed it, was complemented by a revival of political activity among the Nationalist minority in Northern Ireland. When the war ended only two Nationalist MPs were attending Stormont, and organised minority opposition to Unionism was almost non-existent at political level. But after the 1945 Stormont election Nationalists formed the Anti-Partition League which, with a full-time secretary and branches across the North, gave Nationalism in Northern Ireland a degree of organisation and a persistent voice it had hitherto lacked. The policy of Nationalist abstention at Westminster was also ended. Almost immediately a row over the franchise to be used in local elections gave the Nationalist opposition a focal point to concentrate on, and a propaganda weapon to use in Britain and elsewhere in the mounting campaign against partition.[6]

This revived anti-partition activity in Britain and the North inevitably helped stimulate Dublin politicians: the Government of Éire joined in. In June 1947 de Valera called on the British Government 'to make a simple declaration to the effect that they [are] desirous of seeing Partition brought to an end'.[7] This, he said, would make for a solution at the present time. Anti-partitionist temperature in the South was seen in, and raised by, a new party, Clann na Poblachta, founded in the summer of 1946 by Seán MacBride and growing indirectly at least out of the IRA activity of the later 1930s and the war years. Its aims were a formal Republic and a vigorous campaign against partition.[8]

De Valera's snap election of early 1948 was intended to halt the rise of MacBride's party, but had the surprise result of bringing it to power as a junior partner in John A. Costello's Inter-Party Government that ended almost sixteen years of Fianna Fáil rule. MacBride's presence in the new Government, as Minister for External Affairs and as a dominant voice in Cabinet, helped ensure a fresh burst of anti-partitionism and a re-stirring of Unionist anxieties.

Another result of the election was the opportunity for de Valera, out of office, to embark on a major tour of the United States, Australia and New Zealand, rounding off with stops in Burma, Ceylon, India and Italy. Throughout, he denounced Britain, likening its behaviour towards Ireland to that of Stalin in eastern Europe. His attitude towards the Unionists was hard-line nationalism: 'If you don't want to be Irish, we are prepared to let you go and compensate you', was his message, offering wholesale transfer to Britain as his final solution.[9]

More serious than the rhetoric of de Valera out of office was the attitude of Costello in office. In August 1948 he, too, went to North America and immediately alarmed Unionists by linking partition to the question of Éire's participation in any strategic western alliance. Commenting on his press conference on arrival, the *News-Letter*, on 28 August, said: 'The United States is to be given to understand that Ulster alone bars the way to an agreement for strategic purposes in the interests of peace.' Waiting pressmen, the *News-Letter* said, were told that Éire would not consider any such agreement so long as there was partition in Ireland:

> Thus, in two sentences, Mr Costello justifies or condones Eire's neutrality in the recent war, and offers Washington a pretext for urging the British Government to bring pressure to bear upon Ulster.

Over the following week rumour reported that Costello was about to break the last link binding Éire to the Commonwealth by repealing the External Relations Act. It was all, said the *News-Letter* on 6 September, part of a campaign of blackmailing pressure on Ulster. On 7 September Costello made his announcement at a press conference in Ottawa: 'Eire To Sever Last Link' read the *News-Letter* headline the next day. Costello's statement, commented the paper, revealed

> . . . not less clearly than any his predecessors made, the yawning gulf that separates Ulster from Eire, and the futility of his hopes of bridging it by means of threat, or bribe or indirect pressure.

In a sense it was very much in the Unionist interest to have that gulf revealed and deepened, but in 1948 the move to a Republic came at a time of intense anti-partitionist propaganda, with

Unionists unsure of the Labour Government in London, and with an unprecedentedly active and organised Nationalist opposition inside Northern Ireland. For good measure the move by Costello in September 1948 coincided with the 150th anniversary of the 1798 rebellion, marked in Belfast by a ceremony at McArt's Fort on the top of Cavehill, and by the banning of a parade.

Internationally it was a time of great instability and change. The British Empire, as it was still generally termed in Belfast, had seen the departure of Burma; India and Pakistan were independent and might still quit the Empire or Commonwealth; an anti-British party was in power in South Africa. East–West tension meant the threat of war was still present, and Dublin's attitude towards a western alliance had already been put on the table as a bargaining card.

Moreover, the whole theology of Republicanism in Ireland, as Unionists well knew, pointed not towards an acceptance of the yawning gulf, but to constant struggle to achieve thirty-two-county unity. The Costello move, therefore, could easily sound like a threat. Certainly that was the way the Northern Prime Minister, Sir Basil Brooke, chose to represent it. For him the move to a Republic was 'the last stage of that deplorable journey' that had taken the south of Ireland from Free State to total separation.[10] Conforming to the pattern of internal Unionist politics that had been set in 1921–2, he used a perceived threat from the South to establish maximum Unionist solidarity in the North.

The election he called for February 1949 was a direct response to the passing in Dublin, in December, of the Republic of Ireland Act and was a classic confrontation between Nationalism and traditional Unionism, in the course of which the new Northern Ireland Labour Party was eclipsed and Brooke triumphed, Unionists winning thirty-seven seats. If the seats of two independent Unionists in Belfast – more hard-line than the official party, and returned opposed – are added, Unionism was almost back to the position it held in the first Northern Ireland Parliament in 1921. The circumstances of the election and the vigour with which it was fought helped confirm the sterile, sectarian nature of politics in the Northern state at a time when much else was changing, and when the war experience might well have lessened the value of the Orange card to the traditional Unionist leadership. The rise of any significant non-Unionist political movement within the Protestant community was postponed for a decade or more.

A second result of the events of 1948–9 was the guarantee to the Unionists incorporated in the Ireland Act of 1949, affirming that 'in no event will Northern Ireland or any part thereof cease to be part of His Majesty's Dominions and of the United Kingdom without the consent of the Parliament of Northern Ireland'.[11] For Dublin this was an unexpected and highly unwelcome outcome; for the Unionists it was the key assurance they needed, enshrined in the legislation of the Imperial Parliament – they remained a small minority within the United Kingdom, but they now had an explicit guarantee that a decision on the constitutional future of Northern Ireland could be taken only in the place where Unionists had a permanent majority, in the Parliament of Northern Ireland.

Some would say it was ironically appropriate that a rejuvenated anti-partitionism and a precipitate act by a Dublin Government, should lead directly to this legislative guarantee to the Unionists. Not for the first time, Irish nationalism had proved Unionism's greatest support. For Unionists 1949 seemed the last stage of a journey – the final cementing of the partition settlement. What they overlooked at the time was that the guarantee was only as permanent as their devolved parliament.

CHRONOLOGY
1918–49

14 December 1918	General election. In Ireland Sinn Féin win 73 seats, Unionists 26, Irish Parliamentary Party 6.
21 January 1919	Dáil Éireann assembles in Mansion House, Dublin, only 25 Sinn Féin present, many others in jail. Same day ambush at Soloheadbeg, Co. Tipperary, marks beginning of Sinn Féin rebellion, or the Anglo-Irish War.
1 April 1919	De Valera elected President of Dáil. IRA and Sinn Féin in control over much of south and west of country.
25 February 1920	Lloyd George introduces Government of Ireland Bill at Westminster.
10 March 1920	Ulster Unionist Council decides not to oppose Government of Ireland Bill, thereby accepting partition and devolution for Northern Ireland.
June 1920	Serious communal violence in Derry, 18 dead.
July 1920	Communal violence in Belfast. Expulsion of Catholic workers from shipyards and other works. Attacks on Catholics in Lisburn, Banbridge, Dromore.
21 November 1920	Bloody Sunday in Dublin, 11 British officers shot, 12 people killed in reprisal at Croke Park.
23 December 1920	Government of Ireland Act becomes law, proposing devolved parliaments in Belfast and Dublin.
4 February 1921	Sir James Craig accepts Unionist leadership.
5 May 1921	Craig and de Valera meet in secret in Dublin.
24 May 1921	Elections held North and South under the Government of Ireland Act. Unionists win 40 out of 52 seats in North. Craig forms Government. In South Sinn Féin take 124 seats out of 128, all unopposed.
22 June 1921	George V formally opens Northern Ireland Parliament. In South elected Sinn Féin members sit in Dáil and refuse to operate Act.
24 June 1921	Lloyd George invites de Valera and Craig to London for negotiations.

9 July 1921	Truce announced between Crown forces and IRA to take effect on 11 July.
12 July 1921	De Valera in London for talks.
6 December 1921	Articles of Agreement (the Treaty) signed in London between Sinn Féin delegates and British Government.
7 January 1922	Dáil approves Treaty by 64 votes to 57. De Valera subsequently resigns.
14 January 1922	Provisional Government under Collins established in Dublin. British withdrawal begins.
21 January 1922	Craig and Collins meet in London. First Pact.
30 March 1922	Second Craig–Collins Pact agreed but severe communal violence continues in Belfast.
May 1922	Unionist MP Twaddell murdered by IRA. Severe IRA and communal violence in North.
23 May 1922	IRA proscribed in North under Special Powers Act, 500 arrested and interned.
28 June 1922	Four Courts in Dublin attacked, Civil War begins.
6 December 1922	Irish Free State comes into existence.
24 May 1923	De Valera orders his followers to end Civil War.
6 November 1924	Boundary Commission holds first meeting in London.
3 April 1925	General election in Northern Ireland.
28 April 1925	Nationalist members take seats in Northern parliament for first time.
7 November 1925	Findings of Boundary Commission leaked in *Morning Post*. Free State member MacNeill resigns from commission and from Free State Government.
3 December 1925	Tripartite agreement between London, Belfast and Dublin terminates Boundary Commission and confirms existing border.
16 May 1926	De Valera launches his new Fianna Fáil Party.
November 1926	IRA attacks on *garda* stations, 2 *gardaí* killed.
9 June 1927	Free State election, Fianna Fáil narrowly defeated.
11 August 1927	De Valera and Fianna Fáil take seats in Dáil.
16 April 1929	Northern Ireland Parliament abolishes proportional representation.
20 October 1931	IRA and Saor Éire declared illegal in Free State.
16 February 1932	Election in Free State; brings de Valera to power on 9 March.

10 March 1932	New de Valera Government releases IRA prisoners.
16 March 1932	De Valera says he will abolish oath of allegiance, withhold land annuities and introduce protective tariffs.
22 June 1932	Eucharistic Congress opens in Dublin.
30 June 1932	Land annuities payments withheld. 'Economic war' follows.
16 November 1933	Right of appeal from Free State courts to Privy Council abolished.
May 1935	Communal disturbances in Belfast. Also in July.
July 1935	Attacks on Protestant churches and homes in Limerick, Trim and Galway.
18 June 1936	IRA again declared illegal in Free State.
1 July 1937	General election in Free State. Fianna Fáil returned to power; referendum approves new Constitution.
29 December 1937	New Constitution comes into effect – Éire replaces Irish Free State.
25 April 1938	Anglo-Irish agreement ends 'economic war' and returns Treaty ports to Éire.
25 June 1938	Douglas Hyde inaugurated as first President of Éire.
22 December 1938	Internment reintroduced in Northern Ireland.
January 1939	IRA bombing campaign in Britain commences, continuing into 1940.
3 September 1939	Britain and France declare war on Germany. Éire remains neutral.
June 1940	After fall of France, Churchill offers de Valera British commitment to Irish unity in return for co-operation on war. Offer refused.
24 November 1940	Lord Craigavon dies. J.M. Andrews succeeds as Prime Minister of Northern Ireland.
April–May 1941	German air raids on Belfast, almost 1,000 killed.
7 December 1941	Japanese attack Pearl Harbour, bringing USA into war.
26 January 1942	First American troops land in Northern Ireland; de Valera lodges protest.
28 April 1943	J.M. Andrews resigns as Prime Minister of Northern Ireland. Sir Basil Brooke succeeds.
2 May 1945	De Valera calls on German Minister in Dublin to express official condolences on death of Hitler.

8 May 1945	War in Europe ends.
4 February 1948	Election in Éire results in defeat for Fianna Fáil, and election on 18 February of John A. Costello as head of Inter-Party Government.
7 September 1948	Costello, in Canada, announces intention of making Éire a Republic.
21 December 1948	Republic of Ireland Act provides for declaration of Republic.
18 April 1949	Ireland formally becomes a Republic and leaves British Commonwealth.
2 June 1949	Ireland Act declares that, in no circumstances, will Northern Ireland cease to be part of the United Kingdom without consent of Northern parliament.

REFERENCES

KEY TO ABBREVIATIONS

BNL	*Belfast News-Letter (News-Letter)*
BT	*Belfast Telegraph (Telegraph)*
BWT	Belfast Weekly Telegraph
Dáil Éireann, *Debates*	Dáil Éireann, *Parliamentary Debates. Official Report 1922–*
Dáil Éireann, *Minutes of Proceedings*	Dáil Éireann, *Minutes of Proceedings of the First Parliament of the Republic of Ireland 1919–1922. Official Record.* [1921]
Dáil Éireann, *Private Sessions*	Dáil Éireann, *Private Sessions 1921–1922*
Dáil Éireann, *Treaty Debate*	Dáil Éireann, *Official Report, Debate on the Treaty between Great Britain and Ireland signed in London on the 6th December 1921* [1922]
HC	House of Commons, Westminster Parliament
IT	*Irish Times*
NIHC	House of Commons, Northern Ireland Parliament
NW	*Northern Whig (Whig)*
PRO	Public Record Office, London
PRONI	Public Record Office of Northern Ireland
SPO	State Paper Office, Dublin

INTRODUCTION

1 *BNL* 8 February 1921

2 John Morely, *Life of Gladstone* (Edward Lloyd, 1908), vol. II, p. 398

3 Samuel Prenter in S. Rosenbaum (ed.), *Against Home Rule: The Case for the Union* (Kennikat Press, 1970), p. 215

4 Ne Temere, promulgated in 1908, laid down rules for marriage of Catholics to non-Catholics. It soon gave rise to bitter controversy in Ireland, notably the McCann case in Belfast. Motu Proprio, 1911, reasserted the medieval ban on bringing any ecclesiastical person before a lay tribunal without church permission. For details of McCann case *see* William Corkey, *The McCann Mixed Marriage Case* (Dublin, 1911).

5 Major John MacBride, later to be executed as one of the 1916 leaders, led one of the two Irish brigades that fought on the Boer side in the South African War.

6 Phrase is used in Sinn Féin's 'Invitation to elected representatives, the Irish people, January 7, 1919', reprinted in Dorothy Macardle, *The Irish Republic* (Corgi, 1968), p. 847

CHAPTER 1

1 *BBC Northern Ireland Chronology 1924–74* (BBC Information Service, 1974)
2 *Census of Ireland 1911*, vol. III, part 1, [Cd6050] HC1912–13, CXVI, I
3 Figures supplied by *BT*
4 *BNL* 1 September 1922
5 *BT* 8 October 1934
6 Another brother was Commander Oscar Henderson, for many years secretary to the Duke of Abercorn, first Governor of Northern Ireland. *See BNL* 14 April 1930
7 *NW* 24 August 1946
8 *BT* 3 February 1937; information also supplied by Fred Gamble, former *BT* journalist
9 There seems to have been no suggestion that Lynn was removed for political reasons.
10 W.S. Armour, *Facing the Irish Question* (Duckworth, 1935), p. 46
11 *Ibid.*, p. 47
12 Information supplied by Hamilton McDowell and Bruce Proudfoot, both former *NW* journalists
13 *BNL* 4 July 1956
14 PRONI D715/8
15 PRONI CAB 9B 227
16 Information supplied by Bruce Proudfoot
17 Armour, p. 7
18 *NW* 22 December 1924
19 Calton Younger, *Ireland's Civil War* (Muller, 1968), p. 301
20 Michael Farrell, *Arming the Protestants* (Pluto Press, 1983), p. 86
21 G.B. Kenna, *Facts and Figures of the Belfast Pogrom 1920–22* (O'Connell Publishing Co., 1922), p. 25

CHAPTER 2

1 W.S. Churchill, *The Aftermath* (Charles Scribner's Sons, 1929), p. 336
2 *Official Report on Recruiting* (sessional papers, 1921), vol. XX, p. 517(9)
3 *Recruiting in Ireland* (sessional papers, 1921), vol. XXXIX, p. 525
4 *NW* 16 November 1918
5 Andrew Bonar Law in Rosenbaum, p.11
6 Sir Edward Carson in Rosenbaum, pp. 18–22
7 Quoted in D. Fitzpatrick, *Politics and Irish Life 1913–1921* (Gill & Macmillan, 1977), pp. 92–3
8 Maurice MacDonagh, *The Irish at the Front*, Foreword by John Redmond (Hodder & Stoughton, 1916), p. 5
9 *Ibid.*
10 In May 1917 almost the entire leadership of Sinn Féin was arrested on grounds that they were engaged in a treasonable conspiracy with Germany – accusation based on Irish-American contacts with Germany. *See* F.S.L. Lyons, *Ireland since the Famine* (Fontana, 1973), pp. 393–4
11 Macardle, p. 121
12 For example, *BNL* 14, 18 July 1919; 2, 14 August 1919; 30 September 1919; 8 November 1919; 9 January 1920; 13 July 1920
13 *BNL* 3 March 1920
14 *NW* 16 November 1918
15 NIHC, vol. I, col. 307

CHAPTER 3

1 Cornelius O'Leary, *Irish Elections 1918–1977* (Gill & Macmillan, 1979), p. 7

2 Quoted in Macardle, pp. 842–4

3 *Ibid.*, p. 842. Reference to use of 'every means' was deleted by censor in 1918.

4 J.W. Good, *Irish Unionism* (Kennikat Press, 1970), p. 232

5 *BNL* 19 July 1921

6 *BNL* 1 April 1919

7 *BNL* 9 June 1919

8 Macardle, p. 269

9 *BNL* 16 August 1919

10 *BNL* 9 September 1919

11 *Ibid.*

12 *BNL* 6 May 1920

13 *BNL* 19 May 1920

14 *BNL* 7 June 1920

15 *BNL* 9 June 1920

16 *BNL* 8 June 1920

17 *BNL* 9 June 1920

18 *BNL* 10 June 1920

19 *BNL* 8, 9, 10, 11 June 1920

20 Desmond Murphy, *Derry, Donegal and Modern Ulster 1790–1921* (Aileach Press, 1981), pp. 254–5

21 Michael Farrell, *Northern Ireland: The Orange State* (Pluto Press, 1982), p. 26

22 *BNL* 13 July 1920

23 Patrick Buckland, *Irish Unionism*, vol. II (Gill & Macmillan, 1973), p. 122

24 Quoted in Farrell, *Northern Ireland: The Orange State*, p. 29

25 PRO CO 906/30

26 *BNL* 23 August 1920; *NW* 23 August 1920; *Lurgan Mail* 28 August 1920

27 For detailed account of Belfast Boycott *see* D.S. Johnson in J.M. Goldstrom and L.A. Clarkson (eds), *Irish Population, Economy and Society* (Oxford University Press, 1981), chap. 14

28 Dáil Éireann, *Minutes of Proceedings*, p. 191

29 SPO DE 1/2; minutes of Cabinet meeting of 11 August 1920

30 Dáil Éireann, *Minutes of Proceedings*, p. 212

31 *Ibid.*, p. 259

32 *BNL* 2 March 1921

33 SPO DE 2/110

34 *BNL* 13 May 1921

35 *BNL and NW* 30 July 1921

36 Macardle, p. 407

37 PRO CO 762/212, p. 2

38 *Proceedings of the Church of Ireland General Synod 1921*. The Church of Ireland church at Meenglass, Co. Donegal, had been broken into and befouled in April 1921.

39 *BNL* 11 June 1921

CHAPTER 4

1 HC Fifth Series, vol. CXXVII, cols 989–90

2 *BNL* 3 May 1921; *NW* 25 May 1921

3 *BNL* 8 February 1921

4 *BNL* 3 May 1921

5 *BNL* 6 June 1921

6 *BNL* 7 June 1921

7 For example, *NW* 14 May 1921

8 *BNL* 3 May 1921

9 NIHC, vol. I, col. 17

10 *Ibid.*, col. 61

11 PRONI D1415 B/38

12 *BNL* 8 February 1921

13 *BNL* 13 July 1932

14 NIHC, vol. XVI, col. 1031

15 First moves on a truce began as early as December 1920. In April 1921 high-level contact opened via Lord Derby, a leading Conservative and close friend of George V. *See* Lyons, p. 424

16 HC Fifth Series, vol. CXXVII, cols 989–90

17 NIHC, vol. I, col. 298

18 PRONI CAB 4/10/5

19 *BNL* 21 September 1921

20 PRONI D1415 B/38

21 Churchill, p. 290

22 *BNL* 8 June 1921. *See also* W. Alison Phillips, *The Revolution in Ireland* (Longmans, 1923), p. 209

23 Farrell, *Northern Ireland: The Orange State*, p. 41

24 Dáil Éireann, *Treaty Debate*, p. 225

25 Dáil Éireann, *Private Sessions*, p. 29

26 PRONI D1633/2

27 *BNL* 7 June 1921

28 *Ibid.*

29 *BNL* 13 July 1921

30 NIHC, vol. II, col. 53

31 PRONI D1415 B/38

32 PRONI D1633/2

33 *Ibid.*

34 PRONI D1415 B/38

CHAPTER 5

1 PRONI D1415 B/38

2 *BNL* 10 February 1922

3 *BNL* 13 February 1922. The B Specials were travelling by train to Enniskillen via Clones, Co. Cavan. *BNL* account says they were fired upon by uniformed IRA men in Clones station.

4 *BNL* 10 March 1922

5 *BNL* 30 May 1922. Split over Treaty meant anti-Treaty faction generally referred to as 'Republicans' or 'Irregulars'. The fact that in 1922 the army of the Provisional Government was still the IRA did not help Northerners see a clear distinction between pro- and anti-Treaty forces.

6 SPO S 1235

7 *Ibid.*

8 HC Fifth Series, vol. CLIV, col. 1892

9 NIHC, vol. II, cols 748–9

10 Quoted in Sir Arthur Hezlet, *The B-Specials* (Pan, 1973), p. 84

11 *NW* 14, 15, 16 February 1922; 14 March 1922; 3 April 1922

12 PRONI CAB 6/11

13 PRONI CAB 4/48/11

14 *NW* 15 June 1921; *BNL* 29 September 1921

15 NI Senate, vol. II, col. 10

16 PRONI D1633/2

17 *Ibid.*

18 NIHC, vol. II, col. 84

19 *Ibid.*, col. 222

20 Farrell, *Northern Ireland: The Orange State*, p. 57

21 PRONI D1633/2

22 Patrick Buckland, *A History of Northern Ireland* (Gill & Macmillan, 1981), p. 46

23 Younger, pp. 250–51; Leon Ó Broin, *Michael Collins* (Gill & Macmillan, 1980), p. 133; Lyons, p. 457

24 Michael Hopkinson, 'The Northern Question: The Treaty and the Civil War', in preparation

25 *Ibid.*

26 SPO S 1011

27 Dáil Éireann, *Private Sessions*, pp. 18–19

28 St John Ervine, *Craigavon, Ulsterman* (Allen & Unwin, 1949), p. 387

29 Dáil Éireann, *Treaty Debate*, p. 225

30 PRONI FIN 18/1/185

31 SPO DE 1/4, 30 January 1922

32 *Ibid.*, 5 April 1922

33 *BNL* 17 May 1922

34 SPO S 1095

35 Johnson in Goldstrom and Clarkson, p. 306

CHAPTER 6

1 PRONI D1507 1/3/41
2 Buckland, *A History of Northern Ireland*, p. 35
3 Patrick Buckland, *The Factory of Grievances: Devolved Government in Northern Ireland 1921–39* (Gill & Macmillan, 1979), p. 232
4 Ronan Fanning, *Independent Ireland* (Helicon, 1983), p. 36
5 SPO G1/1, vol. 1
6 NIHC, vol. II, col. 512. *See also* David Harkness, *Northern Ireland since 1920* (Helicon, 1983), p. 27
7 Full list given in Ervine, p. 417
8 PRONI D1415 B/38
9 For brief profiles of all members of new parliament *see NW* 23 June 1921. *See also* John F. Harbinson, *The Ulster Unionist Party 1882–1972* (Blackstaff Press, 1973), appendices C and D
10 NIHC, vol. I, col. 29
11 *Ibid.*, cols 64–8
12 *Ibid.*
13 NIHC, vol. II, col. 23
14 *Ibid.*, cols 30–37 *and* col. 320
15 *Ibid.*, cols 320–32
16 *Ibid.*, col. 967
17 NIHC, vol. I, col. 306
18 *Ibid.*
19 *Ibid.*, col. 311
20 *BNL* 1 December 1921
21 NIHC, vol. II, col. 614. *See also* A.T.Q. Stewart, *The Narrow Ground* (Faber & Faber, 1977), pp. 48–52
22 NIHC, vol. II, col. 614
23 *Ibid.*, col. 46
24 John H. Whyte, 'Intra-Unionist disputes in the Northern Ireland House of Commons 1921–72', *Economic and Social Review*, vol. 5 (1973), no. 1, p. 99

25 PRONI D1415 B/38
26 *Ibid.*
27 PRO CO 906/26
28 PRO CO 906/29
29 PRO CO 906/30. S.G. Tallents was a civil servant with a distinguished career: Private Secretary to the Lord Lieutenant 1921–2; attached to Churchill's Irish Committee 1922; Imperial Secretary in Northern Ireland 1922–6.
30 PRO CAB 23/30, 26/22
31 PRO CAB 739/1
32 NIHC, vol. II, col. 920
33 PRONI Cabinet files relating to B Specials remain closed
34 *Census of Population of Northern Ireland 1926. General Report* (1929), p. 1, table XXVII *and Report on Belfast County Borough*, p. 26, table 17
35 PRO CO 906/25; *see also* PRONI D1415 B/38
36 PRO CO 906/25
37 PRO CO 906/30
38 *Ibid.*
39 *Ibid.*
40 SPO S 1011
41 *Ibid.*
42 *Ibid.*
43 *Ibid.*
44 *Ibid.*
45 *Ibid.*
46 *Ibid.*
47 *Ibid.*
48 *Ibid.*
49 *Ibid.*
50 John McColgan, *British Policy and Irish Administration* (Allen & Unwin, 1983), pp. 110–11
51 Hopkinson, 'The Northern Question'
52 SPO DE 261, letter of 8 January 1921

53 *The Times* 31 March 1922
54 NIHC, vol. II, col. 311
55 PRO CO 906/26
56 NIHC, vol. II, col. 595
57 Collins and de Valera agreed that pro- and anti-Treaty candidates would stand as Sinn Féin on a coalition ticket, not against each other.
58 NIHC, vol. II, col. 597

CHAPTER 7

 1 *IT* 8 May 1923
 2 *NW* 4 January 1922
 3 George Seaver, *John Allen Fitzgerald Gregg, Archbishop* (Faith Press, 1963), p. 119
 4 *IT* 20 January 1922
 5 PRO CAB 23/30, 22/10
 6 Macardle, p. 641
 7 *BNL* 2 May 1922
 8 PRO CAB 23(30), 26(22)
 9 *Ibid.*
10 Seaver, p. 121
11 *Ibid.*
12 *Ibid.*
13 *BNL* 13 May 1922
14 PRO CAB 22(30)
15 *NW* 10 June 1922
16 *BNL* 9 June 1922
17 PRO CAB 23/30 (113)
18 SPO S 2112
19 *Ibid.*
20 *Ibid.*
21 *BNL* 5 July 1922
22 *IT* 9 November 1922
23 *Ibid.*
24 PRO CO 45 1192
25 *Ibid.*
26 NIHC, vol. II, col. 1172
27 W.E. Vaughan and A.J. Fitzgerald, *Irish Historical Statistics* (Royal Irish Academy, 1978), pp. 49–69
28 *Minutes of General Assembly of Presbyterian Church in Ireland 1919–1925*
29 PRONI D989C 2/21

CHAPTER 8

 1 PRONI CAB 6/11
 2 PRO CO 906/29
 3 PRO CO 906/30
 4 *NW* 1 February 1924
 5 *NW* 2 May 1924
 6 Craig's administration was criticised over education, temperance, Government extravagance etc.
 7 PRONI D1415 B/38
 8 PRONI CAB 9R/4
 9 *BWT* 24 April 1926
10 *BWT* 12 June 1926
11 *NW* 14 June 1927
12 *NW* 20 August 1927
13 *NW* 16 May 1928
14 *NW* 5, 6 March 1929
15 *NW* 18 April 1929
16 *NW* 13 July 1932
17 NW 15 October 1931
18 *NW* 29 March 1932
19 *Ibid.*
20 *NW* 11 November 1933
21 *Fermanagh Times* 13 July 1933
22 *NW* 13 July 1933
23 PRO PREM 3/131/2

CHAPTER 9

 1 Presbyterian Historical Society, Pamphlet, Box C
 2 Donal O'Sullivan, *The Irish Free State and its Senate* (Faber & Faber, 1940), pp. 90 *and* 95
 3 SPO DE 2/396
 4 Joseph M. Curran (ed.), *The Birth of the Irish Free State 1921–23* (University of Alabama Press, 1980), p. 201

5　F.S.L. Lyons in Francis MacManus (ed.), *The Years of the Great Test 1926–39* (Mercier Press, 1967), p. 97. *See also* Curran, p. 216 *and* Kurt Bowen, *Protestants in a Catholic State: Ireland's Privileged Minority* (Gill & Macmillan, 1983), pp. 324–37

6　Lyons in MacManus, p. 92

7　PRONI D989/C/1/69

8　PRONI D989/B/2/10; after 1922 the Irish Unionist Alliance functioned as a relief organisation working through the Southern Irish Loyalist Relief Organisation

9　PRONI D989/B/1/2

10　*Free State Census 1926* (1929), vol. III, table 7

11　*Statistical Abstract of Ireland 1950* (Dublin Stationery Office, 1951), p. 31, table 34

12　Robert E. Kennedy, jun., *The Irish: Emigration, Marriage and Fertility* (University of California Press, 1972), chap. VI

13　*NW* 31 March 1923

14　*Witness* 29 June 1923; *NW* 28 June 1923

15　*NW* 28 June 1923

16　*NW* 22 December 1924

17　*BWT* 12 June 1926

18　*BWT* 21 August 1926

19　*NW* 21 April 1928

20　*NW* 4 June 1929

21　*Ibid.*

22　*Ibid.*

23　D.H. Akenson, *A Mirror to Kathleen's Face: Education in Independent Ireland 1922–1960* (McGill-Queen's University Press, 1975), pp. 129–30 *and* chap. 8

24　Fanning, p. 57

25　O'Sullivan, p. 165

26　Seanad Éireann, *Parliamentary Debates. Official Report* (1925), vol. V, cols 434–43

27　*IT* 29 March 1923

28　PRONI D989/C/1/69

29　*NW* 7 November 1930

30　Terence Brown, *Ireland, a Social and Cultural History 1922–79* (Fontana, 1981), p. 127. *See also* John H. Whyte, *Church and State in Modern Ireland* (Gill & Macmillan, 1971), chaps 2 and 3

31　Background is given in 'Statement of 1968' (Council of the Irish Federation of University Teachers)

32　*Catholic Bulletin*, vol. XXI (1931), no. 1, p. 2

33　*BNL* 14 July 1931

34　*NW* 13, 17 August 1931

35　*Church of Ireland Gazette* 14 November 1931

36　*See Irish News* 18 December 1931 *and NW* 7 June 1932

37　*NW* 2 July 1932

38　*NW* 13 July 1932

39　NIHC, vol. XVI, cols 1031–5

40　*BNL* 13 July 1933; *Irish Press* 29 October 1931

41　*NW* 28 June 1929

42　*NW* 22 February 1932

43　*IT* 18 March 1935

44　*BNL* 5 June 1934

45　*BNL* 13 July 1934

46　PRONI CAB 9B/227 contains details of east Donegal Protestant petitions; file remains closed

47　*BNL* 16 November 1934

48　*BNL* 7 December 1934

49　PRONI CAB 9B/227. Sir Wilson Hungerford was secretary to the Ulster Unionist Council 1921–41 and a Stormont MP 1929–46

50　*IT* 22, 23, 24 July 1935

251

51 Seaver, p. 126

52 Vaughan and Fitzpatrick, p. 49, table 14

53 *BNL* 8 June 1937

54 NIHC, vol. XIX, col. 1660

55 *NW* 22 April 1938; *see also* O'Sullivan, p. 573

56 *NW* 13 July 1938

CHAPTER 10

1 Macardle, p. 850

2 *NW* 14 August 1924

3 *BWT* 29 May 1926

4 *Ibid.*

5 *BWT* 12 June 1926

6 *BNL* 15 May 1935

7 *69th Report of the Proceedings of the Representative Body of the Church of Ireland*, p. 232

8 *NW* 8 October 1927

9 *NW* 4 November 1932

10 NIHC, vol. XVIII, cols 631–2

11 *Ibid.*

12 PRONI D1415 B/38

13 *Church of Ireland Gazette* 25 January 1929

14 Akenson, pp. 129–30 *and* chap. 8

CHAPTER 11

1 PRONI D1633/3/26

2 *See NW* 17 December 1924; 12, 15 January 1925; 14 February 1925 *and BWT* 17 April 1926; 18 September 1926

3 *NW* 29 January 1927

4 *NW* 6 April 1927

5 For example, *NW* 2 April 1927

6 *NW* 16 July 1931; 5 August 1931; 7 November 1931

7 *NW* 1 September 1932

8 *NW* 5 April 1933

9 *BNL* 5 June 1934

10 PRONI CAB 9B/227

11 *BNL* 20 November 1934

12 *BNL* 19 March 1937

13 *NW* 3 March 1923

14 *BNL* 6 October 1934

15 D.S. Johnson in P. Roebuck (ed.), *Plantation to Partition* (Blackstaff Press, 1981), p. 244

16 *Ibid.*, p. 246

17 PRONI D715/3/54

18 PRONI D715/3/73

19 PRONI D715/6/174

20 PRO T 160/747/F 14026 04

21 *Ibid.*

22 John Bowman, *De Valera and the Ulster Question 1919–1973* (Oxford University Press, 1982), p. 176

23 PRONI D715/11/75

CHAPTER 12

1 PRONI CAB 4/119/16

2 *NW* 16 November 1926; *BWT* 20 November 1926

3 *NW* 30 July 1927

4 J. Bowyer Bell, *Secret Army: History of the Irish Republican Army 1916–79* (Academy Press, 1983), p. 65

5 *BNL* 28 March 1934

6 *BNL* 9 April 1934

7 *BNL* 15 July 1935

8 *BNL* 22 July 1935

9 *NW* 29 July 1937

10 *NW* 4 February 1938

11 *NW* 15 December 1938

CHAPTER 13

1 Bonar Law in Rosenbaum, p. 12

2 Thomas Jones, *Whitehall Diary*, ed. Keith Middlemas (Oxford University Press, 1971), vol. III, p. 147

3 Curran, chap. 14

4 *The Free State* 11 November 1922
5 Dáil Éireann, *Debates*,
  vol. XV,
  col. 739
6 O'Sullivan, pp. 559ff.
7 *Ibid.* pp. 532 *and* 563
8 Harkness, p. 113
9 *Ibid.*, p. 115
10 F.W.F. Smith, *Frederick Edwin, Earl
  of Birkenhead* (Eyre & Spottiswoode,
  1959), p. 383
11 PRONI D989/C/1/69
12 *NW* 7 November 1930
13 *NW* 5 March 1932
14 Bowman, pp. 110ff.
15 Dáil Éireann, *Debates*, vol. CVII,
  col. 91
16 *BNL* 20 July 1936
17 Bowman, pp. 160ff.
18 *Ibid.*, p. 116
19 *Ibid.*, p. 218
20 *Ibid.*, p. 231
21 *Ibid.*, p. 272
22 *Ibid.*, p. 229
23 *Ibid.*
24 PRO PREM 3/131/2
25 *BT* 29 June 1940
26 PRONI D1415 B/38

6 *NW* 6 June 1922
7 Ervine, for example, p. xi
8 *NW* 28 August 1933
9 PRONI CAB 8A/5
10 Irish Trades Union Congress,
  founded in 1894, continued to
  include Northern members after
  partition; a Northern committee was
  formed in 1943
11 PRONI D715/7
12 Fanning, p. 178
13 *New Northman*, vol. V (1937), no. 1
14 *New Northman*, vol. VI (1938), no. 3
15 In 1938 Hugh Montgomery was a
  retired army general. Son of a
  Unionist Senator, he himself had
  resigned from the party in the
  mid-1930s. As an advocate of better
  relations within Northern Ireland,
  and between North and South, he
  was the main force behind the
  formation of the Irish Association. A
  brief account of its beginnings is
  given in a pamphlet by Mary
  A. McNeill, circulated privately
  in 1982.
16 *New Northman*, vol. VI (1938), no. 3

CHAPTER 14

1 James Stephens, *The Insurrection in
  Dublin* (Sceptre Books, 1965), p. 93
2 *Ibid.*
3 Roland Gaucher, *The Terrorists*
  (Secker & Warburg, 1968), p. x.
  Gaucher dates first use of terrorism
  on a methodical basis in pursuit of a
  political goal to Russia *c.* 1879
4 Harold Jackson, *The Two
  Irelands – a Dual Study of
  Inter-group Tensions* (Minority
  Rights Group, 1971)
5 *See BNL* 7 June 1921 *and* NIHC,
  vol. XXI, col. 1228

CHAPTER 15

1 Maurice Moynihan (ed.), *Eamon
  de Valera: Speeches and Statements*
  (Gill & Macmillan, 1980),
  pp. 461–2
2 Robert Fisk, *In Time of War:
  Ireland, Ulster and the Price of
  Neutrality* (Brandon, 1983), p. 282
3 William A. Carson, *Ulster and the
  Irish Republic,* Introduction by
  David Gray (Cleland, 1956), p. ix
4 NIHC, vol. XXVI, col. 646
5 Harkness, p. 188
6 *Ibid.*, p. 114
7 Dáil Éireann, *Debates*, vol. CVII,
  col. 80

8 Seán MacBride 1904–88; son of
  Major John MacBride, who was
  executed as one of the leaders of the
  1916 Rising. He was a member of the
  IRA in the early 1920s and opposed
  the Treaty; IRA Chief of Staff
  1936–7; entered the Dáil in 1947

9 T. Ryle Dwyer, *Eamon de Valera*
  . (Gill & Macmillan, 1980), p. 133
10 *BNL* 15 September 1949
11 Ireland Act 1949, Section 1(2)

SELECT BIBLIOGRAPHY

NEWSPAPERS

Belfast News-Letter
Belfast Telegraph
Belfast Weekly Telegraph
Church of Ireland Gazette
Irish News
Irish Times
Northern Whig
New Northman
Witness

PRIMARY SOURCES

Public Record Office of Northern Ireland:

Carson papers, D 1507
Lady Craig's diaries, typed extracts 1905–40, D 1415 B/38
Londonderry papers, D 3099
Lady Spender's diaries, 1914–41, D 1633/2
Sir Wilfrid Spender, Financial Diary, 1931–44, D 715.
  Availability under review by Northern Ireland authorities at time of
  writing and not accessible. Indirect access only.

Government Records:

Cabinet conclusions, 1921–40, CAB 4
Cabinet papers: CAB 9A (Finance); CAB 9B (Home Affairs);
  CAB 6 (Police)
Ministry of Finance papers, FIN 18
Prime Minister's papers, PM 6, 7, 9, 10
(Note: many of the above documents, like the Spender Financial Diary,
  were withdrawn from access in the mid-1970s. The period of closure
  for some has been extended; others are under review.)

Public Record Office, London:

Cabinet papers, conclusions, CAB 23
Colonial Office, CO, particularly papers of S.G. Tallents,
    CO 906 and 739
Dominions Office, DO
Home Office, HO
Proceedings and Memoranda of Cabinet Committees, CAB 27
Treasury, T

State Paper Office, Dublin:

Cabinet files, S series, particularly S 1011, North East Advisory Committee
Dáil papers, DE 2
Minutes of Dáil Cabinets, DE 1

BOOKS, ARTICLES AND PAMPHLETS

Akenson, D.H. *A Mirror to Kathleen's Face: Education in Independent
    Ireland 1922–1960,* Montreal, McGill-Queen's University Press, 1975
Akenson, D.H. and J.F. Fallin. 'The Irish Civil War and the drafting of the
    Irish Free State constitution', *Éire-Ireland,* vol. V (1970)
Armour, W.S. *Facing the Irish Question,* London, Duckworth, 1935
Beckett, J.C. *The Anglo-Irish Tradition,* London, Faber & Faber, 1976
Beckett, J.C. 'The Anglo-Irish tradition in literature', *Lagan,* no. 2 (1944)
Beckett, J.C. 'Northern Ireland', *Journal of Contemporary History,*
    no. 6 (1971)
Bell, J. Bowyer. *Secret Army: History of the Irish Republican Army
    1916–79,* Dublin, Academy Press, 1983
Bew, Paul. 'The problem of Irish Unionism', *Economy and Society,*
    vol. 6 (1977)
Bew, Paul, Peter Gibbon and Henry Patterson. *The State in Northern
    Ireland 1921–72,* Manchester, Manchester University Press, 1979
Bowen, Kurt. *Protestants in a Catholic State: Ireland's Privileged Minority,*
    Dublin, Gill & Macmillan, 1983
Bowman, John. *De Valera and the Ulster Question 1919–1973,* Oxford,
    Oxford University Press, 1982
Boyce, D. George. *Englishmen and Irish Troubles,* London,
    Jonathan Cape, 1972
Boyce, D. George. *Nationalism in Ireland,* Dublin,
    Gill & Macmillan, 1982
Brown, Terence. *Ireland, a Social and Cultural History 1922–79,* London,
    Fontana, 1981
Buckland, Patrick. *Irish Unionism,* vol. I, *The Anglo-Irish and the New*

Ireland 1885–1922, Dublin, Gill & Macmillan, 1972

Buckland, Patrick. *Irish Unionism*, vol. II, *Ulster Unionism and the Origins of Northern Ireland 1886–1922*, Dublin, Gill & Macmillan, 1973

Buckland, Patrick. *The Factory of Grievances: Devolved Government in Northern Ireland 1921–39*, Dublin, Gill & Macmillan, 1979

Buckland, Patrick. *James Craig*, Dublin, Gill & Macmillan, 1980

Buckland, Patrick. *A History of Northern Ireland*, Dublin, Gill & Macmillan, 1981

Buckland, Patrick. 'The unity of Ulster Unionism 1886–1939', *History*, vol. 60 (1975)

Clarkson, L.A. *see* Goldstrom, J.M. and L.A. Clarkson (eds)

Curran, Joseph M. (ed.). *The Birth of the Irish Free State 1921–23*, Birmingham, University of Alabama Press, 1980

Elliott, S. *Northern Ireland Parliamentary Election Results 1921–72*, Chichester, Political Reference Publishers, 1973

Ervine, St John. *Sir Edward Carson and the Ulster Movement*, Dublin, Maunsel Press, 1915

Ervine, St John. *Craigavon, Ulsterman*, London, Allen & Unwin, 1949

Fallin, J.F. *see* Akenson, D.H. and J.F. Fallin

Fanning, Ronan. *Independent Ireland*, Dublin, Helicon, 1983

Farrell, Michael. *Northern Ireland: The Orange State*, London, Pluto Press, 1976

Farrell, Michael. *Arming the Protestants*, London, Pluto Press, 1983

Fisk, Robert. *In Time of War: Ireland, Ulster and the Price of Neutrality*, Dingle, Brandon, 1983

Gibbon, Peter *see* Bew, Paul, Peter Gibbon and Henry Patterson

Goldstrom, J.M. and L.A. Clarkson (eds). *Irish Population, Economy and Society*, Oxford, Oxford University Press, 1981

Harbinson, John F. *The Ulster Unionist Party 1882–1972*, Belfast, Blackstaff Press, 1973

Harkness, David. *The Restless Dominion*, London, Macmillan, 1969

Harkness, David. *Northern Ireland since 1920*, Dublin, Helicon, 1983

Hezlet, Sir Arthur. *The B-Specials*, London, Pan, 1973

Johnson, David. *The Interwar Economy in Ireland*, Studies in Irish Economic and Social History, no. 4, Dundalk, Dundalgan Press, 1985

Kenna, G.B. *Facts and Figures of the Belfast Pogrom 1920–22*, Dublin, O'Connell Publishing Co., 1922

Kennedy, Robert E., jun. *The Irish: Emigration, Marriage and Fertility*, Berkeley, University of California Press, 1972

Laffan, Michael. *The Partition of Ireland 1911–1925*, Dundalk, Dundalgan Press, 1983

Lawlor, Sheila. *Britain and Ireland 1914–23*, Dublin, Gill & Macmillan, 1983

Lyons, F.S.L. *Ireland since the Famine*, London, Fontana, 1973

Lyons, F.S.L. *Culture and Anarchy 1890–1939*, Oxford, Oxford University Press, 1982

Macardle, Dorothy. *The Irish Republic*, London, Corgi, 1968. (First published by Gollancz, 1937.)

McColgan, John. *British Policy and the Irish Administration 1920–22*, London, Allen & Unwin, 1983

MacDonagh, Oliver. *Ireland: The Union and its Aftermath*, London, Allen & Unwin, 1977

MacDonagh, Oliver. *States of Mind*, London, Allen & Unwin, 1983

MacManus, Francis (ed.). *The Years of the Great Test 1926–39*, Cork, Mercier Press, 1967

Miller, David W. *Queen's Rebels: Ulster Loyalism in Historical Perspective*, Dublin, Gill & Macmillan, 1978

Murphy, Desmond. *Derry, Donegal and Modern Ulster 1790–1921*, Derry, Aileach Press, 1981

O'Halloran, Clare. *Partition and the Limits of Irish Nationalism*, Dublin, Gill & Macmillan, 1987

O'Leary, Cornelius. *Irish Elections 1918–1977*, Dublin, Gill & Macmillan, 1979

O'Sullivan, Donal. *The Irish Free State and its Senate*, London, Faber & Faber, 1940

Patterson, Henry *see* Bew, Paul, Peter Gibbon and Henry Patterson

Roebuck, P. (ed.). *Plantation to Partition*, Belfast, Blackstaff Press, 1981

Rosenbaum, S. (ed.). *Against Home Rule: The Case for the Union*, New York, Kennikat Press, 1970. (First published by Frederich Warne, 1912.)

Seaver, George. *John Allen Fitzgerald Gregg, Archbishop*, London, Faith Press, 1963

Stephens, James. *The Insurrection in Dublin*, Dublin, Sceptre Books, 1965. (First published by Maunsel Press, 1916.)

Stewart, A.T.Q. *The Narrow Ground*, London, Faber & Faber, 1977

White, Jack. *Minority Report: The Anatomy of the Southern Irish Protestant*, Dublin, Gill & Macmillan, 1975

Whyte, John H. *Church and State in Modern Ireland*, Dublin, Gill & Macmillan, 1971

Whyte, John H. 'Intra-Unionist disputes in the Northern Ireland House of Commons 1921–72', *Economic and Social Review*, vol. 5 (1973)

Whyte, John H. 'Interpretations of the Northern Ireland problem', *Economic and Social Review*, vol. 9 (1978)

Wilson, T. (ed.). *Ulster under Home Rule*, Oxford, Oxford University Press, 1955

Younger, Calton. *Ireland's Civil War*, London, Muller, 1968

ACKNOWLEDGEMENTS

The co-operation of the staffs of the Public Record Office of Northern Ireland, of the Public Record Office at Kew, and of the State Paper Office in Dublin Castle is gratefully acknowledged.

Crown-copyright material in the Public Record Office is reproduced by permission of the Controller of Her Majesty's Stationery Office.

Dáil records and other material in the State Paper Office are reproduced by permission of the Director.

Material in the Public Record Office of Northern Ireland is reproduced by permission of the Deputy Keeper of the Records. Permission to use material from particular PRONI collections is also acknowledged: Brian Dingwall to quote from the diaries of Lady Spender; Viscount Craigavon to quote from the diaries of Lady Craigavon; and the Ulster Unionist Council.

261